C000258294

GUNNING FOR THE ENEMY

OTHER BOOKS ABOUT BOMBER COMMAND
BY MEL ROLFE PUBLISHED BY GRUB STREET:

To Hell And Back
Hell On Earth
Flying Into Hell

GUNNING
FOR THE ENEMY

Wallace McIntosh, DFC AND BAR, DFM

MEL ROLFE

GRUB STREET · LONDON

Published by
Grub Street
The Basement
10 Chivalry Road
London SW11 1HT

Copyright © 2003 Grub Street, London
Text copyright © 2003 Mel Rolfe

British Library Cataloguing in Publication Data
Rolfe, Mel
  Gunning for the Enemy: Wallace McIntosh, DFC and Bar, DFM
  1. McIntosh, Wallace. 2. World War, 1939-1945 Aerial operations, British
  3. Airmen Great Britain Biography
  I. Title

ISBN 1 904010 45 8

All rights reserved. No part of this publication may be reproduced,
stored in a retrieval system, or transmitted in any form or by any
means, electronic, mechanical, photocopying, recording, or otherwise,
without the prior permission of the copyright owner.

Typeset by Pearl Graphics, Hemel Hempstead

Printed and bound in Great Britain by Biddles Ltd, Guildford and King's Lynn
www.biddles.co.uk

In memory of Christina McIntosh

CONTENTS

ACKNOWLEDGEMENTS

I thank Wallace McIntosh for his unwavering patience in dealing with my innumerable questions, many of which I asked in infuriatingly different ways several times in an effort to winkle out further bits of important information I believed to be lurking in the more remote corners of his memory.

The following all contributed information or help in my preparation of *Gunning For The Enemy*: Pete Barber, Peter Bark, Dr John Cook DFC, Jean Craig, Robert Craig, Betty Elmer, the late Ron Emeny, Jessie Field-Richards, Friends of Metheringham Airfield, Raymond Glynne-Owen, the *Grantham Journal*, Ivar Grey, George Hall, Frank Haslam, Stan Hauxwell, Angela Hickling, Angela Holmes, James Hood, Kevin Mapley, Gordon Moulton-Barrett, the *Northumberland Gazette*, Harry Orchard, Stan Reed, Fred Richardson DFC, Russell Richardson, Tom Rogers, Frank Sim, Ken Smith, the *Spilsby Standard*, Roy Stephenson, Steve Stevens DFC, Katharine Stout, Dave Stubley, Larry Sutherland DFC and Bar, Robert Tuxworth, Arthur Watson, Graham Wheat, Vera Willis (née Tomlinson), Ron Winton, and Carl Wolter.

Considerable thanks are again due to my dear wife, Jessie, who has kept me on track for a fifth book about men who flew with Bomber Command. Her sub-editing service is, as ever, unmatched and immaculate, reading carefully through every chapter several times, sorting out grammatical howlers and, when asked, finding appropriate words which I could not extract from the murky black hole of my mind.

CHAPTER ONE

HARD TIMES

The vast armada of bombers moved over Germany like a raging thunderstorm, blasting through a shuddering night as black and inhospitable as death. The 191 Lancasters, 124 Halifaxes and eighty-one Stirlings, carrying enough bombs to tear the heart and soul out of a city, bore inexorably towards their target, Berlin. They flew in a stream through a long howling corridor several miles wide, 8,000ft between the highest Lancasters and the lowest Stirlings, each bomber with the additional awesome burden of high-octane fuel and several thousand rounds of .303in ammunition.

These flying coffins were crewed by around 2,770 men, forty-five of whom would be dead within an hour. None considered himself brave or heroic, yet they all faced death or serious injury every time they took off on a gruelling bombing operation.

There were any number of ways that a man might be killed in Bomber Command. His aircraft might be caught in the intense barrage of shells being pumped up by enemy gunners on the ground or from flak ships, both guarding important targets or key routes across occupied Europe. Luftwaffe fighters, swifter and more-heavily armed than their prey, caused carnage among lumbering bombers. They could also become unfortunate casualties of mid-air collisions, or be bombed by their own aircraft flying at a higher altitude. Then there were the loathed pimps of the air war, the powerful searchlights fluttering, whirling and stabbing about the sky, seeking victims to lock on to and plant their fatal kiss as a lure for the predatory fighters.

It was 27 March 1943. Crushed into the mid-upper turret of a 207 Squadron Lancaster, cocooned in constricting layers of flying gear, his ears violently assaulted by the four great pounding Rolls-Royce Merlin engines, Sergeant Wallace McIntosh rested his forefingers lightly on the two triggers of the twin Brownings. He peered anxiously into the deep virtually impenetrable darkness. It was his twenty-third birthday. Having rejected the offer of a lively piss-up later in the mess he was celebrating instead by flying to the Big City where he could be assured of a warm welcome. Having not seen another bomber since crossing the English coast two hours ago, he felt alone in a world impregnated by noise and saturated by murk. Unseen except as a great mass rolling across German radar screens, they might have been trapped inside a huge echoing unlit subterranean cavern.

Their aircraft droned resolutely on towards the German capital as McIntosh and rear gunner Sergeant Grant Booth continually rotated their turrets, peering intently into the thick unyielding darkness, searching for the blurred movement of an approaching enemy fighter, intent on blowing them to pieces. It was like looking for a smear of black paint splashed aimlessly on the canvas of the limitless night sky. The air gunners were the vigilant defenders of their Lancaster and, after a few trips, could be identified by the premature crinkles around their eyes.

Outside, at 20,000 feet, the temperature was minus forty degrees. Inside his turret, despite an electrically-heated flying suit, McIntosh shivered. If you wanted a peaceful and comfortable war you did not join a Bomber Command aircrew.

The previous day McIntosh had stood quietly at a field gate with his skipper, Sergeant Fred Richardson, where they absently watched cattle languidly munching grass, before continuing their stroll to a pub in the Nottinghamshire village of Langar, near the airfield. Tonight they had flown into the devil's playground.

Bomber aircrews came from every segment of life. The majority wanted no more than to fight for their country, give Hitler a bloody nose, and kill Nazis. There was also a small sprinkling of spoiled sons of rich or titled families, seeking adventure and stories to titivate society beauties. Others came from poor backgrounds, aspiring for a better life, not too disturbed by rumours that their significant improvement in circumstances might end in sudden death.

Few would emerge at the end of the war with such distinction as Wallace McIntosh, who had been brought up in the most grinding poverty among people whose only ambition was to survive until tomorrow. His prospects took off spectacularly when he joined the Royal Air Force and became an air gunner. But it was a fluke and the threat of being court martialled which led him to become a member of a bomber crew.

* * *

A ferocious blizzard swept the north-east of Scotland on 27 March 1920 when a young woman, warmly wrapped and heavily pregnant, stepped nervously from Logiereive Farmhouse. She closed the door and hurried, head down, swishing purposefully through the thick snow across the yard, pausing at a stone barn into which she disappeared. The farm stood a mile or so outside the village of Tarves on the narrow drift-blocked road to Ellon, north of Aberdeen.

Lizzie Hendry was nineteen. Small and pretty, with lustrous hair as black as freshly-laid tar, she had an impish sense of humour. But she was not laughing now. This was the moment she had dreaded for months and although she would have welcomed the comforting presence of her mother, Lizzie knew this was one ordeal she must face alone. She settled stoically into an old chair and waited, holding her swollen stomach.

Later that day she emerged from the barn carrying her baby, wrapped in a blanket. The farmer and his wife, who employed her as a domestic servant, sent for Doctor Munro who was forced to leave his pony and gig in Tarves and take a precarious walk along a stone dyke to see his patients. The baby would be named Wallace McIntosh.

Within three days Lizzie Hendry had reluctantly decided to continue working at the farm without the encumbrance of her first baby. When her parents heard that in her dilemma she was thinking of getting the baby adopted they walked without hesitation four miles from their modest home near Ellon along the choked and frozen lane to Logiereive Farm. The horror and shame of seeing a grandchild taken into an orphanage or a house full of strangers was unacceptable despite the obvious difficulties of rearing him themselves.

They brought the youngster up with as much pride and love as if he were their own, despite their perilously impoverished circumstances. His mother would marry the baby's father, Wallace McIntosh Senior, the following year and bear him another ten children, but twenty-four years passed before she saw her first-born again.

Young Wallace was born into a hard world in which agricultural workers in Scotland were treated like serfs, occupying the bottom rung of a rickety employment ladder. The estate owners and farmers held all the cards. They had the land and the jobs and controlled the destiny of those who worked for them, not hesitating to cast out those who did not conform.

The boy's grandfather, Alexander Hendry, a skilled stockman, suffered badly from rheumatism. His fragile health often meant he could not work for more than two or three weeks at a time, and eviction from another miserable little tied cottage inevitably followed.

Wallace's grandmother, Elizabeth Knox Hendry, claimed to be a direct descendant of the sixteenth century Scottish Protestant reformer John Knox. She was no less devout than her illustrious forebear, always attending church on Sundays, wherever they were living. This little family were frequently on the move looking for a place to stay, and work for Grandpa when he was fit.

They expected no handouts and got none. Days, weeks, months and years followed with grim predictability in which nothing turned up to ease their constant battle to stay alive. The man's poor health made the daily grind an even greater struggle, but somehow, they kept going. And now they had another mouth to feed. Adjustments had to be made to their own frugal diet and while making sure they always had enough milk for the baby, not many weeks passed before he was introduced to the unrivalled nourishment of porridge.

He called them Grandma and Grandpa, but to him they were an exceptionally warm and loving mixture of grandparents and parents. In his eyes, at first, he was their only child even though, occasionally, some of their own children came calling. The boy was not yet aware of their extreme poverty because most of his friends came from families similarly afflicted.

The Hendrys were not unfamiliar with struggle. They had had seven children, including a pair of twins, all brought up on farms, leaving school and branching out on their own after their fourteenth birthdays. All were hard workers, a credit to their parents.

Young Wallace's father, Wallace McIntosh Senior, who topped six feet, was dark-haired and handsome, with a twinkle in his eye reserved for similarly twinkling young women. He had been a soldier in the First World War and before the second conflict worked on farms as a horseman. Later as a labourer, he helped lay the runways at Dyce which opened officially as an airfield on 4 July 1934, and was home to Fighter Command's 612 Squadron at the outbreak of war. Later it was the base for a variety of units. It is now Aberdeen Airport.

Wallace McIntosh Junior would be touched by death long before he joined the RAF. He was five when three tragedies created turmoil within the family. Firstly, his friend died of measles after they had moved to Altens, near Nigg, south of Aberdeen. McIntosh recalls:

'It was terrible at five to be hardened to seeing death. I was taken to see Billy's body at the horse-drawn caravan in which he and his parents lived. He had cotton wool in his nose and I thought: "Now why would that be?" It intrigued me later because I didn't see it in the other two.'

Shortly afterwards, Wallace and Alistair Chalmers, also five, were playing happily on the seashore at Kineff when the other boy was caught by a wave and drowned. In the distress and panic of the moment, it was Alistair's three-year-old sister, Isabel, who ran for help. When he was fourteen Alistair's parents, who had moved to Kent, sent Wallace a Bible which he carried through the war and still keeps, a treasured possession.

The final appalling act in the trio of traumas followed when Aunt Mary, aged seventeen, his mother's sister, died in agony from terrible burns after her clothing had been set ablaze. Flames had leapt in a blow-back from a big kitchen range stove she was trying to light early one morning at Slains Park Farm, near Kineff, Kincardineshire, where she was employed as a housemaid.

Now in his eighties, McIntosh says sombrely: 'She was my grandparents' youngest child, the only one still living with us at home in a cottage on the farm. I remember Farmer Forbes' horse and trap taking my grandparents to see her at Stonehaven hospital, where she died later the same day. I was lifted up to see poor Mary in her coffin.'

His early years were spent travelling with his grandparents from farm to farm, living in an assortment of wretched hovels. Water was fetched in a pail from wells or burns up to half-a-mile away. They washed outside, no pleasure in the depths of a freezing Scottish winter.

The boy's staple diet was potatoes, and brose. Brose, or porridge, was a bowl of oatmeal on which boiling water was poured, briskly stirred and sprinkled with salt. Sometimes the juice of a boiled turnip or kale was added to liven it up and, for a treat, a spoonful of black treacle, diluted in warm water.

McIntosh, recalling those dismal meals, says: 'I had brose three times a day for years on end. It was a meal which began with cattle drovers who carried oatmeal on their backs and a bowl of carved wood. They supped from a spoon often made from a cow's horn.'

Even so, he still starts every day with a good bowl of porridge, prepared with hot milk and plenty of sugar. But not brose, which belongs to his childhood. They also had broth, and meals were occasionally supplemented by the flesh of animals and birds poached by his grandfather and later, by himself. He could steal, kill and butcher a young sheep in a field before he was twelve.

Neither grandparent had been born into such poverty, although both had known nothing but hard times. Both were articulate and could read and write, but they had been caught up in a downward slide from which there seemed to be no escape. Life was tough, survival their most pressing ambition. Although they felt shame at their miserable situation, his grandparents had the tenacity to keep going. They retained their dignity and were always heading for better times. Their clothes may have been ragged and patched, but they were clean. The couple passed on to the boy their wisdom, gleaned from years of wrong moves and thwarted ambitions, much of which he remembered and used to shape and enlighten his own life. Apart from teaching him right from wrong they explained how when you were poor and made a mistake it was more likely that severe punishment might follow than if you were well off and, consequently, of greater importance.

Grandma told him: 'Always look your best, you never know who you may meet. First impressions are important.' Another invaluable tip was: 'Never be last because they are the easiest caught.'

His grandfather's advice was more practical: 'Always carry a piece of string, it will do to lace up a boot. Carry a knife and you can skin a rabbit or cut a sheep's throat. And always have a shilling, it's handy if you need a quick exit on a bus.'

The boy was prone to sore throats and Grandma's infallible treatment was tying the socks he had worn that day around his neck in bed at night. It is a remedy he has used effectively in adult life.

They had few possessions apart from a few paltry sticks of furniture. McIntosh says:

'The main things they had were their two chairs, and there was a little stool that Granny sat on with her knees up because she was always either sewing, knitting, or making clothes, something for me. Always for me. People gave her clothes and some she cut down. She used to repair my boots with leather. She had a last and hammer. In later years Granny couldn't knit because of rheumatism in her fingers.'

Their proudest possession was a small chiming clock which stood on an old pine dresser. If sold the money might have fed them for a month or more, but they needed something from better times to cling to. Grandma's life savings, a ten shilling (50p) note, was hidden inside the clock for use only in the most dire emergency. McIntosh never knew if the money was used during their roughest experiences, nor what happened to the clock after the old people died.

Young Wallace's world was bounded by the fields, woods and rolling hills he could see from his home, wherever that might be, and a vast intriguing sky which stretched to infinity. There was a great profusion of wildlife. Horses and carts occasionally clattered by in the lane and familiar farm workers waved to the wee absorbed boy crouched by the verge playing happily with an empty matchbox on a string, which could be a lorry plunging through the grit and grime, a battleship ploughing over rough seas, or a car taking him and his grandparents to the seaside, the latter one of his impossible dreams.

He mostly made his own toys, trucks roughly carved from wood, although there were sometimes magical days when Uncle Jimmy Hendry appeared with wonderful presents like a rubber ball or a tiny racing car purchased from Woolworths.

He saw one or two single-engine aircraft blundering across the sky. To him they were a curious sight, frightening birds and stampeding cattle. Nothing more than that. Not yet.

Wallace adored his grandparents and they gradually built their lives around him. Grandma Hendry was tall, lithe, full of good humour and common sense. She could also be unexpectedly fiery, standing up to anyone who made the mistake of believing she was an ignorant peasant woman by arrogantly trampling over her or her family. Less forthright, her husband was sometimes embarrassed by the unquenchable spirit which wagged her lacerating tongue, although secretly proud that she had the guts to stand up to the overbearing presence of authority.

Grandpa, known to everyone as Sandy, was broad and stocky with a twirling black moustache. He chewed tobacco and smoked his pipe until the choking fumes filled the small parlour and his wife banished him outside to the doorstep.

'When Grandpa ran out of tobacco I had to run to the nearest shop to get two ounces of Mitchell's Three X Bogie Roll. He was a hard-working man and my grandmother kept things tidy with what limited facilities she had. They turned me out the best that they could.'

Among his more distressing early memories are those of his grandfather, tortured by rheumatism, struggling to walk in a cottage which forever seemed to stink of boiling potatoes and Sloan's Liniment. There was no shelter working in the fields during heavy rain and the boy often saw his grandfather stagger in after a long day and sit exhausted beside a fire, his saturated clothes steaming, triggering another painful bout of rheumatism. His grandmother, who brought in shillings by cleaning other people's houses, was once seriously ill with influenza and her distressed little grandson ran a mile to the nearest farm to summon the doctor.

Wallace McIntosh was thirteen-and-a-half when he left school and started working full-time. Earning a living was not new to him. He had first been paid years before for doing odd jobs at various farms while attending fourteen different schools. Thin and wiry he had tremendous stamina, built up by running through fields, tramping the hills of Aberdeenshire and Perthshire, and walking miles to and from his lessons, barefoot in summer, to save on boot leather.

Young Wallace loved the freedom of the countryside and one fine spring day he impulsively decided to make a short detour into a wood on his walk of over three miles to Crathes school near Banchory. It did not feel like playing truant which was something bigger and braver boys did, but Wallace had the riches of two slices of bread and syrup in a paper bag, his feet were propelled by skittishness, and birds called joyously to him from the trees. Where there were birds there would be birds' nests, and at seven he was something of a specialist, with fifty-two different eggs in his collection. If he could also surprise a dozing pheasant and return home with that tucked down his shirt *and* a bagful of eggs to eat his grandparents would be proud of him.

They were not proud, they were outraged. Wallace had planned to stay in the wood until it was the normal time for leaving school, but time passed slowly for a boy who quickly ran out of things to do. When he walked into their cottage on Kilduthie farm without eggs or pheasant it was only midday. McIntosh has never forgotten the only beating he ever received from his grandfather. He says: 'Next day the teacher asked where I had been and I told her I'd been playing truant, it was no use telling a lie. She said I was a naughty boy and took a note of it.'

Wallace clearly had the instincts for rebellion, while eventually realising that his naughtiness might upset and reflect badly on those he most cared for.

The boy was seven when he first heard about the existence of Christmas. The Hendrys could not afford to celebrate the festive season and anxiously tried to explain that occasional bad behaviour was not the reason why he did not receive presents. He was ten or eleven before he was given his first Christmas stocking containing an apple and an orange, but birthdays meant nothing until he became an airman.

Grandpa's health broke at Kilduthie, eviction followed and he was lucky to be offered a job in Perthshire. His grandson recalls the excitement of the move.

'The estate of R Wymess-Honeyman, a linoleum magnate, had a recruiting campaign, my grandfather was interviewed in Aberdeen and offered a job. It was quite an event, part of a big exodus of people to Perthshire, a daring adventure. We were given tickets to go by railway to Perth, the first time I'd been on a train. Several families were taken in wagons from Perth to near Grandtully, south of Pitlochry beside the river Tay. We lived in isolation up in the hills in a corner of The Lurgan, a big, otherwise empty, house, which had a lovely view over the Tay valley, but this was a case of the estate getting labour cheap. Once they had you there you couldn't run away. This was common practice in those days.

'The place was infested with pheasants and rabbits. I snared rabbits and hares, and caught pheasants at night. I was a good poacher. A hogget, a young sheep, was the easiest thing to get, it would walk up to you. I cut its throat, then skinned it. No one could see me out there in the wilds at night. It was a very dicey thing to do, but this was the time of The Depression, it was food and I carried it home on my shoulder. There wasn't much between skinning a big hare and skinning a sheep. The only thing was you had to bury out of sight the fleece, rabbit skins and pheasant feathers. You couldn't burn anything because of the smell and poaching was a serious crime.

'My grandfather was once apprehended while catching a rabbit and had to humbly beg the pardon of the Laird of Haddo, near Tarves, or lose his job. That was at a place which teemed with rabbits that were not worth a penny and ate everybody's vegetables. But we had to be kept in our place by these people with power.'

Much of Grandpa's work was seasonal and there were usually jobs to be found in Perthshire for someone willing to tackle anything. In the spring he would row boats, or pull nets for gentlemen fishing for salmon. His wife cleaned cottages occupied by the fishermen and, in late summer, by wealthy folk who swarmed north for grouse shooting. McIntosh recalls:

'People got jobs beating, carrying, and looking after ponies that brought down the bodies of deer which had been shot. Potato planting kept Grandpa busy on farms in April and May. After that came the singling and hoeing of turnips. Then came the start of harvesting fruit crops. Perthshire was famous for its raspberries. Peas and strawberries followed, then lifting potatoes.'

At The Lurgan, however, he looked after a flock of sheep and cattle at an out farm. Mrs Hendry also milked two cows, making butter and cheese for sale. The cows were perks, together with sacks of potatoes, oatmeal and coal.

Wallace had a walk of over four miles to Grandtully school. On stormy days he arrived soaking wet, hoping that one of the teachers would be thoughtful enough to make a big pot of soup for lunch. Such thoughtfulness broke down when he was pushed to the end of the queue where the soup was thinnest, because he was not expected to be a long-term pupil.

Aged ten, Wallace offered his services as a beater at the grouse shoot on the Wymess-Honeyman estate from 12 August. While providing his own packed lunch he was paid about 1s 6d (7.5p) a day as one of up to thirty beaters waving little white flags and yelling to scare grouse forward to the rich guests waiting in the butts with their guns and loaders. As the day wore on the boy was tired and his bare bony legs were scratched raw from the rasping heather, but he was earning money and Grandma proudly tied sacking from his ankles to his knees to protect them next day.

It was a cold spring day when the work ran out for Sandy Hendry and they were given short notice to leave The Lurgan. The only accommodation they could find, thanks to a shepherd friend, was a disused and damp wooden shed, set in the corner of a field three miles away on the other side of the Tay. They had reached rock bottom.

That night Wallace's grandmother heated two bricks in a fire built outside the shed, wrapped them in hessian and placed the hot bundle at the bottom of the boy's bed, which was like a large pillow, or tyke, filled with chaff. Little comforts were important when spirits were low.

He huddled beneath the single blanket, clad in underpants, a semnit (vest), and sweaters – knitted by Grandma – which multiplied as the weather grew colder. Going to school he drew on trousers, another jersey or two, a baggy old jacket and heavy boots. He was much older before he wore his first shirt. The boy fell asleep listening to his worried grandparents murmuring at the other end of the shed that their circumstances could only improve.

Wallace walked to school as usual next morning with warm brose in his stomach and encouraging words from Grandma in his head. 'You need education, Wallace,' she had said gravely. 'It will help get you out of this into a better way of life.'

Without a penny coming in they lived mainly on oatmeal and potatoes, although Wallace often slipped out quietly, returning later with a snared rabbit or a fish or two.

During the next two or three weeks the boy's diet was given a welcome boost from an unexpected quarter. He still went to Grandtully school, but along a different road, beside which stood the nobly-turreted Grandtully castle, the seat of the Stuart family since the end of the 14th century. Returning one day he noticed a young woman dressed in the black and white uniform of a maid standing self-consciously in the road near the castle. Smiling she handed the surprised boy a small package wrapped in paper. Inside was a ham sandwich, which he wolfed down eagerly. Thereafter, two or three times a week, whatever the weather, a maid from the castle would be waiting to hand over a gift of food, which might be a chicken leg, a chunk of ham, a portion of corned beef, or sandwiches.

He never discovered the identity of his Good Samaritan and has since often wondered who took pity on the solitary waif, suspecting it might have been Lady Stuart herself who spotted him trudging home. Curiously, about fifty years later, McIntosh won a competition to spend a week as a guest at the castle, and he slept in the late Lady Stuart's room.

In a week or two they heard of a two-room thatched cottage which stood empty on the Dundee-Perth road in the village of Glendoick. One room had an earth floor, and although Mr Hendry was ill again, he laid flagstones, and they considered their new home, with its stout walls, sound roof and large garden, was a palace compared to the shed.

When his health improved he was employed by a farmer to sort and clamp potatoes. Wallace's grandmother was also working and the boy, now aged ten, became an important breadwinner, helping during potato harvesting, and gathering raspberries. He was never idle and their living standards began to improve.

'The potato farmer recommended my grandfather for a more permanent job which had a cottage attached at Candy Farm, near Glenfarg, south of Perth. It was a nice cottage and Grandma remarked that it was the first home she had lived in with running water. It only had one tap in the scullery, but it was better than slopping about with buckets. I was eleven when we moved there. I had my happiest days at Glenfarg.'

Farmer Gow, a kind man, in his late thirties, took an interest in the little family offering them a pig to keep in the sty in the back garden. They gratefully accepted the animal even though up till now they could hardly feed themselves. McIntosh says it was a wonderful place for a young lad growing up.

'A burn full of fish ran through the farm, which was hoatching, or swarming, with rabbits and there were plenty of pheasants and hares. The River Farg ran within 150 yards of my new school and salmon came up from the Tay to spawn around September and October. During the lunch break I ran to the river, girdled about under the banks and whipped out a salmon.

'Mr Gow was a charming man. My grandfather was looking after cattle and Grandma worked every second morning at The Big Hoose. Mr Gow invited me to go shooting rabbits with him one Saturday afternoon. It was, popping off rabbits, that I discovered I was a first-class shot. Some time later the farmer surprised me by buying me a brand new 410 double-barrel gun. Every Saturday morning he gave me a box of cartridges and said: "I want to see you come back with twenty-five rabbits, but don't look at the pheasants, *I* shoot them". I did nick one or two pheasants, but killed as many rabbits as I could carry, sometimes several outside a burrow with one shot.

'I went tramping off in the hills looking for birds' eggs with my friends, the brothers Bill and Bunt Deas, whose father had a small joinery business in the village and was fairly well off. Lapwings' and seagulls' eggs, pigeon pie and crow pie were eaten at the time.

'I was never a brilliant scholar and when I left school the parting words of the headmaster, Mr Henderson, were not encouraging. He said: "Well Wallace, I think you'll just manage to count all the money you'll ever make."

'Mr Gow gave me a job and a wage of five shillings (25p) a week. I thought I was a millionaire. He grew a lot of potatoes, stored in clamps in the corners of fields nearest the roads, to make it easy for them to be loaded on to carts or lorries. I arrived on frosty mornings with a sack over my head picking potatoes with frozen fingers. I fed and cleaned out cattle and pigs, chased the cows out after milking night and morning, and chopped down trees. After two years I decided it was time to move on. I always wanted to better myself. I could see how poor we were and wanted a way out.'

He dreamed, as all children dream, of being someone special, of being a hero. Of being grown up and seeing adults nudge their scowling offspring to whisper: 'That's Wallace McIntosh. You could be like him when you grow up if you really put your mind to it.'

As a present for his first job away his grandmother gave him a kettle, a pot, and a heavy cast-iron pan for his brose. He worked for a solicitor who kept a hobby farm, Flock House, near Kinross where Mr Robertson, the unloved farm bailiff, yelled angrily if he saw a worker straighten his back for more than a few seconds.

One freezing day when the yard was covered in ice the boy slipped, breaking his leg in two places. He was laid on an old door, carried into the modest bothy where he lived, and left alone in agony. Much later, desperate for a leak, he urinated where he lay. When ambulance men arrived after four hours their saturated and malodorous patient had become seriously disenchanted with his employer.

After five weeks in Perth Royal Infirmary, he returned to Candy Farm to work for a while until leaving to become an assistant gamekeeper, winning prizes at clay pigeon shooting for a big estate. He remembers rowing boats for people fishing on the Tay and says, chuckling: 'One thing which interested me was how the women could sit in a boat for seven or eight hours without having a piss. The men just pissed over the side.'

Other jobs followed at different farms and he became interested in boxing, twice earning 10s (50p) for going three rounds with a hard-boiled fairground pug at a boxing booth in Perth. Boxing at ten stone, he knocked out his first six opponents after joining promoter Jimmy Blair's stable. He and five other boxers squeezed into a little car travelling to different venues all over Scotland every Saturday.

He was invited to turn professional, but the boxing was interfering with work and, at eighteen, after occasionally getting off his bicycle to watch twin-engine Ansons taking off and landing at Perth's Scone airport, he first thought about joining the RAF.

At this stage he thought less of the aircraft and more of the cheerful young airmen he had seen in uniform strolling about Perth, apparently without a care in the world. Men who did not have to worry about feeding themselves and having a few bob in their pocket. This could be an escape route for him.

CHAPTER TWO

THREE SQUARE MEALS A DAY

Aged eighteen, Wallace McIntosh's modest ambition was to have a regular job which paid a reasonable wage and offered three square meals a day. With that in mind he cycled on an old groaning bicycle nearly thirty miles to Dundee early in 1939 to join up and be part of the war that everyone was saying was inevitable.

He was working at a farm near the Perthshire village of Rhynd. The job was dull and he found his rut getting depressingly deeper. While daily becoming more detached from his childhood the adulthood of his dreams seemed more remote than ever. An entire lifetime to be spent on the land loomed massively in his mind.

His grandparents had retired, and were now living on the first floor of The Cross, a small dour house in Errol on the other side of the Tay. Still poor, they lived on the basic state pension, but were settled at last. They had to watch their pennies, but at least they had pennies to watch. The days spent trudging about the countryside searching for work were over, and their seven children were settled and doing well and they had brought up a fine grandson for whom they had high hopes.

McIntosh was now a slim lad of about five foot seven, weighing ten stones with blue-grey eyes which radiated humour, and sharp wits. His thick black hair and handsome intelligent features had almost certainly attracted the attention of several pretty young women, but he was shy, uncertain in their company and generally steered clear of them.

The first Forces recruiting office he found in Dundee was for the Royal Navy, which he used as a practice run before seeking the Boys in Blue. The Navy, however, quickly sent him on his way with a dismissive flap of the hand and a disdainful sneer. The RAF dealt with him no less severely, while offering him the courtesy of an explanation for their total disinterest by listing his singular lack of education, and qualifications and having no fixed abode.

A large beaming Black Watch sergeant boomed: 'We'll take you, son.' But McIntosh shook his head politely and returned to Rhynd sadly, his future in ruins, his thoughts dislocated, and the arduous cycle ride home appearing to be twice as far.

Despite the cold rejections he still nurtured an overwhelming desire to be in the RAF and to find the elusive security he craved. He went to see the Rev J L

Fyfe Scott, minister of St Adrian's parish church in Rhynd. Fyfe Scott was a kindly man who, after losing both legs in the First World War, became a restless champion of the underdog. McIntosh played the accordion at the church's monthly socials and they occasionally chatted about his eagerness to get away in search of a better life. The youngster had always been impressed by the older man's willingness to listen and was delighted when the priest said he would write a letter for him to take to the recruiting office. Fyfe Scott believed the RAF's main reason for rejecting him was because McIntosh did not have a permanent address. And although the lad had no examination certificates to flutter self-confidently under the critical eye of someone who had the power to change his circumstances, he could read, write and do his sums as well as any of his parishioners. There was more to him than could be adequately explained in a dry official certificate. He was quick to learn, resourceful, and would not let anybody down.

With a paternal twinkle in his eye, the compassionate priest told him he could say he lived at the manse. Back in Dundee an RAF sergeant read Fyfe Scott's letter, extolling the many qualities of the young man, rubbed his chin thoughtfully and said that because there was no proof his education was up to the standard required by the RAF for anything better, the only job which might be available to him would be general duties. If this interested him he would have to come back for a proper interview and medical.

It was enough. The venerable bike seemed to have sprouted wings as, overwhelmed with joy, McIntosh flew back to the farm where he worked like two men until his interview in Dundee came and went without a hitch. He then waited impatiently for the official letter with an enclosed rail warrant and the instruction to present himself at the reception centre at RAF Uxbridge where he would be kitted out.

He cycled to Errol bearing the incredible letter with 'OHMS' stamped at the top of the envelope and, eyes shining, told his proud grandparents: 'That's me finished with the land.' And they immediately celebrated with a cup of tea. Both old people knew this was an admirable move, but Grandma wept because she knew nothing about the Air Force and worried about the looming war, although the youngster reassured her that he had a ground job. Flying was not even a distant possibility.

In October 1939, McIntosh set off excitedly for Uxbridge, Middlesex, which seemed a terrible long way south when he looked reflectively out from the steam train snorting aggressively over the beautiful rolling Scottish countryside he knew so well.

Although he had an inkling that general duties in the RAF would not involve him in making any major decisions or shouldering any real responsibility, his optimism was sky high. He knew he would start as a dogsbody, but he was a hard worker, and not content to shuffle around for ever among the also-rans. He was on the way up. A new secret ambition, conceived on a perfect day that saw him travelling across the border into England for the first time, was to be, as soon as possible, promoted to corporal.

Uxbridge was a huge camp, teeming with airmen, most of them sprogs who had left home, probably for the first time, feeling anxious, awkward, uncertain of what would be expected of them. McIntosh was slightly apprehensive certainly, but not having lived anywhere for long enough that he could call a real home – although he would miss the wise counsel of his grandparents – he never suffered from homesickness. In future, wherever he was stationed was home. He quickly made friends who, after they had penetrated his crushed and vibrating Scottish syllables, enjoyed his abrasive wit and lively conversation. He chuckles softly at the memory:

'Uxbridge was quite an eye opener for me, although I was prepared for anything. Some of the guys who joined up with me were so dim, it was obvious they had never been over the doorstep. I wasn't streetwise, but I was pretty sharp and had moved about a bit. My adrenaline was flowing. There was always an air of expectancy, something bigger was going to be round the next corner. I had always been looking for something different and I had found it. It was an exciting time to have landed in the RAF. I thought: "This is my niche. This is me. I'm actually going to see Britain." I never thought of the world.'

The month before Wallace McIntosh joined the RAF in search of three square meals a day and something different, England declared war on Germany. At the time Bomber Command was gaining experience for bombing operations at night over Germany by dropping propaganda leaflets, McIntosh entered an Uxbridge dining hall for his first evening meal and found out what a fork was used for. In his previous life, he had used only a spoon and his fingers.

The food in the RAF was good, varied and plentiful. Even the porridge was tastier than anything he had eaten in Scotland. He was amazed to discover that he could eat as much as he wanted and, for the first time in his life, there was sugar to sprinkle on it.

Kitted out, he was posted to Padgate, Lancashire, where he and his unworldly sprog companions encountered drill and physical training instructors, and education officers, who were hell bent on turning squalid and ignorant young men into citizens of whom King George VI would be justifiably proud when he woke up every morning.

They were roused at the crack of dawn, hustled across vast parade grounds, encouraged to leap over wooden horses in a gym, yawned wearily in classrooms, while attempting to learn about the British and RAF constitutions, perking up when being warned about the hideous dangers of loose women and venereal disease. Even more importantly, they were urged to spend many absorbing hours polishing the dull scratched toecaps of their boots until they reflected their own glowering faces, to press their trousers so the creases looked capable of cutting down trees, and keep their billets so glitteringly clean that inspecting sergeants and officers recoiled from the radiance which threatened to damage their eyeballs.

Although disdainful of the tedious procedure of discipline and its wretched conformity, Aircraftman Second Class McIntosh stoically suffered the square-bashing and the RAF's obsession with spit and polish. Having been sufficiently disciplined at an early age he only needed telling to do a thing once and he would get on with it. It was hardly surprising that he resented the mindless repetition of 'left-right, left-right', 'at ease' and 'attenshun'. Never happy in the grip of conformity he conformed without openly criticising the tried and tested methods, for he loved his new life, but regarded the drill NCOs with contempt.

'Most were as thick as shit,' he growls scathingly, grinding up and spitting out the husks of another shuddering memory of overbearing bellowing NCOs. Yet, perversely, he accepts that they had an important part to play in turning out reliable and conscientious airmen. And a man who had recently discovered the delights of three square meals a day was not going to rattle the cage.

But he fiercely resented being called 'Jock', which he considered to be a derogatory and inflammatory name used by bog-ignorant Englishmen who believed every Scotsman to be another wild-haired, half-witted, bagpipe-torturing, porridge-slurping descendant of the least articulate and civilised man who had been misguided enough to follow Bonny Prince Charlie into battle. McIntosh preferred to be called 'Wallace', although 'Mac' was acceptable, but not 'Wally', for in Scotland china wally dogs, wearing foolish grins, stood on either end of thousands of mantelpieces.

On nights off airmen flocked to an underground dance hall at Warrington and danced to the exhilarating music of Nat Bookbinder and the Chapters.

At the end of these intriguing few weeks some young men went on to train as aircraft fitters, wireless operators, armourers, clerks and any number of other important tasks which would help Britain win the war. McIntosh was now deemed fully qualified to take on a miscellany of RAF general duties and odd jobs, any of which he could have done more than adequately without setting foot in Padgate.

This meant he would carry out guard duties, help the guardroom by escorting prisoners, load trucks, deliver rations and messages, in fact do, without complaint, anything that could be dreamed up by the officers. He was still at the bottom of the pile as he had been ever since he was born, but he was now at the bottom of a different pile. A pile with prospects. That was the difference.

Posted to the operational station of Linton-on-Ouse, near York, one of the RAF's more modern airfields, he felt as if he had been moved closer to the war because based here were 51 and 58 Squadrons and the men who flew the Armstrong Whitworth Whitley twin-engine bombers. AC2 McIntosh had nothing to do with the aircrews who were still regularly bombing the enemy with leaflets, but he spent many hours standing beside their precious aircraft toting a loaded Lee Enfield rifle, making sure that foreign agents did not sneak in and sabotage or steal an aircraft which really did have the unnerving reputation among the men who flew it of being The Flying Coffin.

Once he peeped into what he had believed to be an ordinary shed behind the mess and discovered perspiring officers clad in white singlets and shorts thrashing a small ball against a concrete wall. He had never seen a squash court before and while humble airmen were not allowed to join the officers in their play he thought it seemed to be a game which, given the chance, he would enjoy.

As an airman he took part in any sport that he found listed on the notice board in the airmen's mess. He boxed a little, played football and cricket, enjoyed athletics, anything which involved using up the tightly-coiled energy which was contained in his restless slim frame.

Hungry for education he joined evening classes, saturating his brain cells with anything that was on offer, mainly English language and mathematics. He was given sums and misspelled words to work on in his spare time.

'Things happened so quickly to me it wasn't real,' he says. 'I had luck ride with me all the time. But I always say you make your own luck. Luck doesn't come along and tap you on the shoulder.'

One of the characters at Linton was the stocky Sergeant Casling, who was in charge of the RAF service police, the SPs or Snowdrops. He later became the station warrant officer at Linton. McIntosh remembers him with a slight tremor: 'He once gave me a terrible bollocking for not saluting an officer in front of the guardroom. He made me practice my saluting fifty times. I became quite good at it.'

McIntosh was among ten general duties airmen posted to Harrogate and billeted comfortably at the fashionable Lancaster hotel in Cold Bath Road. Having settled in they were taken to the town's police headquarters and each given a .45 revolver and six rounds in a little cotton bag. They were taught how to shoot, but not told who or what they would be required to shoot.

This was at a time when hundreds of civil servants were being evacuated from London and despatched 200 miles north to Harrogate where they took over many of the hotels. The accident branch of the RAF was also moved from Whitehall to the attractive spa town.

It was soon made clear that the airmen had been given the not insignificant status of escorts to several thousand files, riding imposingly in vans which clattered busily up and down the Great North Road between London and the West Riding of Yorkshire. The dusty piles of documents had to be counted with earnest precision in and out of the vans, while the gunmen stood by, for if one was missing an Air Ministry inquiry would be speedily launched and heads would roll. The little convoy stopped at RAF Wittering on the way south and on the return, but whoever drew the short straw had to stand guard all night over the important cargo.

The civil servants, mainly women, quickly made themselves at home, whooping it up at regular dances in The Crown Hotel to which the young airmen were invited. One night McIntosh and three friends had left The Crown and were ambling over an expanse of open ground, known as The Stray, towards their own hotel, when they noticed two police cars and an ambulance parked outside the Lancaster. They learned from the crowd of bystanders that an RAF corporal had been killed after plunging down the hotel's lift shaft.

The unfortunate man had come from the Isle of Lewis in the Outer Hebrides, and next day McIntosh and another Scot from among the guardians of the files were ordered to escort his coffin, with full military honours, to Harrogate railway station. They accompanied the coffin on the train to Glasgow where the corporal's body was met by a grieving relative and representatives of the RAF. The two general duties men, having completed their gloomy duty, returned to Harrogate.

McIntosh was also among a dozen men posted in the early summer of 1940 to Drem, a big fighter station east of Edinburgh, in an area notable for its grouse shooting and fishing, but McIntosh had no time to pursue his former interests. Nor were they greeted with great whoops of joy at the guardroom, for they were not expected and no one knew what should be done with them. This happened occasionally during wartime in the RAF when great droves of servicemen were shuffled between stations and the original reasons for postings were lost or forgotten. A wretched clerk's indecipherable scrawl on a form might send an unsuspecting airman to a station hundreds of miles from his intended posting, but the only excuse anyone could think to give him was: 'It's one of those things, there is a war on, you know and anyway, you did join the RAF to see the bloody world.'

At Drem admin officers and senior NCOs shouted down telephones and banged a few heads together in an effort to find the original paperwork while clerical assistants fixed the weary new bods up with a meal and accommodation and attempted to think of something for them to do.

They were given beds for the night, but next morning, as no one could think of a sensible reason for keeping them at Drem, the dishevelled unwanted group were put on a lorry with their kit and driven to the ground radar site at Cockburnspath, Berwickshire, nine miles south-east of Dunbar on a headland overlooking the North Sea. Cockburnspath was a satellite of a big radar station at RAF Dronhill, which stood further south, on bleak Coldingham Moor overlooking the 400ft cliffs of St Abb's Head, and was itself administered by Drem.

It is possible that more security guards were required at that time at Cockburnspath, where around fifty radar specialists were stationed. Their top secret work was all hidden away from prying eyes in an underground installation which the inquisitive McIntosh would several times try unsuccessfully to visit. The only sign that betrayed Cockburnspath as somewhere unusual in those early months of the war was what to McIntosh looked like a big chicken coop covered in wire going round and round above ground.

He was not downhearted when he discovered that he was to be assigned to guard duty within sight and sound of the sea in a scenic part of Scotland. The new arrivals were placed in civilian digs a mile away at the tiny village of Cockburnspath and McIntosh found that his good fortune continued to blossom, when he and another general duties airman, Hector Baikie, were moved into the comfortable detached house owned by an enterprising middle-aged couple, Mr and Mrs Cribbes. They were the sort of people a still-growing young man with a bottomless pit for a stomach might choose to be his surrogate parents. They ran the butcher's, baker's and grocer's shops, and the post office. McIntosh, licking his lips at the glorious memory of Mrs Cribbes' large wholesome meals, says:

'They were wonderful people and had no family. Mr Cribbes was a quiet man. He was the baker, always up early, we hardly ever saw him, but she was a friendly sort, most attentive to your food and your clothing, which she washed and ironed, although she was not required to do so. If you were coming off night shift after guard duty she was always there with an excellent hot meal. She was house proud, often telling us to change or clean our shoes when we came into the house, but it was what I call gracious living. And, of course, everything was paid for by the RAF. Wonderful, just wonderful, a very long way from that miserable shed near Grandtully.'

Scots in the Forces far from home occasionally received little gifts from groups of kind-hearted women in villages north of the border. They made up parcels of knitted socks and balaclavas, one or two baked dumplings, cakes and scones. These were popularly known as Jock's Boxes and McIntosh received three early in his RAF career from the Women's Rural Institute at Tarves.

The Army was also stationed at Cockburnspath. Middle-aged veterans of the First World War manned four guard posts outside the twelve-foot high wire fence which surrounded the base compound. Accommodated in their own hut, they considered the station a soft posting, often turning up for the 10pm shift after sinking a few ales at Cockburnspath Hotel. They knew the work going on here was secret, but perhaps thought the remoteness of the base had adequately established its own protection. The guardroom inside the compound was operated by RAF service police. The Army and RAF liaised in matters of security. An RAF corporal was always on duty with a soldier at the main gates.

The following year McIntosh was promoted to corporal a good deal more quickly than he had anticipated. At first contented with his job he was gradually putting on weight and muscle, looking forward to one day getting a third stripe. Still a country boy at heart he enjoyed being on guard duty when it involved walking leisurely alone across the headland at dawn, looking down from a spot which he regarded as his own slice of heaven upon the beautiful Pease Bay where porpoises could often be seen playing in the sea.

It was here that he saw for the first time Spitfires from Drem flying in the distance. Fighter units from the south were sent for rest periods to Drem and occasionally used for coastal patrols, which were rather less lively than what the pilots had been used to. He imagined them streaking above Kent and Sussex, engaging and knocking down innumerable enemy bombers. While accepting he would not be considered to train as a fighter pilot McIntosh decided he could do more for the war effort by being an air gunner. Like so many young airmen he wanted to kill Nazis, but knew he would not get a chance to do that here. He sent off the first of several applications to re-muster as an air gunner, and waited. He had become an expert at waiting.

Pease Bay was sheltered by great cliffs and nearby was the tiny village of Cove where a handful of cottages clung precariously to the rocks, and there were caves, once used by smugglers. Top brass thought the long wide sandy beach, pierced by outcrops of large rocks, could be an ideal landing area for Germans and mines were laid outside the picturesque harbour from which a few fishing boats cautiously plied their trade. More rational folk believed the enemy were not so stupid they would be tempted to invade Britain by ferrying forces across 400 inhospitable miles of the North Sea.

One of McIntosh's jobs was regularly to inspect the four guard posts, making sure the men on duty remained alert and had not been lulled by the tranquillity of this quiet backwater into thinking that nothing unpleasant could ever happen there. Vigilance had not always been uppermost in the minds of the guards at this small but important station. However, McIntosh always carried a loaded rifle or a .45 revolver on his rounds.

The base's commanding officer was not challenged one night when he appeared unexpectedly at the main gate. He found the guards enjoying an extended tea break away from their post and, incandescent with rage, he whipped up enough fear for them to believe that Adolf Hitler, after working overtime at the Chancellery, had pinpointed Cockburnspath as first choice to receive the mighty spearhead of his invasion.

A few nights afterwards the super-efficient officer, not entirely convinced by the cringing apologies and promises of the shamefaced guards, sneaked in to catch them with their heads down again. They were ready for him. He was later said to have been slow at giving the password. A shot rang out and a guard's bullet smashed into the officer's shoulder. The incident was hushed up, but not that efficiently. Villagers were still chuckling about the CO's surprise sixty years later.

McIntosh was between guard posts doing his rounds one night when, as usual, he paused on the cliff top and looked down on Pease Bay. He saw something unusual bobbing in the bay, edging towards Cove harbour. It was a mine which had become detached from its moorings in the rough sea. He says:

'It was a great black sinister brute of a thing with the horns sticking out. If it had hit the breakwater it could have blown the whole harbour and little village to bits. We got through to the coastguard who sent a firing squad to sink it. A buoy was put in to warn off boats. I was congratulated by the coastguard for spotting the mine and later mentioned in Despatches.'

After the initial excitement of this incident had faded a second act of alertness by the corporal was met with a marked lack of enthusiasm at the base. A twin-engine Dornier 17 bomber created a stir one night in the spring of 1941 when it lost altitude and circled Cockburnspath displaying more than what could be described as mere inquisitiveness, before dropping a stick of bombs on fields between a farm and the base.

Three nights later McIntosh was talking to a soldier at the main gate when another lone Dornier slunk in over the North Sea and began slowly circling the station. McIntosh recalls the bomber getting closer, continuing to circumnavigate the headland, its ugly snarling engines drilling wickedly into the minds of people below, creating increasing unease and tension.

Much of the camp, including the Army guards, stared into the dark sky, half expecting the aircraft to come bursting out of the dark and blow them to smithereens. The soldiers clutched their rifles which were as useless as peashooters in this grimly unpredictable situation. In any case, everyone had been warned against firing indiscriminately at enemy aircraft to avoid revealing the position of the station. Two Lewis machine guns, with full magazines, mounted near the main gate on a pillbox, ostensibly for the defence of the base, were unattended.

Corporal McIntosh listening to the circling bomber thought it possible the pilot was lost. Maybe he had missed his target and was looking for an alternative to bomb. Even more unnerving, did he realise that a secret radar station lay below and was holding fire until he could bomb with pinpoint accuracy?

Waiting was unnerving too. McIntosh wondered if they were expected to hang around uselessly until the Dornier released its bombs. Thoughts raced through his mind, building up into a turmoil of anxiety and impulsiveness as he heard the bomber turn to swing in again. Everything happened in the fierce heat of a moment as McIntosh sprinted to the Lewis guns, with the cry in his ears of the Army guard: 'Oh, my God!'

The airman leaped up on to the pillbox and as the Dornier came over he turned one of the guns towards it, firing a long burst until it moved towards the sea, dropping its bombs a quarter-of-a-mile away into a field belonging to farmer James Hood, of Cove Farm House, who also owned the land on which RAF Cockburnspath stood.

It was the first time McIntosh had fired a gun since blasting rabbits with a twelve-bore in Perthshire. He believes the German pilot had not expected to be fired on and had jettisoned his bombs in fright before beating it back to Germany.

Corporal McIntosh listened to the ground-shaking thumps of the exploding bombs, smiled at the gaping guard, turned away from the gun feeling inordinately pleased with himself, and promptly fell off the pillbox, crushing his nose. He got up in a daze to hear the wail of a hand-cranked siren and men shouting. SPs were demanding to be told what had happened and the Army guard hovered, hunched and frightened.

A short time later a truck roared through the gaping gates and RAF service police reinforcements jumped out in a tidal wave of importance. They arrested two other airmen and McIntosh, whose grotesquely-swollen nose was still pouring blood. The other pair were released as McIntosh's nose was inadequately treated from the first-aid box in the guardroom.

Told he could face a court martial, his new world was disintegrating as he was pushed back in the truck which sped off to Dronhill where he was held briefly at station headquarters. Shaking his head wanly, he says:

'Everyone had been panicking at Cockburnspath. This was a new situation for them and they couldn't deal with it. Certainly, it was made clear to me several times that I should not have been firing that gun, simply because it was not my job, although it seemed to be a perfectly sensible thing to do at the time with an enemy bomber flying unchallenged above the station and the pilot taking his time to decide where he should drop his bombs.'

He was taken to Drem after being driven to Cockburnspath village to pick up his belongings and tell Mrs Cribbes: 'I don't think you'll be seeing me again for a wee while.'

Taken in front of Drem's adjutant he was told the threatened court martial had been quashed. A report of the incident had been given Group Captain Atcherley, Drem's commanding officer. Atcherley, a distinguished pilot who had flown in the Schneider Trophy air race, flung the paperwork to one side and growled: 'Scrub this bloody nonsense, there's a war on. We'll take the man off the station.'

McIntosh's stream of applications to be re-mustered to aircrew had not gone unnoticed at Drem. The group padre, who knew him well, asked: 'Do you think the time you have been at Cockburnspath is playing on your nerves?'

McIntosh replied: 'I want to get away. I'm fed up with the place. I want to get on bombers and be part of the war.'

His posting was handled swiftly. He was sent to Turnhouse, a fighter station, near Edinburgh. There was hardly time to put down his kitbag before he was admitted to Astley-Einsley hospital on the Braid Hills outside Edinburgh where his crumpled nose was scrutinised. A large piece of bone was removed by an Army surgeon, Major Guthrie. Years later McIntosh enjoyed delighting and horrifying his grandchildren by pushing the filleted organ flat against his face.

Wearing the light-blue uniform and red tie of a wounded serviceman McIntosh was among six convalescing servicemen released into the community for a day. Given free passes they took a bus into Edinburgh and headed for Darlings, a high-class silk merchant.

'They were wonderful people who every Wednesday gave a party and high tea to invalids. Cream buns, all the fancy drinks and a lovely feed. And then a bit of entertainment, occasionally a conjurer. It lasted about an hour-and-a-half.

'Three of us came out on to Princes Street. There were gardens below. We had walked on to Hanover Street and were standing there. Three wounded servicemen. One of them said: "Hey! Wallace. These three dames coming down here are having a hell of a look at us." He was right, and one of them, an ATS corporal came straight across to me.'

She was dark-haired and good looking. McIntosh, still shy of girls, hesitated as the young woman fixed him with a gaze which could not easily be ignored and said:

'Are you Wallace McIntosh?'

'Yes, why?' he replied, cautiously.

'I'm your sister, Flora.'

There was an awkward pause as the other pair, an airman and a soldier, exchanged puzzled glances, wondering how a man could forget he had a sister, while McIntosh, blushing furiously, suffered a temporary attack of lockjaw. They went to a canteen in the gardens and ordered tea and buns and Flora told her brother a little about the family he had never seen.

One brother, Gordon, was in the Royal Engineers, the other, Edward, was serving with the RAF Regiment. Both would survive the war. A second sister, Lizzie, was also in the ATS. To this day McIntosh does not know how a sister he was unaware of could so easily pick out a brother she had not seen on a busy Edinburgh street.

After ten days in hospital and an aircrew medical in Edinburgh McIntosh returned to Turnhouse in mid-afternoon. He picked up a railway warrant at the guardroom and, with another handful of men, caught the midnight train to London, where they found a bus which called at the Aircrew Reception Unit at Lord's cricket ground in St John's Wood.

CHAPTER THREE

THE SHARPSHOOTERS

Service police patrolled Horseforth Avenue, Bridlington, in well-polished clomping black boots every night shortly before the 10pm curfew which had been imposed by avuncular RAF chiefs seriously concerned about preserving the innocence of young men undergoing initial aircrew training in the Yorkshire market town.

Horseforth Avenue was one of several prim streets in Bridlington which had been commandeered for the RAF and while it was not thought the heady stench of rotting seaweed drifting in from the beaches late at night would alone seriously affect a wholesome airmen's ability to soak up knowledge, that and the town's pretty young women, persuaded on to a secluded stretch of sand in the blackout might have combined to distract them from learning with total commitment how to win the war.

For McIntosh, accommodated with eight other airmen in three rooms at a big house on the avenue in the late spring of 1942, Bridlington, built round a busy harbour, was not too dissimilar to a sort of Padgate-on-Sea.

Out of bed early every morning to march up and down the promenade, they were taken steaming back to their billets and given a minute or two to change into navy blue shorts and white singlets, before being harried, puffing and cursing, round the resort's streets. They ran along the beach which, unlike some stretches of sand in England, was not covered by great coils of barbed wire in defence against Hitler's invading hordes. They learned to run on hard wet sand recently vacated by the sea rather than the dry stuff above the water line which drained energy and made them wish they had thought more seriously a few weeks ago about their immediate future.

There were more lectures in English and arithmetic, and they learned how to strip and reassemble a .303in Browning machine gun until it could be done in their sleep, while gradually getting to grips with the strange dots and dashes of the Morse code, with the key and the Aldis lamp.

'Somebody was at the top of the Spa ballroom flickering away with an Aldis lamp, while the rest of us were on the beach trying to figure out the message. Naturally you would have some prick who knew Morse inside out and everybody would gather behind him writing it all down as he called out the letters. Until the corporal instructor shouted: "Shut up! You clever bastard." But we all managed to pass. I enjoyed everything, except the drill which was

27

mindless. I volunteered for all the PT displays doing hand stands, leapfrogs and all that crap to get excused from doing fire duties. Six poor sods were stationed on the Spa roof all bloody night in case of fire.

'Bridlington was a lovely town and had great bands. We went dancing every night at the Spa – which is where we had all our meals – or another ballroom farther along the front. I had become interested in girls by this time. I didn't fancy any, but enjoyed dancing with them.'

McIntosh and his eight companions were frequently absent from the billet after 10pm, but they were never hauled into the guardroom to explain their flagrant disregard for standing orders. At first they feared a large SP might be waiting for them at the house in the small hours twirling his revolver, fixing them with a menacing glare. Much later, some believed that even the SPs shared a revulsion for orders which restricted the boundless hormonal energy of young men who might be dead before the end of the year. Such restrictions were acceptable provided they could be routinely ignored.

McIntosh took a step nearer to getting to grips with the Germans on 27 September 1942, when he was posted from Bridlington to 4 Air Gunnery School, Morpeth, seventeen miles north of Newcastle Upon Tyne.

He saw his first Blackburn Botha taking off from Morpeth before being driven through the station gates. He watched it almost lovingly from the back of a truck, knowing this would be the first aeroplane that would lift him off the ground and help turn him into an air gunner. It waggled its wings, rumbled off towards the North Sea with another bunch of trainees and he had to get involved in more mundane matters like humping his kitbag off the transport, signing in at the guardroom and finding the Nissen hut which would be his home for the next few weeks.

He quickly realised that this was a very different Air Force to the one he had experienced at Cockburnspath.

'The people I was with were more interesting for one thing. I had got into a routine at Cockburnspath which involved little more than getting up in the morning, having breakfast, going up to the main gate and listening to tales of woe from somebody and funny stories from the Army guys, and standing around at the top of the cliffs. After eight hours it was back to my billet and asking Mrs Cribbes what was for pudding, then off to the only pub, Cockburnspath Hotel, for a lemonade, because I didn't drink beer in those days. There was nothing exciting about Cockburnspath. The people underground were doing a marvellous job, but the rest of us didn't seem to be taking part in anything.

'At Morpeth I was with fellows who had been to public schools and university. There was a sprinkling of men who had re-mustered from other RAF trades. They all wanted to do their bit. With my background I was really chuffed to be there and found I could take everything in my stride. When I went to a lecture I absorbed it. Some chaps worried over little things and swatted up at night on things like aircraft recognition, whereas I could relax, although we were being pushed as hard as hell.

'You didn't get to know people well here, but I had one good pal on the course, John Macmarine, who had just come back from Ethiopia where he had been a leading aircraftman armourer, flying as a gunner in open cockpits. The armourers had to fly when they were short of aircrew. It was pretty rough and although they were only meant to be peace keepers he told me about when they machine-gunned bandits on the side of the hills. When you went to Ethiopia you were pretty much stuck there. He reckoned the only way he could get home on leave near Dumfries was to re-muster as aircrew, which is what he did.'

At the end of May 1942, the RAF launched its first 1,000-bomber raid. Forty-one aircraft were lost, but damage to Cologne was widespread. Nearly 500 Germans were killed, 5,027 injured, and 45,132 bombed out of their homes. Similar operations were mounted that summer against other German cities, including Bremen and Essen. The war was hotting up and McIntosh desperately wanted to be part of it, but not in a Botha.

The Botha had been built as a reconnaissance bomber early in the war, but its twin 880hp Bristol Perseus X engines were under powered and although 580 aircraft were produced and some used operationally they were turned over to training duties from 1941 to 1944.

McIntosh became fond of the aircraft, although his affection for it probably originated from the excitement of scudding through the sky with Polish pilots who endeavoured to put a bit of zip into an otherwise boring job which had become a glorified taxi service for sprog gunners. Most of the Botha pilots were Polish, who had a reputation for liking women and booze, but they ached for their devastated country and feared for loved ones left behind. Many had narrowly avoided death in their escape from the Nazis and had no fear of danger, taking a wicked delight in livening up another dull trip with dash and, occasionally, recklessness.

Experts at low flying, pulling up sharply before smashing into cliffs, beating up church steeples and airfields, they brought apoplexy to the purple faces of top brass. The mad high-spirited antics of Polish pilots presented some trainees with more heart-stopping and bowel-loosening moments than they would ever experience on bombing operations. Not surprisingly, McIntosh, a free spirit who kept any unconventional instincts under control, thought they were great pilots.

There were few opportunities for killing Germans at training units, while mistakes could lead to tragic accidents. Two Bothas collided at Morpeth after one took off from the wrong runway on 16 November 1942 when, incredibly, only one man died. But on 29 March 1943 no one survived the midair collision of two Bothas.

The garrulous McIntosh picked up useful information while talking to other airmen more advanced on the course. He was advised to get into the dorsal turret first.

'This was helpful gen, because it meant I avoided going into a turret full of vomit. Four or five gunners normally went up together and we took it in turns to go into the turret. Very often a couple could not hang on to their breakfast or lunch. The smell in that aircraft was abominable and some poor bastard had to hose-pipe it down after we'd landed. I wasn't a bossy boots, but I always made sure I was first to fire the Brownings so I was in the fresh air, before going forward to sit beside the pilot for the rest of the flight and admire the view. I was very badly sick the first time I flew, but never again.

'A lot of money was spent developing the Botha as a dive bomber for the Royal Navy in the late 1930s, but it was a total bloody disaster because they couldn't pull out of dives very well, and we lost a few. Three were lost when I was there, including one which crashed on the runway. A lot of chaps died during training, it could be a very hairy business. But the Botha was not that manoeuvrable and fancy stuff was ill advised. But in straight and level flight it was fast and better for training than an Anson or an Oxford, which it could easily beat up. We got up to 275mph in a Botha, which had the same fully-hydraulic Frazer Nash turret that was the mid-upper turret in the Manchester and early Lancasters. That was useful for those of us who later went on to Lancasters.

'The Botha had two .303in Browning machine guns in the dorsal turret and one in the nose which was never armed. At first we did familiarisation, air-to-sea firing which helped get us acclimatised to the noise, the turning of the turret and pressing the triggers to fire a couple of hundred rounds into the sea. You watched for the splashes as the bullets ripped into the water. Later we had a target in the sea, and then we fired at a drogue, usually pulled by a Martinet, sometimes an Anson. We normally flew about 400 to 800 yards from the drogue.

'There was nothing that told you in the air if you were hitting the drogue, but we all had our own colour which was on the tip of the bullets and they left marks which could be counted. I was pretty sharp. I knew that if you fired a great bloody burst you were bound to hit it with maybe two out of fifty shots. But if you took nice careful aim in short bursts you would get two or three bullets on each time. That was the secret. I always got a score up in the eighties and finished second in my course. On aircraft recognition I was absolutely red hot, so much so that I was called in to instruct the Americans between my tours.

'Going up in an aircraft for the first time was exciting to a certain extent, although not as much as it would have been had I flown a couple of years before. It was the sort of thing which I had expected and dreamed about for some time. I flew with nine different pilots at Morpeth, most of them Poles, all mad bastards, but tough guys who could really handle an aircraft. They loved to fly and were great fliers. They didn't fly with a crew, just the trainee gunners. They jumped in and cried out: "Come on lads, be seated." They'd be taxiing down the runway before the door was closed.

'They were durable and obstinate guys, most of whom had fought their way out of Poland. Any who were caught risked being crucified because they were hated by the Germans. I don't know what the hell we would have done without them because they were doing a tremendous job while relieving some of our own people to fly against the enemy. But it was a miserable job for them day in, day out, up and down. It was no more exciting than getting in a bus and spending the whole day shuttling backwards and forwards into Newcastle. Flying started at 8am and lasted during all hours of daylight. It was a long day for the pilots.

'They didn't want to be hanging about up there and often said: "Get the bloody firing over bloody quick then we go for a ride." So we'd fire off our rounds and go hare-assing across the sea, beat up Morpeth and Alnwick, dart up the Northumbrian moors, along the Borders over the hills and heather, starting at 200ft then going right down on the deck.

'And all the time the pilot would be talking. They talked about the scenery, the speed they were doing and asked if everybody was okay. They were also preoccupied with what had been left in the back of their aircraft. "Come on boys," they would say. "Own up, who's been sick in the bottom of my aeroplane today. Do it in your battledress, but don't leave it in the aircraft. I don't mind you leaving money or fags, but not sick."

'I often drank with the Poles who all liked a dram. They told me about their country and how beautiful it was, especially the Tatra mountains, which stood in the south, below Kraców. They were very fond of the mountains of Scotland too, but said I must one day try to see the Tatras for myself. Many settled down here, marrying British girls, but I often wonder what became of the Polish pilots who took me up at Morpeth, including Sergeants Switalski, Szeckalski and Jadliszkie.

'A typical day at gunnery school would have about an hour on aircraft recognition, which was very important. They occasionally slipped in aircraft to fool you, like the Blenheim or Beaufort, which could be mistaken at a distance for the Junkers-88 because they all had the twin engines and the single fin and rudder. We covered tactics, gun sights and air-sea rescue with dinghy drill. This was important because if you came down in the sea and were still in one piece you needed to know how to get out of the aircraft, into a dinghy, and how to survive until, hopefully, you were rescued.

'We did our dinghy drill in a Newcastle swimming pool. The instructor said: "We're running late. Bloody well hurry up, the pubs close in half an hour." We had to put on the Mae West, turn the dinghy over, and get in and out of it. It took twenty minutes and there was nothing enthusiastic about it.'

None of the chaps anticipated ever coming down in the drink. This was an inconvenience that always happened to other fellows, like death and serious injury. Aircrews had a touching faith in their pilot whom they expected would extricate them from every kind of serious trouble. However badly they were shot up they would limp bravely back over enemy territory, wind whistling through great holes punched in the fuselage, both wings hanging on by scraps of groaning metal, to land at the nearest English airfield, just as the remaining engines consumed the last pint of fuel and died, drawing awed glances from passing sprogs.

What they did not know was that unless they had a combination of amazing luck and a truly gifted pilot a ditching aircraft would hit the sea with the force of a speeding heavy truck smashing head on into a concrete wall. It could break up and sink in seconds, taking dinghy and crew with it.

Baling out of a disabled aircraft was another potential hazard which was often treated by instructors with less zeal and resourcefulness than might have been expected. McIntosh was taught in a classroom, thick with cigarette fumes, the theory of how best to jump out of a crippled aircraft while attached to a parachute. The smiling instructor, with a flow of old jokes to lighten the situation, held a parachute up in front of his class, which he clipped to a harness in a demonstration of measured coolness, which did not suggest they would only be needed in a life or death situation. He said: 'If you are leaving the aircraft from the rear turret fall out backwards. Baling out from the tail door roll out and pull the D-ring after counting ten.' A piece of cake.

No one told the recruits what it was like standing at the escape hatch at 20,000ft with a great torrent of burning fuel reaching out from a wrecked engine to beyond the rear turret. Nor did the instructors offer advice for anyone who might enjoy the blessed relief of landing safely only to encounter the ultimate horror of being captured by a maddened crowd of baying German civilians, armed with bricks and pitchforks, wanting to exact immediate revenge on anyone who might have been responsible for reducing their homes to rubble.

Instructors were restrained in telling McIntosh and his fellow trainees at Morpeth no more than that they were getting into a dangerous occupation. They did not reveal that the odds were stacked heavily against their survival. Of the sixty-one trainees photographed on his air gunnery course at Morpeth in September 1942 McIntosh believes no more than six were alive at the end of the war.

The art of gunnery was a complex subject but by the end of the course they had amassed piles of notes having learned about such things as the trajectories of bullets, cone of fire, and different tracer bullets used for night raids and day sorties.

McIntosh does not remember much about passing out from Morpeth except that they enjoyed a dinner of hot pot that night in one of the town pubs and their NCO instructors dipped into the kitty for more than their fair share to convert into pints of beer.

He passed his final examination with eighty-four per cent, earning the remarks: 'Intelligent and confident', and signed by the chief instructor, Squadron Leader L A Simpson. McIntosh recalls his relief and surprise.

'Everybody was under so much strain with the hope of passing the course and the expectancy of where we would be posted. We all thought we were going to OTUs to join up with a crew on a Wimpey to train for five weeks and then graduate to a squadron. Instead, we bypassed the OTUs.'

Now he was a qualified air gunner, proudly displaying sergeant's stripes and a half-wing, with exactly eleven hours' flying experience. The gunners' names and the groups they were being posted to were read out slowly by a squadron leader to men who were pleased to have passed the course but anxious to know where they would be based. Most were despatched to Stirling squadrons in 3 Group. McIntosh, with his inquiring and cynical mind speculated that if so many new men were needed for Stirlings it was almost certain these squadrons were losing a lot of bods. He was relieved to be among the dozen posted to 5 Group, which was equipped with Lancasters.

In November he went straight to 1485 Bombing Gunnery Flight at Fulbeck, between Lincoln and Grantham. This was 5 Group's small specialised gunnery school which was used to pep up air gunners. He was there six days flying in Wellingtons with former Lancaster pilots, working hard on air firing and fighter affiliation.

Assessed as above average he was posted after the intensive training to 1654 Heavy Conversion Unit, Wigsley, during a period of stormy weather, and crewed up as a mid-upper gunner in D Flight with twenty-year-old pilot Sergeant Fred Richardson, a Yorkshireman.

Wigsley was east of Lincoln, just inside the Nottinghamshire border. It had not been designed with the comfort of young gentlemen in mind. McIntosh, shuddering, describes with characteristic bluntness the bleak station which opened nine months before he arrived, as 'a miserable shit hole'. It was as if the primitive conditions were deliberately created in the curious belief that airmen who were almost permanently cold, wet and uncomfortable would be good aircrews. They buckled down and did their jobs, but it was not easy.

'It seemed unreal that we were expected to live in such inhospitable accommodation. It was a terrible place, so bitterly cold as winter set in. There were no liberty buses and we didn't go out anywhere. The huts were bad and we had hardly any coke to put on the fires. The dispersal points were so far from the billets and the bloody mess appeared to be miles away. You seemed to be continually walking. We called it Stalag Luft Wigsley. It was overcrowded and full of clapped-out aircraft, which were no longer considered good enough for operational flying. We staggered back after training each night through snowdrifts, arriving soaking wet at our cold billet, where we had no coke and no wood. To get the place warm we tore down and broke up some of the rafters, and set fire to them in the stove.'

Crawling into their frozen beds there was little to look forward to next day because there was a shortage of Lancasters as Bomber Command struggled to build up the squadrons. Instead, they flew in worn-out Manchesters, the twin-engine aircraft from A V Roe, which was converted into the rather more successful Lancaster.

McIntosh wangled four days' leave to dash up to Scotland and get married on 2 December. He had met Betty Fleming in Cockburnspath at a dance in the village hall. Small, pretty and dark-haired she had been keeping house for her uncle at his farm. McIntosh's first real girlfriend, she was eighteen.

Richardson arrived at Wigsley from OTU needing only a flight engineer and mid-upper gunner to complete his crew. McIntosh recalls the curious business of crewing up:

'A lot of different chaps, including gunners, engineers and pilots, all of us sprogs, were put into a big room and we milled around together. None of the instructors or senior officers got involved. We were just left to sort ourselves out. I was looking for someone who I thought I would get on with. I started speaking to a rear gunner then his pilot, Fred Richardson, came along. We just gelled and suddenly, Fred had a mid-upper and an engineer, Dinger Bell. It was as simple as that.'

From Glusburn, in the West Riding of Yorkshire, Fred Richardson had matriculated in 1937 from Keighley Boys' grammar school with distinction in French and German. In early 1939 he was a progress chaser at a vitreous enamelling plant in Keighley, and did part-time duty with the Home Guard. Aged eighteen it was time to volunteer for the armed services. He says:

'My best pal, Geoffrey Dickinson and I decided we wanted to be in the Fleet

Air Arm, him as a pilot and me as a navigator. We were interviewed in Gosport, Hampshire, but were not accepted, presumably we had the wrong background and had only played second XV rugby at school. We volunteered for the RAF and were both sent to Cardington, Bedfordshire, in March 1941 to be kitted out.

'When we said we wanted to become "a crew" we were told the chance of one being trained as a pilot and the other as a navigator and being assigned together to the same squadron was virtually impossible, so we both decided to train as pilots. We stayed together until September that year when we reached the aircrew receiving centre in London, but Geoffrey was sent to the East Riding of Yorkshire to start his flying training and I was soon shipped off to Canada before being sent to 1 British Flying Training School at Terrell, Texas, about thirty miles east of Dallas.'

Richardson qualified as a pilot in May 1942 and his report included the encouraging words 'tempering dash with discretion'.

Too young to vote, but old enough to die for his country, Richardson nevertheless commanded respect from his crew. The strict discipline he imposed on them in the aircraft quickly bound them together as a competent team. From this discipline sprang mutual trust which was essential in the smooth running of an operational bomber, almost certainly more successfully than if they had flown with a happy-go-lucky skipper who wanted them to think he was a good egg.

His smooth boyish features masked a strong and determined character which impressed Flight Sergeant Middleton, the big pilot instructor at Wigsley, who reported that Richardson would try everything he was asked to do without question. This included cutting out one engine above the canal between Boston and The Wash, and flying on for a bit before re-starting it, displaying an astounding confidence at the controls of the creaking Manchester. Richardson's confidence soon spread to the men sitting behind him.

Middleton, who had completed a tour of operations on Wellingtons and Manchesters, enjoyed low flying and occasionally took them on a guided tour tucking the aircraft in a few feet above the same canal, grinning broadly as shrieking men and women threw themselves angrily into the bottom of barges, before bursting straight out above Mablethorpe or Wainfleet where he seemed to let the aeroplane pull itself up.

One night in the winter of 1942 they were called into the crew room and told a big operation was planned and all training crews at Wigsley would be involved. McIntosh recalls the tension, apprehension and excitement:

'Middleton told us: "Christ! This must be Berlin, one of those high-profile raids with a maximum effort." We were given a Lancaster to take to Swinderby where we were told to harmonise the guns. All the ammunition was put in, with the different tracer, the ball and the high tensile. The Lancaster we were given had seen better days. It was suffering badly from stress, in no better shape than the Manchesters we'd been flying.

'We had everything geed-up ready for an op and then, at the last minute, thank God, it was cancelled. Half those fatigued old training aircraft would have struggled to get to the target wherever it had been. But even on operational Lancasters I have seen rivets dancing and popping out of the root of the wings. It used to shake me to see the wings flex, especially during takeoff with a full bomb load. The point of the wing flexed about 3ft 6in. It was metal bending and you were sitting on it.'

Their first training flight at Wigsley was on 10 December and others quickly followed. Training was intensive. A lot of money had been invested in training crews and Bomber Command wanted its money's worth. Much of it was repetitive, but continual practice should make a man competent in any career which he is following.

Aircrews not only had to face many dodgy moments on a sortie over enemy territory. Taking off and landing were critical tests of a pilot's ability in the early days. Consequently, they had to endure numerous long sessions of circuits and bumps; taking off, landing and lifting off again. They had night-flying tests, cross-country exercises and bombing practice, often carried out over Wainfleet Sands on the Lincolnshire coast. One trip was to familiarise the flight engineer with the controls to enable him to take over if Richardson was killed, injured, or taken ill. It was unlikely that he would be competent to land the Lancaster, but it had been known for engineers or other members of the crew to safely put down a bomber after their skipper had been put out of action.

That Christmas was bleak, cold and covered by snow. McIntosh recalls:

'On Christmas Eve we played cards right through until Christmas Day lunch. It was snowing like hell, you'd get soaking wet and miserable walking the two miles back to the billet. We knew it would be a stand down on Christmas Day and at least it was warm in the mess where we smoked, talked and played shoot pontoon, which the Canadians loved. We had the occasional game of darts and Bing Crosby was belting out "White Christmas" from the radio.'

Exercises continued after Christmas, despite the wretched weather. McIntosh remembers sitting in his turret waiting for snow to stop falling.

'It was on 30 December, snowing like the devil. We were more or less grounded, but they could not afford to have a backlog in training, they had to keep the thing going. We remained sitting at our positions with the engines ticking over and I was playing "Auld Lang Syne" on my mouth organ in the top turret. The snow stopped, the runway was cleared and we went up for bombing and air firing practice. I fired 200 rounds, air to sea. We were up for 3hr 45min, came back, landed, and stumbled off to our frozen billet.'

On 14 January 1943 Fred Richardson and his crew were posted to 207 Squadron which was then based at Langar, about fifteen miles from Nottingham.

CHAPTER FOUR

HIGHLY-TUNED SPROGS

They arrived on 207 Squadron from their separate training stations pumped full of useful information. They were probably full of themselves, too. No longer the useless sprogs from the earliest days of service life when they knew nothing, they were now clued up and keyed up, ready to kick Hitler's backside. Yet it took little time to discover, to their chagrin, that they were regarded as the greenest novices on the squadron, for however much they knew about navigation, Morse, gunnery, how to fly an aircraft, and the rest of it, they knew sweet Fanny Adams about what it was really like going on a sortie. How would they feel going into battle with a full load of bombs over Germany through intense flak and being chased by screeching murderous fighters seeking to blast them into the outer reaches of hell? That was the real test when sprogs had to grow up and be counted among the statistics of the living or the dead.

Their total lack of operational experience was painfully obvious when the six who were NCOs presented themselves, white-faced and anxious, displaying crisp white stripes and nicely-creased trousers in the sergeants' mess at Langar for the first time.

The early months of 1943 were the most harrowing time of the bombing war when, routinely, bright-eyed young men, believing themselves to be immortal, went off one night and were never seen again. It was Bomber Command's equivalent of going over the top in the First World War.

The new boys regarded with surprise the assortment of aircrews, sagged, crumpled as corpses in armchairs, some with their faces covered by newspapers, a few feebly nursing glasses of beer, all looking as if they had not slept for a month or more. Within a few weeks Richardson and his six-man crew, cruelly short of sleep, would be looking no less wretched after spending many exhausting hours flying over Europe and laying waste to German cities. All this time hundreds of good men were being lost, making room for January's new boys to become – with a considerable amount of luck – March's veterans. Within a day or two they all knew of several aircrew who had been killed. The longer you were a survivor in Bomber Command, the more men you had known were dead.

A bomber aircrew was a team and when the men in it worked well together they became closer than brothers. But if one member of that team was flawed in any way the crew became weakened and the chances of them getting safely through a tour of operations were severely reduced. The pilot was the master key to having a satisfactory crew and bringing them together as a team. A weak pilot, who panicked in a crisis, could not respond instantly to a fighter attack, was a constant moaner, or someone who recklessly cut corners, rarely made it through a tour, which meant his crew were doomed as soon as they joined him.

Good crews were airmen who had taken aboard and valued every aspect of their training. They were highly-tuned fellows who knew their job inside out, looked out for each other and were proud to be part of Bomber Command's war machine.

Fred Richardson was a good pilot. Unprepossessing at 5ft 8in and nine stone he was quietly confident.

'Fred was a very strict and firm skipper, but fair and extremely calm, which was important in a pilot. I often felt he had a tough time because not all his original crew lasted the whole tour. And at this time we had very few navigational aids compared to later on. Gee was good and H2S was perfected during my second tour. Mind you, in my opinion, our eyes were the best radar we could have. The intelligence we were given about enemy fighter stations en route and where flak ships were lying would also improve later in the war. The weather was very hit and miss at a time when we needed a reliable forecast, knowing whether we could expect icing, for instance.

'A lot of people never came back to tell us about icing because their aircraft, having iced up, became heavy, slow and uncontrollable and went straight into the deck. It could be very frightening flying high in winter and coming out of icy cloud to hear the loud thumps of ice as they smashed into the tailplane. Ice had built up on the leading edges of the wings then broken off. At first we thought we'd been hit by flak or cannon shells. We normally came down to melt the ice. By the end of the war most aircraft had a rubber gadget fitted on to their leading edges which expanded and contracted to crack the ice.'

Richardson remembers his crew as 'on the whole, very good. The trouble was I didn't have a complete crew all the way through.'

It was not easy to blend such a disparate collection of backgrounds, characters and temperaments into a workmanlike crew. It took time and there was not much of that available on the over-stretched squadrons. It was a lot to ask of an inexperienced pilot to work miracles with men who were mostly older than himself, some being sensitive individuals who might still bear grudges stacked up against overbearing and aggravating schoolteachers, besides getting them safely to and from a grim assortment of fanatically-defended targets. But youth was the norm in Bomber Command, they all had to muck in and, hopefully, develop the wholehearted press-on spirit encouraged by senior officers.

Not everyone mucked in as willingly or as competently as their skipper would have wished. Richardson's first navigator, for instance, was not the ideal man for the job as he explains:

'While we were still at 29 Operational Training Unit, North Luffenham, we went on a night exercise which sent us over the middle of the North Sea. The idea was that you fly out there and after a certain length of time you turn south, then west, and when the navigator said: "You can come down to 1,000ft now", I said: "Fine."

'I brought the aircraft down, but instead of us going over Flamborough Head we were heading up the Hull estuary with barrage balloons literally all round us. They looked like small Zeppelins. Very dodgy. Full throttle and rapid upward acceleration was immediately required.

'I got rid of him shortly after we got on the squadron. He joined another crew who used to drink before they took off. The pilot, a Scot, forgot to take the pitot head cover off one night, they crashed on takeoff and were all killed.'

Richardson flew on A Flight with another four navigators including Flight Sergeant Vince Cairney, who came from a crew which had been dismantled after their pilot had finished his tour. Cairney only needed a few more trips before he had earned a long rest from bombing, just as his new skipper had got used to him.

He was later replaced by Flying Officer Ken Newby who had been posted from 617 Squadron and claimed to have flown with Dambuster pilot Guy Gibson. In his late twenties, Newby, who sported a large black moustache and smoked a pipe, was a quiet stocky man who lived in Bradford.

McIntosh recalls Newby with affection:

'Ken was well-heeled, his family were in the textile trade, but he was a nice chap and if we went anywhere he always insisted on paying for the first round. He didn't splash his money about although he did talk about holidays in Spain he had enjoyed before the war. Spain, Jesus! Where's that?'

An outstanding and confident navigator, Newby always sat down at his position in the aircraft with the casual air of a man arriving at his office. He just needed a bowler hat and furled umbrella to complete the picture.

He was a natural, reading navigational charts, swiftly working out positions and new courses as easily as more humble bods could recite their multiplication tables. It was comforting for a pilot to know that his navigator was on the ball, instead of worrying whether he would end up over the target or at the opposite end of Germany. McIntosh again:

'In dicey moments Ken could tell Fred quickly where we were and what new course he should be on. Once the aircraft was badly on fire and they had a job getting it out. Three voices spoke at once. "Bombs gone!" "Fire extinguishers!" And: "Two seven oh!" In other words the bomb aimer had got rid of the bloody bombs, the flight engineer had the extinguishers on and the navigator was telling Fred to get the hell out of it. Coming back there was no sense in hugging danger. Get in, get out. And if you were over Germany and wanted to hit England, two seven oh was the course to be on.'

The wireless operator, Flying Officer Ken Gray, a Canadian with a James Stewart drawl, aged about twenty-eight, was slim, gaunt, efficient, fond of a drink, warm-hearted and, like most of his crewmates, rather quiet.

Flight Sergeant Sammy Craig was not quiet. The thick-set Northern Irishman, who had a fine mop of wavy blond hair, came from Cloughmills, near Coleraine in County Antrim, where his diminutive father was the village school's headmaster. As a young man he lived for sport and had represented Northern Ireland in schoolboy rugby internationals. He studied dentistry at Queen's University, Belfast, for a year before joining the RAF in 1942, refusing to allow his active service to be deferred. His crew regarded him fondly as the wild Irish boy.

At twenty, he was Richardson's second bomb aimer and, after a night in a pub, the effect of alcohol was to apply a flaming torch to the fuse of Craig's fiery temper which often exploded back in the billet where his pilot was among many to be involved in brief brawls with the short-tempered Ulsterman. Richardson says:

'There were a lot of fights, but they were never that serious. Sammy would let fly with one punch and that was usually the end of it. He'd probably fall off the bed afterwards.'

Yet there was more to the high-spirited Craig than his inability to control the demons of booze. For Sammy Craig, who regularly flew at 20,000ft while lying on his belly peering down into the sky through the bomb aimer's compartment, was terrified of heights and could never steel himself to climb a ladder.

His widow, Jean, recalls his extreme agitation in their car on a family holiday, years after the war, when negotiating a narrow winding road which became increasingly more precipitous on a hill on the Outer Hebridean Isle of Lewis.

He never conquered his acrophobia and although he had briefly mentioned his fears to his crewmates which, in itself took immense courage, no one realised the superhuman effort that was needed by Craig every time he climbed into a plane. Nor could they imagine the dark thoughts which haunted him at times when there was a good chance he might be forced to bale out from a crippled aircraft.

McIntosh occasionally saw Craig look into the sky before an op and murmur: 'Jesus! Away up there again tonight.'

Craig innocently added to his pilot's problems when he went on leave. Living so far from the airfield he was allowed an extra two days for the journey between Langar and Cloughmills. Occasionally, the bomb aimer was away when they went flying, either on an operation or an exercise, and Richardson was given a spare bod, never popular for pilots who struggled to maintain a consistent crew and never knew if the new man would let them down.

The rear gunner, twenty-one-year-old Sergeant Grant Booth, a good-hearted Canadian, always shared the parcels of goodies he had sent from home. A heavy smoker himself, he cracked open the pack of 200 cigarettes for the others to dip into. There were cakes, too, and lumps of biltong – hard dried beef – which they chewed with relish. Whenever their aircraft was attacked by enemy fighters Booth and McIntosh worked together as a deadly team.

Their first flight engineer, Sergeant J K 'Dinger' Bell, whom McIntosh best remembers as having a big nose, only lasted a few sorties and was eventually posted to 97 Squadron. He was replaced by the dark-haired Ralph Fairhead, a Londoner, with a black Clark Gable moustache, who had previously been in the same crew as Vince Cairney. A former Halton brat who had trained for ground crew, he had re-mustered to aircrew. McIntosh remembers him as 'an absolute gentleman', a bit dour, but a chap he would not hesitate to turn to if he had a problem.

Richardson remembers Wallace McIntosh as a fine gunner and for his dry sense of humour. In the curious way one's memory has of tenaciously clinging to inconsequential fragments from the distant past, he has total recall of a NAAFI waggon arriving at dispersal during breaks in flying tests and his mid-upper, eyes gleaming mischievously, exclaiming: 'Mun, have a cuppa tea and a wad', in his unique interpretation of a Yorkshire accent.

There were no giants among Richardson and his crew, most of whom stood at around 5ft 8in when they joined the RAF. The one exception was McIntosh whose slim rejoicing body had responded so positively to the unexpected intake of regular nourishing food that, having gained a stone in weight, he now stood a fraction under six feet.

As a bunch of men they were not pre-eminent among their peers. Unspectacular, but generally efficient, sticking as close to King's Regulations as seemed sensible without leaving themselves open to horrid accusations of toadying up to the squadron commander, and hoping for the best. They were not marked out as obvious candidates for an early chop by the cynical prophets who reckoned they could tell instinctively as soon as they walked through the door whether a new crew would be killed within their first two or three ops. Nor was it possible to tell whether Richardson and his crew were destined to be long-term survivors. A chap needed considerable luck to be a survivor in Bomber Command and most of the time luck depended a good deal upon outside forces, largely those operated by the Germans. Richardson said: 'We all knew our jobs and got on with them. It was a complete team effort.'

McIntosh's grandmother wrote to him regularly and sent well-wrapped parcels of knitted socks and warm blue V-neck sweaters, but he had little time to reply. There was so much to do, so much to absorb in the new environment.

Langar airfield, which stood between the Nottinghamshire villages of Langar and Harby, opened in 5 Group in September 1942 with the usual three runways, 207 Squadron moving in on the twentieth from Bottesford, where its Manchesters had been replaced by Lancasters. It was the only operational squadron to be based at Langar where major repairs and reconditioning on the bombers were carried out on the same site by A V Roe, manufacturers of the Lancaster.

McIntosh felt comfortable at Langar where the crew's NCOs lived in a wooden accommodation hut, heated by a big black stove, although it was a long walk from the mess. Two other crews shared the billet. He says:

'I liked Langar because, having been a country bumpkin, wandering about all over the countryside, it was marvellous to go to places like Nottingham and the big football grounds. I was a great football fan and headed for Nottingham regardless of whether it was Notts County or Nottingham Forest playing. I was seeing different things even though I had been in the Air Force a while. This was new; this was big, and I had a shilling or two in my pocket. Newark was a nice little town and we had great pleasure going there just to visit the pictures, or have a meal and a drink and come back to camp on the bus.

'There were fewer aircrew at Langar, where we knew everybody, than at Spilsby, where we moved later. But there was nothing very jovial about Langar at that time where hardly anybody finished their tour from the New Year through until June. We lost an awful lot of people very early in their tours. Some of these poor guys came here after long training stints then one op and bang. It was a sort of Elimination Waltz in which you hoped you were left dancing at the end with the one girl on the floor.

'We had a good mess with a nice lounge and big windows which looked right over the airfield. We could see our aircraft, K-King, away in the distance, sitting right up against the road. Our dispersal was the one nearest the village. I often sat in the mess and saw someone going up for a test. There was always something happening. And although chaps were dying we had some extraordinarily happy times in the mess, often talking about nothing at all, as if we were living ordinary lives.'

However, there was nothing ordinary about the lives of Wallace McIntosh and his crewmates who, in common with all aircrew, were volunteers. No one in the RAF was press-ganged into flying in bombers, although their unwritten brief was, quite simply: kill or be killed. They never considered themselves to be professional assassins, but that is what they were and they were good at their jobs, as were the crews of German fighters. That, after all, is what war is about. The madness of war decreed that the opposing sides should hunt down and kill thousands – even millions – of their enemies.

Bomber Command was like a large family firm which traded in death and destruction. Business was booming. A quiet night in a village pub with your mates could be followed twenty-four hours later by the horror of a battle to the death in the sky. But more work was needed before they would be sent up on that first op. Richardson and his crew spent many hours training above the East Midlands during the cold early weeks of 1943. Skills needed to be honed, while gradually adjusting to the versatility of the Lancaster and gauging how far the big bomber could be pushed in an emergency.

The squadron had Mark I and Mark III Avro Lancasters at Langar. Both had 1,640hp Merlin engines. The Mark Is were made by Rolls-Royce, the Mark IIIs were Packard-built in the USA. The aircraft were otherwise identical. Maximum speed at 19,000ft was claimed to be 270mph, cruising at 210mph.

The Lancaster, with its four booming engines, looked like a massive aerial battleship although inside, the fuselage was as cramped as a long gloomy cigar-shaped corridor, packed tightly with equipment which caused continuous difficulties for men trying to get to or from the cockpit. Not an inch of space was wasted and only vital apparatus was aboard, allowing the maximum number of bombs to be carried.

The main obstruction was the loathed main spar which held the huge wings to the fuselage. It was difficult enough to climb over it to get to your position wearing flying gear and a parachute while the Lancaster was immobile on the ground. But in the dark with the aircraft badly damaged, diving helplessly towards the ground, possibly on fire while leaking fuel swilled about your feet as you were glued to the side of the fuselage by G-force, it became a nightmare of hellish proportions.

The pilot sat with a clear view twenty feet off the ground on the port side of the cockpit where an astonishing range of dials, gauges and controls greeted him as he took up his position. The flight engineer was a sort of pilot's special mate, closely monitoring the mass of equipment in addition to numerous other jobs, which included looking after fuel management, helping his skipper and peering out of the cockpit looking for trouble which could appear without warning at any moment.

He had the hinged dickey seat to the right of the pilot, although engineers often stood for most of the trip. The navigator sat alone with his charts, flight plan, protractor and dividers at a little desk in a curtained-off compartment behind the pilot. Aft of the navigator, checking his equipment, was the wireless operator in the Lancaster's only cosy berth, in front of his transmitter/receiver, beside the warm air inlet. Sammy Craig reached his position by squeezing under the engineer's seat and crawling down a hole in the metal floor to his bomb sight and release gear. On some clear nights he manned the twin Brownings in the front turret.

The bomber was a fighting machine, not designed with the comfort of its crew in mind. Roy Chadwick, the designer, had given the legendary Lancaster a vast 102ft wingspan, which could carry a heavier load of bombs than any other wartime bomber. The lack of comfort and low temperatures, particularly in the gunners' turrets, probably had the effect of more easily maintaining the crew's vigilance during a night sortie than plush interior fittings, snug central heating and easy chairs. The Lancaster was eventually the mainstay of Bomber Command, with a total 7,377 being manufactured, equipping nearly sixty squadrons.

In the middle of their steady preparation for that first sortie, McIntosh and Booth were unexpectedly catapulted into the war. On 4 February 1943 they were drafted into a crew which had both gunners off sick. Suddenly the war, which that morning seemed as remote as ever, had arrived with a shuddering jolt. Scheduled training was postponed as they prepared to be confronted by the real thing.

The two men were to be spare bods for a crew which did not welcome the pair with open arms although they needed them for that night's attack against Turin. But twenty-five-year-old Sergeant Pete Evison, their temporary skipper, who had been on a handful of sorties, was friendly enough. It did not seem long since McIntosh had ventured out of Scotland for the first time. Now, on this cold winter's night he was to fly across Europe. He was excited and apprehensive, for no one could adequately explain to a young man what it was like attacking and being confronted by the enemy for the first time, although he was told that the Italians were usually a much softer touch than the Germans.

McIntosh recalls little about the outward flight. His logbook records that they took off from Langar at 6.20pm. A total 188 aircraft headed for Turin that night and they were among 156 who would bomb the target, causing widespread damage. Three Lancasters were lost. McIntosh says:

'Pete was a pleasant chap. They were short of gunners on the squadron at this time and he was desperate to get two that night. Rather than bugger about taking one from here and another from there they took two from the one crew. Fred wasn't very pleased and neither were Grant and myself really because we had all been coming together nicely as a team. It was always difficult flying with a strange crew and Fred was aware that we could both be lost on that raid. We could have refused but it wouldn't have done us any good and if we'd decided not to go with them there's no bloody doubt it would have been held against us.

'Going to Turin was all right. It was quite picturesque going over the Alps. We bombed an aircraft factory from 20,000ft, although it was saturation bombing, bombing the city really. It was coming back when the trouble started. They were arguing noisily about the course we should be on after we'd left the target. It was a lovely clear night and I couldn't understand what the problem was. We had got to Turin without any trouble. The wireless operator seemed to have the most to say. He was an Australian, a dominant fellow. They were a mixed-up crew and I felt sorry for the pilot who had all these jabbering chaps around him each acting as if he was the skipper.

'Then over the French border Grant picked up a Messerschmitt Bf-109 that was following us dead astern and these guys all panicked. They were arguing loudly with each other about what to do next. As the wireless operator and the navigator all threw their bit in I thought poor Pete wouldn't know what the hell to do. It was bad discipline and I didn't feel comfortable flying with them. Nor did Grant. We normally never spoke to one another on our aircraft unless it was an emergency.'

The fighter followed Evison's Lancaster R5504 EM-P for about ten minutes and immediately after it disappeared a violent combat broke out behind Evison's aircraft. It was likely that the German pilot had attacked someone else having realised he had been spotted which, in an instant, had removed all the sporty one-sidedness from the situation. It was easier for a night fighter to notch up kills by attacking bombers which were blissfully unaware of any danger. A quick kill, then away for another one or two before supper. Nippy German fighters shot down high numbers of lumbering Allied bombers.

Agitation increased on the Lancaster when they ran into a severe electrical storm over France.

'I was quite frightened seeing the props whirling with sparks and static electricity running up and down my two gun barrels,' says McIntosh. 'It was also dancing on Booth's Brownings. The pilot told us over the intercom what was happening and we lost height trying to get out of it.'

Evison's Lancaster, running out of fuel after flying too fast or too high, plus the inconvenience of being led hopelessly astray by careless navigation, was diverted to Exeter where they landed with frayed tempers and less than half-an-hour's juice in the tanks. They had been in the air 7hr 40min. They were debriefed, given a meal and beds.

In bed that night McIntosh decided that if Evison asked for him again he would refuse to go, whatever the outcome. His excitement before taking off for Turin had been obliterated by the lack of professionalism displayed by the pilot and his crew in whom he had no confidence. The weather closed in later and they were unable to return to Langar until the morning of 7 February, a 1hr 25min flight which was uneventful. On 3 March Pete Evison and his crew were shot down and killed on a raid against Hamburg.

In the meantime Richardson, a good well-organised pilot, and his crew were blending together quite well, looking forward to their first sortie. In the next week the training hotted up with two bombing exercises off the Lincolnshire and Scottish coasts, a night-flying test, and a 4hr 50min cross-country run on the night of 11 February, which took them over Scotland at 20,000ft.

'The cross-country was to be as near to operational circumstances as possible. The navigator and wireless operator had particular things to do and we indulged ourselves with a couple of corkscrews just to keep our hands in. The following night we went on a bull's eye, a precision bombing exercise, which lasted 4hr 30min. We felt good.'

Next morning Richardson's name was on that night's operational list in the crew room. This would be his second op for all sprog skippers flew on their first raid as second dickey with an experienced pilot. Richardson had been to Nuremberg with Pilot Officer Charlie Soutar, an Australian. The boyish Richardson was elated to be in charge of a Lancaster. He says:

'I felt that I had achieved something, got somewhere and, I suppose, it was character building, but although I was very much a new boy on the squadron only one pilot on 207 ever offered me any advice. He said: "Fred, fly high, fly fast, and weave like fucking hell." That was Bill Ottley who was killed that May flying with 617 Squadron on the Dambusters' raid.

'I had done a leaflet raid over Paris, piloting a Wellington when I was on the OTU, but Nuremberg was a bit hairier than that. Flak was hitting aircraft at our height in front of us and we didn't like it. I thought all trips were going to be like that but they never were, although we had a few dodgy ones.'

Even though Richardson and his gunners had experienced one op tonight was different because this was what they had been working towards. But McIntosh would not yet fulfil his ambition of bombing Germany because their target, they learned at briefing that afternoon, was Lorient in the west of France.

'The whole station swung into action when ops were on. The first briefing was for the pilots and navigators. The others had their own separate briefings, and the gunners had a little chat with the boys in the gunnery section before joining everyone in the main briefing room. A sheet was pulled off a large map of western Europe on a board which stood at the far end of the room and we saw a tape leading from Langar dropping south and ending at a point on the Breton coast of France. Lorient, that was our target. We were told what was expected of us then the met officer spoke for a couple of minutes, but these guys were never very accurate. The intelligence man said something, and he didn't know a hell of a lot either. Then it broke up and we went away to the mess for a meal and waited, chatting to each other or writing letters.

'When it was time I went to the locker room to pick up my flying suit. I always had number eleven. The suits were brand new when I joined the squadron, number eleven was given to me and I stuck to it. I already had my leather helmet which I carried everywhere. I wore an electrically-heated suit over my RAF trousers. Over that went my gunner's Taylor flying suit which had big buoyancy pockets in the knees, elbows and collar, like a built-in Mae West. If you came down in the sea you were supposed to float. It was difficult to get on and Booth pushed mine up and over my shoulders and I did the same for him. We looked a bit like dead yellow whales.

'Under that lot I always wore a big white warm jersey, and the lucky grey, maroon and white scarf my grandmother had bought for me, and which I still have. I wore white silk gloves next to my hands and heated gloves on top of those. Finally I drew on a pair of big leather gloves, but I often flew without these because I needed to have plenty of room to move my trigger fingers. I had ordinary socks underneath, some of which were recommended by fishermen, and squeezed on my slip-on flying boots.

'While I was at Langar a consignment of ladies' stockings arrived for gunners to wear to help keep out the cold. We were told they were very good. They were dished out and some swore that they were really comfortable although our crew didn't wear them. I believe some Americans who manned their aircraft's waist guns, which were in exposed positions, wore women's silk stockings.' It is possible that scores of air gunners went to war wearing women's stockings although some might have ended up being treasured presents for wives and girlfriends.

'I tucked my escape kit into a pocket. It was a box which held things like silk maps, a compass, French francs, a tin of Tree-Sweet orange juice, Horlicks tablets and Beech Nut chewing gum. We picked up our 'chutes from the WAAFs in the parachute section and were ready to go. Our timing was usually so good that the pilot, navigator and the others were coming past as we staggered outside.

'We checked that the crew were all there and waited for the first transport to take us to our dispersal point. Sometimes it was a big lorry carrying a couple of crews, but normally it was a small one-crew Commer or Bedford van with a tarpaulin roof, driven by a WAAF.

'The navigator had a big green pouch for his maps and equipment. The wireless operator stood with a box at his feet. It was his job to pick up the pigeons. They were cooing gently. You don't hear much about the pigeons but they were very important, although they stopped using them later on. Sometimes they hadn't turned up and a little truck would drive round dispersals handing them out. They were stowed in their box in the aircraft near the navigator. The theory was that if we ditched in the sea or crash-landed somewhere we could send a message back by pigeon. They would fly back to their individual owners who lived near Langar. A lot belonged to miners who were keen pigeon fanciers. If we were attacked during a raid, back at base we looked to see if their box had been hit. The wireless operator took them to debriefing where they were picked up by whoever was looking after them.

'The ground crew were waiting at the aircraft which had been bombed up earlier that day, the ammunition belts were full and enough high-octane fuel had been pumped into the six wing tanks to get us to Lorient and back with a bit in reserve. Fred went slowly round the bomber looking at the wheels and so on to make sure that everything seemed okay. Then he removed the red cover of the pitot head which was in the nose of the aircraft. That was most important. When you are tearing down the runway it gives you your air speed.

'On another sortie, mentioned earlier, the unfortunate aircraft, with a full load of bombs, started its run before somebody noticed the pitot head cover was still there. They started flashing the Lanc and the pilot began slowing up, realised he was not going to stop before the end of the runway and opened up.

But he couldn't get enough air speed. They went a few feet over the end of the runway, crashed and blew up. There wasn't much of them left. The pilot's wife, who was standing on the Langar perimeter road, watched the bomber take off and come down again.

'We climbed into the aircraft and I went into the mid-upper turret after hanging my parachute on a bracket below. Grant hung his inside the fuselage, it would have been impossible to operate the guns with our parachutes strapped on. I had a hinged canvas seat which I pulled open and had a wriggle around to get comfortable because there wasn't much room. I got my hands on the Brownings to make sure I had sufficient movement. My finger would be on the trigger the whole time during an operation.'

Routine took over as covers protecting tyres from engine oil were removed and the trolley accumulator was plugged in beneath the aircraft to conserve its batteries. The four cold engines were started in sequence, coughing and spluttering, then Richardson and his engineer started carrying out a seemingly endless list of pre-flight checks which included altimeter, temperatures, pressures and oxygen regulator. McIntosh and Booth checked their guns and moved the turrets. If the sortie was to be extra long bowsers went round topping up fuel tanks after the run up.

The crew left the aircraft, smoked one or two cigarettes and chattered about nothing in particular. A Very pistol flare went up, signalling they were close to takeoff and they ambled round the aircraft and urinated on the back wheel. This became a symbolic act among many aircrews. When seven men were to be closeted in an aircraft for several hours at a time, none was that keen on making a mid-flight visit through a dark throbbing aircraft to the Elsen, the chemical toilet at the back. It was symbolism wrapped up in sound common sense. Pissing presented difficulties to both gunners who had to reach inside three sets of flies and stand in a curious crouch to avoid saturating at least one pair of trousers. At 20,000ft in the dark these problems were multiplied.

The pilot signed the required chit for taking over the aircraft, handed it back to Sergeant Ken Maynard, who was in charge of their ground crew, and the seven fliers climbed aboard, having stowed their cigarettes in a pocket, together with lighters, all of which had been officially banned from the bombers.

They switched on the oxygen before taking off. McIntosh explains: 'Some chaps switched it on at four or five thousand feet, or higher. You needed it at 10,000ft, but we turned it on while we were on the deck because it kept us fresh and alert. It remained on all the time.'

The oxygen would also clear the heads of anyone foolish enough to take his seat suffering from a monumental hangover: 'I've known of blokes who have had a heavy night who've gone out to an aircraft, switched on the oxygen for ten minutes and come back in better shape.'

If there were any jitters among the crew that night it did not show and McIntosh describes what they were probably all feeling: 'We took off as if it was a normal cross-country. It was our job. This was what we were paid to do. There was little sense of apprehension. If anyone was scared they didn't mention it. No one ever did. It was not the thing to do.'

CHAPTER FIVE

INTO BATTLE

The Lancasters, heavy with bombs, ammunition and hundreds of gallons of fuel, waddled clumsily along the 50ft-wide perimeter track like fat old women tottering on tiny bunioned feet in too-small shoes with bulky bags of shopping. Taxiing was a skilful business, using brakes, rudders and subtle bursts of power directed carefully into the outer engines. Aircraft had been known to stray from the concrete and get bogged down in the grass, interrupting an entire squadron's takeoff.

Later, Fred Richardson would earn the awesome reputation of being the fastest pilot taxiing on the squadron. The saying on 207, conveyed as quickly as possible to new chaps, was: 'For Chrissake, get in behind Richardson. Don't go in front of him, the bugger'll catch you up.'

No one, certainly not the other rear gunners, wanted Richardson's four props whirling murderously about their ears, fanning their Lancaster's blushing backside. The former pilot cannot today, at eighty, offer any more intriguing explanation for his spirited dashes around the perimeter than that he did not like hanging about and wanted to get off the ground as soon as possible.

Lining up at the head of the runway the Lancasters, each weighing nearly thirty tons, seemed to be arrogantly sniffing the air as they waited patiently in turn for the red light from the controller's zebra caravan to turn green. The ground shook as their engines echoed harshly over the damp airfield where well-wishers, including other aircrews not on ops, ground crews, a few WAAFs, including intelligence officer Flight Officer Joyce Brotherton, and admin bods, huddled into warm coats to wave the bombers on their way.

One by one an aircraft's engines were run up against the brakes before leaping forward under full power to thunder down the runway, almost to the end, dragging themselves into the air when often they appeared to have left it too late, inflicting mild convulsions on those watching. As the sound of the engines faded and the airfield was plunged into an uncomfortable silence the spectators drifted away, some into the messes, some to Nottingham, others to work as yet uncompleted. It would be a long night.

The green flashed and Grant Booth cried: 'All clear behind,' in case somebody who had just taken off was hurtling in for an emergency landing. Wallace McIntosh and some of the others waved at the small crowd beside the controller's caravan as they began pounding down the runway, the engineer holding the throttles wide against the stops. The mid-upper waited for the clink as the wheels came up, the aircraft lurched slightly when the flaps came in and they could relax a little as Langar fell away into the darkness. Taking off with a full bomb load was the moment McIntosh dreaded. If an engine failed or if they slipped off the runway it could be curtains for everybody.

Richardson hauled the bellowing W4171 off the ground at 7.15pm and began climbing. He wanted to get high, the higher the better. Bombing from the moon would have been perfect, but they felt safe enough at around 20,000ft, even Craig. It was an illusion, really, for the flak could still reach them, as could the waiting German fighters, but psychologically, they were more comfortable at that height, danger appeared to be further away, and their continued indestructibility seemed more assured.

'You were climbing like the clappers until I heard Fred revving back and knew we were up and safe and setting course. The only thing you didn't want to do was prang into somebody else in the circuit. And our circuit may have overlapped another airfield's especially if several hundred bombers were out that night.'

A total of 466 bombers – 164 Lancasters, 140 Wellingtons, ninety-six Halifaxes and sixty-six Stirlings – headed for Lorient where, earlier in the war, the Germans had established an operational base for U-boats which were a continual menace to Allied shipping in the Atlantic.

Maintaining radio silence the stream of bombers reached their operating ceiling and headed for the target, but not straight towards it, they needed to confuse the German controller with one or two dog legs to make him think they were flying elsewhere and, perhaps, send his fighters off on a false errand.

From the moment their bomber left the ground Richardson's two gunners became the aircraft's eyes. Other crew members also kept watch during an operation, but the gunners were expected to spend the whole trip searching the night sky for German fighters. It is difficult to imagine how RAF air gunners maintained their vigilance for hours on end. Their turrets were constantly on the move as they peered into the inky black night searching for something alien, something different, something which might already have marked them out as a possible target.

They hoped they would see nothing, while knowing that if they missed a dim movement which was a marauding fighter closing in for the kill they might all die. One gunner blinking at an inopportune moment could condemn seven men to extinction. McIntosh and Booth knew this. So did their skipper and the rest of the crew. It was a fearful responsibility and had to be their obsession. McIntosh sometimes had tears in his aching eyes from the constant searching which, combined with the excruciating cold, made him aware of his vulnerability. He quickly wiped the tears away with the back of his gloves. Search, search, search. Tiring, but it must be done and could save their lives.

'If you see, you have a chance. If you don't see, you have no chance, it's as simple as that. Even if your eyes were bursting out of your head it paid you to keep searching. Not everyone did. I've heard of gunners falling asleep in their turret. I know of some who, when they started to go below oxygen height would have a cigarette. Bloody crazy. You are not concentrating if you're smoking.

'It sounds boring, but I was absolutely focused on my job and that was to defend that aircraft to the best of my ability until we got back to dispersal. My motto was: *"See, but don't be seen."* It is possible that thinking became sluggish because of the cold, but I was tensed up, did not want to make mistakes and so was full of concentration.

'I had tremendous night vision which is what an air gunner needed. My vision is very good, even today, at picking up an aircraft in the sky. I was once told that I would make a good tennis player because I had an eye for the ball. I think you can train your eyes, but I could pick up any movement, just a movement.'

Flak was heavy and searchlights swept the sky as they came in straight and steady over the target. At this moment the Lancaster was a sitting duck for flak or fighters, but McIntosh, his eyes boring into the sky from all sides, did not see any enemy aircraft. The bomb doors were opened by Sammy Craig whose instructions never varied:

'Bomb doors open, master switch on, bombs fused and selected.' His words were repeated calmly by Richardson. Craig, lying prone, his thumb pressed lightly on the bomb tit release button, guided his pilot in.

'Left, steady, left, steady, steadeee, right, hold it . . . Bombs gone!' At 17,000ft the aircraft jerked a little and then, as more terrible seconds crept by, they remained straight and steady until the photoflash had allowed the automatic camera to record the effect of their exploding bombs. After the photoflash burst into the sky the pilot dipped the nose and began diving.

'He dived to get the hell out of it,' says McIntosh. 'I thought it was great, exhilarating. I felt very secure and thought: "There's no bugger going to attack or get me at this speed." We touched 360mph going down over the Bay of Biscay before Fred levelled out at around 6,000ft and we cruised back home, still searching the sky, until a voice in the cockpit announced that we had crossed into the West Country.'

They emerged from the aircraft wearing broad grins. The trip had taken 6hr 55min. McIntosh and Booth, delighted to be with their own crew, had noted the startling difference in discipline and attitude from their first op as spare bods. They enjoyed a smoke in the frosty air, told their loyal ground crew – shivering in their leather donkey jackets and oil-streaked overalls, who were delighted to see them back – that the aircraft was in good shape and undamaged, and waited for the truck to take them to debriefing as the four cooling Merlin engines ticked and tocked.

The raid had caused severe damage to Lorient which had already been badly battered by earlier raids. Some 1,000 tons of bombs fell that night, the town's heaviest hammering of the war. Three nights later it was blasted again by Bomber Command, the last in a series of attacks on the town after which Lorient was said to be knocked flat and deserted.

The effect of the raid could not be established until next morning when the bombers' photographs had been developed and Richardson was pleased to discover that they had a good aiming point photograph. In the meantime, debriefing officers wanted to gather in as much information about the raid as possible from the aircrews. Information about the bombing itself, and the

amount of resistance put up by the Germans. What was the flak like? Did they
see any fighters? How many of our kites did they see going down?

The truck pulled up outside the intelligence section's Nissen hut where fair-
haired Joyce Brotherton was one of a team of debriefing officers. Forty-three-
year-old Brotherton had been a school teacher at Fulbeck, north of Grantham
before joining up. She was known variously by the aircrews as a matronly
figure and a mother hen who showed genuine concern for everyone who had
risked their lives on the latest op, and for those who had not come back. After
the war she wrote down her memories of 207 and 44 Squadrons in an
unpublished book, *Press On Regardless.*

The warmth of her character led to Brotherton being adopted as 207
Squadron's talisman. She could usually be found among well-wishers standing
at the controller's caravan, waving cheerfully to departing crews. Her value to
the squadron took on a special significance one filthy wet night when she
decided to remain in the warmth of the mess instead of shivering in the rain on
a wind-swept airfield. That night the squadron lost several aircraft. Brotherton
was so appalled, and concerned for the young superstitious airmen who
remained, that she never missed another operational takeoff, whatever the
weather, when she was on the station.

'After being debriefed we chatted to other chaps when we were waiting on
the bus to take us to the mess for our early breakfast of bacon and eggs. What
sort of a trip did you have? See any fighters? Oh yeah, that's another one in.
That sort of thing. For us there was a little elation at returning off our first trip
together, but we didn't show that.'

It was a question of not showing yourselves up as sprogs while straining
your ears to pick up any little tips for survival or for putting one over on the
Germans.

'We walked back to the billet. By now the adrenaline was no longer
pumping. We'd quietened down. That was the sortie finished. I went to bed and
slept easily because I was very tired. My eyes were tired from searching for
bandits. It had been a long trip, but there would be much longer ones to come.
Benzedrine tablets to help keep you awake and alert were handed out before a
raid, but we didn't use them. I didn't fancy any of the after-effects. Besides,
some chaps took Bennies, the op was cancelled and they were left as high as
kites in the billet, unable to sleep. It was their fault not waiting to take them
until they took off.

'It wasn't easy getting used to the sorties and the extraordinary things we
had to do, but you got into a rhythm and a routine. You knew you had thirty ops
staring you in the face, you accepted that and got on with it, but we couldn't
afford to have any weak links. I was not normally afraid of anything except
being hit by flak. I hated the bloody flak. If a piece of flak had your name on
it that was it, because you could do nothing about it. At least you had a chance
with fighters.'

On 16 February they were briefed again to attack Lorient, but the sortie was
aborted because of engine trouble before they got to the target. They returned
to Langar having been airborne for 3hr 40min. Ten days passed before their
next op which was to Cologne. They took off at 6.55pm in Lancaster ED554.

A year before on St Valentine's Day, Bomber Command had received a new directive for area bombing on German cities. The main thrust of bombing operations was to be made against built-up areas, rather than strategic individual military or industrial targets, to shatter the morale of the civilians and, hopefully, bring an earlier end to the war. McIntosh remembers the trip clearly because it was their first visit to the Ruhr.

'It was the first real target. The Ruhr, Happy Valley, was everyone's hot spot. It was quite straightforward with reasonably good visibility, although we encountered flak going in towards the target. The target that night was the city of Cologne, make no mistake about that. We went straight in and dropped our bombs from 20,000ft. It was the first time I had seen a German town burning and it looked good.' Total casualties in Cologne were 109 dead, over 150 injured and 6,322 lost their homes.

Ops were much more traumatic than McIntosh had anticipated, especially in the Ruhr. He had not realised there would be so much flak, so many fighters and such a high number of bombers on fire with men trapped inside falling earthwards, and towns consumed by flames.

'It was frightening and horrifying and I was part of it, but I told myself that if I was going to survive I had to detach myself from it, and that is what I did.'

Of the 55,500 men who died while flying in Bomber Command about 18,000 were air gunners. This should not be a surprising statistic. They sat in hideously exposed positions, almost as if they had been planted there to draw the wicked fire of the German fighters away from the bombers' wing fuel tanks and the crowded thirty-three-foot long bomb bays. The Germans regarded them with a healthy respect for although the RAF gunners' .303in Brownings were no match for the more heavily-armed enemy aircraft, their bullets could still kill a man and bring down a fighter.

The Germans favoured surprise attacks, darting in from the rear, blasting at the unprotected bellies of the bombers. Many tail-end Charlies, not surprisingly, thought the Germans were first trying to kill them, breaching the Lancaster's first resistance, before snuffing out their aircraft. Not so. It was just unfortunate that the rear gunner was in their line of fire. The fighter pilot's ambition was to knock down as many invading bombers in a night as he could. They enjoyed the prestige of being acclaimed as fighter aces.

The mid-upper gunner had the best all-round view, although many men died in the top turret when their bomber caught fire and flames rushed below through the fuselage.

'It was bloody cold being a gunner,' says McIntosh, who can still shiver grimly at the memory of squeezing into a wartime turret. 'If it had not been for the electrically-heated suits we'd have had it. But the cold and the cramped conditions never bothered me. Some chaps had occasional problems with their flying suits but my number eleven always worked well. We got into some dodgy situations which caused apprehension, but I never let it cross my mind that I wouldn't be back. When we climbed into the aircraft we were totally focused on coming back and nothing was going to stop us regardless of what the hell was thrown at us. We were prepared for any emergencies and any unusual situation and I think that is why we got through.

'There were very few veteran gunners at Langar at this time who might have passed on a few tricks of the trade, but I observed all that I could. An old pilot there, who might have been about twenty-five, told me: "Experience comes through operations". And there's no question that he was right. You could teach chaps everything, but the situation in the air on a sortie was entirely different. Each operation was different. Each crew faced different experiences to the others every night. Experience was the only thing providing that you had done your homework and you were prepared for the unexpected. It was the unexpected that you were looking for all the time.

'And we were weaving – banking from side to side – all the time during a sortie. Fred weaved in a V so we could see underneath the aircraft which was most important. Grant and I were looking, so was Sammy who had his face down on the perspex panel in the nose. We knew that was the area where the fighters would attack, but it was a tiring manoeuvre for the pilot and there was always a danger of straying a few degrees off course. It was great to look down the side from the top turret. Grant, in the rear turret, was looking level and down, Sammy Craig in the nose and I were looking underneath and if there was someone in the astrodome, normally the flight engineer, he would be looking to see if anything was happening above. We started weaving as we came up to the Dutch coast and while crossing Germany. Coming back we stopped weaving over the Channel after leaving the flak ships behind.'

Two nights after tasting the delights of Cologne they were sent to France again. The target was the port of St Nazaire on the Loire, south-east of Lorient. Lifting off from Langar at 6.45pm they joined another 436 aircraft in hammering a second U-boat base. Five bombers were lost in a raid which caused considerable destruction. Many bombs struck the port area and over half the town was destroyed. Richardson encountered no real problems on this op, nor on the sortie on 3 March when they were sent north to Hamburg. The German inland port would be more menacing when they revisited the city that summer.

Next morning spirits were high when they left on their first leave from Langar. McIntosh picked up his railway warrant and a pass for six days at the orderly room.

'The train was packed as usual, and I stood in the crowded corridor from Grantham to Edinburgh. A soldier said: "You're going home on leave, son?" I said: "Yeah, not so much of the 'son', I was in Hamburg last night." He was a sergeant, an old sweat. He never spoke to me again.'

He arrived in Errol at his grandparents' home on 5 March where next day his first child, Frances, was born. Since their marriage his wife, Betty, had been living with McIntosh's grandparents on the second floor of the small terraced house in The Square. When he was home McIntosh lived with his wife and daughter in one room. The one other room served as the kitchen/scullery and the Hendry's bedroom. Heating, cooking and lighting was by paraffin stoves and lamps. Water was carried into the house from a tap outside in the yard where stood the toilet and big wash-house which had a fire-heated copper for washing clothes. Toilet and wash-house were also used by other families. Before his marriage McIntosh had climbed the narrow winding stair to sleep in the small attic, lit only by a skylight, now used for storage. It was a far from ideal arrangement putting McIntosh's relationship with Betty under great strain.

Bearing in mind the precarious nature of her grandson's employment, the level-headed Mrs Hendry thought it would be wise to have Frances baptised before he went back to war. Within three days of the birth she summoned a Church of Scotland minister to their tiny home and he performed the ceremony with Betty, still in bed, holding the baby.

Whenever McIntosh went home he almost expected his grandparents to have changed to reflect his new circumstances, although he was relieved that they had not. They were enjoying the present as a breath of fresh air, although it was less easy for older people to shake off a miserable past than it was for the young. They were inordinately proud of their grandson, but he had joined a world of which they could never really be a part and the gap between his way of life and theirs was continuing to widen. No longer tired he welcomed his return to Langar where he had good friends and camaraderie which he had missed and there was the expectancy of going on more ops.

Back at Langar they were flung into a succession of night flying tests, bombing exercises, and formation flying, the last of which no one enjoyed for everybody was so bad at it, not returning to operations until 22 March when they were sent back to St Nazaire.

At briefing the weather man said thick fog was expected to creep through Nottinghamshire later that night and on their return they should be prepared to be diverted to Lossiemouth in the north of Scotland. This was a prospect they viewed with dismay, even McIntosh preferring the cold comfort of his billet at Langar to the uncertain flatlands of Morayshire, and the ritual drenching of the back wheel was conducted with more vehemence than usual.

Richardson was at the controls of ED550 K-King when they pulled away from Langar at 7.30pm. Over 350 aircraft set off for St Nazaire, although 3 Group recalled all but eight of its sixty-three Stirlings before they reached the target. The remaining 283 accurately bombed the port area. They included K-King of 207 Squadron which roared back over the Channel expecting to receive a call to take them on the long haul to Lossiemouth.

They were near Plymouth when wireless operator Ken Gray picked up a signal telling them to divert to Netheravon, Wiltshire. Richardson remembers the difficulties of that night:

'We managed to find the area but couldn't get any reply from them. Eventually Boscombe Down picked up our call and suggested we diverted to them. As we came in to land I could see that although the runway was lit up it was uneven grass, not Tarmac. We landed at 12.28am, were directed to a dispersal point and left the aircraft there overnight.

'When we got back to the bomber in daylight we found we'd been parked nose down on a very steep slope at the bottom of which was one of Boscombe's special experimental planes. If our brakes had failed we would have gone straight through it.'

Sorties now came thick and fast. On 26 March they went to Duisburg. Richardson had to abort the raid after a bad fire had put one engine out of action giving the pilot enough doubts to pull out before getting to the target.

The next night McIntosh celebrated his twenty-third birthday by flying to Berlin for the first time. They were in W4171 while their regular aircraft was being repaired. Just before midnight, nearly three hours after takeoff, Ken Gray murmured over the intercom: 'Happy Birthday, Wallace.' The wireless operator demurred from wishing the gunner many happy returns in case it brought bad luck to them all.

Nine aircraft: four Halifaxes, three Lancasters and two Stirlings did not get home that night. Richardson's Lancaster made it back to Langar, but only after a couple of breathless skirmishes.

Leaving the target which they had bombed at 20,000ft they were attacked by a Messerschmitt Bf-109 which hurtled in from the rear. McIntosh, recalling a spectacular surge of adrenaline, says:

'It was a big city to go across and I was surprised that it seemed to be defended less intensely than targets in the Ruhr where you were passing over a lot of territory and knew that flak would be thrown up at you all the time. Then we were attacked by the night fighter.

'He was above us during the attack. We dived and came up then he went down and was below us when Grant Booth let rip from the rear turret. The fighter caught fire and exploded. We were untouched.

'About a minute later, just as we'd straightened up after losing about 4,000ft we were attacked by another 109. It came in from the rear and we both fired away at him. I could see Booth's tracer going right through the fighter then he disappeared underneath us and was invisible to me, but Booth had nailed him. We claimed it as damaged and it was later confirmed as destroyed.'

That night's target had been the centre of Berlin but the raid was accepted as a failure with both areas marked by the Pathfinders falling short of the city. W4171 had been airborne for 7hr 55min.

By their tenth sortie, on 29 March, Richardson and his crew were considered to be veterans. Their main qualification for such lofty status was that they were still alive, having joined the squadron less than three months ago. They were tired veterans, inured to the constant pounding of four engines in their ears, the rattle of flak against their aircraft, the intense cold, the lack of sleep, and the enemy's obsession to shoot them out of the sky. Now, back in their favourite ED550 EM K-King, they were told to return to Berlin. It was their longest trip so far: 8hr 20min.

The attack against the German capital was unsatisfactory with most bombs from over 300 aircraft falling in the countryside while getting there was not made any easier by icing and the met men's wind forecast being wide of the mark. The Pathfinders' marking was too far south, the main force arrived late and twenty-one aircraft were lost.

'I believe that March to May 1943 were the roughest months I can remember. The flak was heavy and the losses were high. You just carried on, night after bloody night, not wanting to hear too much about the statistics, really. It was quite traumatic at that time. In those days we were maybe only putting out eight or nine aircraft for an op because there was a shortage of bombers, so many were being shot down and crews killed. If you lost two that was a hell of a lot. And everyone was so young. Today they would appear in a juvenile court if they made a mistake or upset someone.'

The Richardson crew had not been long at Langar before familiar faces disappeared from the mess and new ones, fresh-faced and eager, turned up, the odds heavily stacked against them being alive in a month or two. In March 1943 twenty-six aircrew from 207 Squadron were killed, another thirteen became prisoners of war, and two successfully evaded the Germans to find their way back to England.

No counsellors were available sixty years ago to deal with traumatised aircrew who were left to cope with the horrors of war the best they could. Occasionally men cracked up on squadrons after sustaining the constant stresses of operational bombing. Instead of being pitied and helped to rebuild their dilapidated emotions many were treated harshly. The dreaded letters 'LMF' – Lack of Moral Fibre – were stamped at the end of their logbooks, they were usually reduced in rank, often to AC2 when they were given the filthiest most humbling of jobs at another RAF station. Some, whose nerve had gone, but were highly regarded, were protected by their skippers or squadron commanders, allowed to keep their rank and dignity and given ground jobs elsewhere. Wallace, who agrees with many Bomber Command veterans about the insensitive treatment of broken men, says: 'They were treated pretty rough, which was totally unnecessary and so humiliating. Men like that should just have been taken off operations without any recriminations.'

The Battle of the Ruhr, which ran for a year from the spring of 1943, was in full swing on 3 April when Richardson's Lancaster was among 348 aircraft sent to bomb Essen, home of the giant Krupp armament complex.

Richardson did not make it to Essen after a mechanical failure caused the starboard outer engine to be swamped by fire which the engineer could not put out with the extinguishers. The pilot said: 'Okay, we're going down, we'll blow it out.' McIntosh says:

'My heart dropped when they couldn't get the fire out. Flames from the engine were going past the tail plane, it was very frightening. When Fred said he was going down my mind, for a second, flashed up all kinds of images and I even thought: "Is he going to try and land this thing with the engine burning?" Then I realised why he was diving and G-force was pinning me to my seat. The fire went out but we had lost so much height and were well off track that Fred decided to abort the op.'

The burned-out engine had worked the mid-upper turret and a frustrated and fuming McIntosh was forced to spend the rest of the flight peering out as an unarmed observer. Shortly after they had landed the crew were told they would be up again the following night.

Thick cloud and strong winds made marking difficult on 4 April for the Pathfinders over Kiel which endured an onslaught from nearly 600 aircraft, but little damage was done to the seaport on a night which McIntosh regarded as a straightforward op with little to report apart from a lot of flak coming up as they cleared the German coast.

Four nights later they returned to the Ruhr. Their target was the industrial city and river port of Duisburg.

'It was a tough trip. There was very heavy flak being pumped up from a city which always seemed to take us ages to go over. We appeared to be sitting there for ever and not making much progress. The city was covered by cloud this night but we went to Duisburg several times. I liked it when the lights from the fires below were behind me and we were on our way home.'

They were touching 200mph and while Duisburg seemed to be drawing them into eternity it seemed they were only crawling and he almost felt that someone should get out and push them along more quickly.

They went back to Duisburg twenty-four hours later when cloud cover was still in place and, like the previous night, bombs were widely scattered.

The raid on the Italian port of La Spezia on 13 April was more successful, although the flight was exhausting for the crews. Richardson's Lancaster, ED600, left Langar at 8.20pm and touched down there at 6.50am. McIntosh recalls:

'There was a lot of flak there, that was all, but you had to watch out for fighters on the way back. Ju-88s particularly floated about north of Italy which was a famous corner for them. We had a good aiming point photo of shipping in the harbour so we must have hit something. This was the only time I had a smoke on the aircraft. I just had a couple of puffs about half-an-hour from Langar. We were all very tired.

'By the time we had been debriefed, taken for our breakfasts, and walked a mile and a half to our billets, it must have been nearly lunchtime. Then we were called out again in mid-afternoon. We were on again that night having had very little sleep since getting back from La Spezia.'

It was not easy, even for young men, to shake off the heaviness in their heads as they took off at the uncivilised time of 10.15pm for Stuttgart. It was like a dire non-alcoholic hangover. Wallace McIntosh took deep breaths of oxygen to fight off any inclination for his eyes to close and was soon back in normal search mode. He later described this sortie as 'a hairy kind of a trip'.

They had bombed the target and were pointing to the west when a Ju-88 showed an unhealthy interest in putting them to sleep for good.

'He came in from dead astern, then dodged off to have a look at us, came back underneath and was picked up by Sammy Craig. We assumed it was the same fighter because all this happened within the space of five minutes. He attacked us from the rear again, disappeared, and came in off the port side, almost level with our Lanc. The navigator looked out of the astrodome and could see him when he came in the last time on the port side.

'Grant certainly rattled his stuffing I can tell you. He got a great shot at him as he banked in and I was also pouring bullets into the fighter. We were down to about 6,000ft when he went away in definite trouble. We assumed he had been badly hit and claimed it as a probable. Later several other bombers confirmed at debriefings that it had been shot down and the probable became a definite.'

Their job done they roared back to England. They remained alert but their mood was lighter. Half-way across the North Sea, at 8,000ft, Fred Richardson's voice over the intercom was chirpy.

'Okay boys, time for a fag.'

CHAPTER SIX

JOINING THE TOFFS

A curious spluttering burst through the intercom as they headed smartly away from the burning Prussian town of Stettin. It was the sort of noise a man might make who, having fallen asleep in a deep soothing bath, had been propelled forward and under by the magical properties of an unsatisfactory dream before swallowing a large bar of soap. The sound turned into mangled gurgles of disbelief, then a loud roar of exasperation, and at last a withering complaint, impregnated with much outraged suffering, from Sammy Craig.

'*Fred*, I'm soaking wet.' Having allowed his skipper a distracted moment to digest this morsel of the bomb aimer's extreme discomfort in the nose of the Lancaster Craig added, plaintively: 'Can you go up a bit?'

On 20 April 1943 they had left Langar at 9.30pm and headed north with over 400 aircraft hugging the sea. There were two targets that moonlit night. One was Stettin which, with its shipbuilding yards, stood on the Oder, thirty miles from the Baltic. The second, eight miles south of the Baltic, was the port of Rostock, on the Warnow, home to the Heinkel factory. They turned east across the bottom of Denmark and began following the contours of the land until more than eighty Stirlings turned south over the Baltic to bomb Rostock. The others, Lancasters, Halifaxes and Stirlings, continued east.

'Early in my first tour I didn't like dark nights because it was so difficult to see anything. I liked to see everything around us. People used to run shit scared of moonlight. I didn't, I loved it because we could see – and it was a fifty-fifty battle then. There's nothing worse than the enemy you can't see. It was a lovely clear night and we were right down on the deck over Denmark, to avoid the enemy radar. Christ we were low, and really pelting on, we were even going underneath Stirlings. Mind you, I might have enjoyed low flying more if I'd been in the cockpit and could see where we were going. If we'd hit anything there was no way to escape for Grant and I. But Fred was an expert, my God he could really put her down. I could see the outline of villages and houses quite clearly.

'German gunners in flak towers on the mainland were actually firing down at some of our bombers. There was a lot of light flak, but none of it caught us. A Stirling was shot down 300 yards behind us as we were crossing one of the Danish islands. We also passed a Stirling, a big black monster, on our starboard side, slightly above us, about 500 yards away. There was a burst of fire from the ground and whup! The shells raked into it, turning it over and the bomber smashed into the deck, exploding in a ball of flames. The crew didn't have a hope in hell. We knew fighters wouldn't be about because we were so low, but we still kept watch on both beams and above.'

With experience McIntosh became more comfortable on sorties shrouded in the darkest night and the following year, on daylight raids, he decided that on the whole he felt rather more secure on night operations.

Heading for Stettin at a height of less than 200ft the pilot needed all his concentration to keep the Lancaster out of trouble. He was helped by the flight engineer and the bomb aimer who teamed up to give their skipper early warnings of church steeples, rises in the land, and the glint of high-tension electric cables strung out like giant garrotting wires between high-stepping pylons. Fred Richardson recalls leapfrogging the cables and how the amazing Lancaster responded to his touch of the controls, even with its belly packed with heavy high explosives. They came under fire from ships and from two flak towers which stood on either side of a channel. One bomber crashed into a windmill.

On the ground Danes stood in their gardens, staggered by the noise and sight of the passing Allied armada of airborne battleships, waving them on to their unknown destination as the bombers turned south at 200mph over the Baltic Sea, soon climbing to a bombing height of around 7,000ft.

Turning into the target, where opposition was fierce, they saw a Ju-88 on the starboard beam 700 yards away chasing another Lancaster. The raid claimed twenty-one aircraft, but it tore out 100 acres of the centre of the town where many industrial buildings, including a chemical factory, were left in ruins and 586 people were killed. In the other raid, Rostock was hidden by a dense smoke screen, bombing was scattered and eight Stirlings were lost.

Away from the target they dropped to fifty feet over the Baltic, nearly low enough to trail a baited fishing line from the aircraft, probably whipping up an impressive wake behind them. It was not difficult to maintain this height. It was moonlight and the pilot could see the water.

Shortly afterwards Sammy Craig received his unexpected shower as the four big propellors sucked up the icy spray from the choppy sea and whipped it on to the underside of the Lancaster. The water squirted in through the sealing around the escape hatch.

At first Richardson was sceptical of Craig's claim. 'Bloody impossible,' he growled unsympathetically. Then, a little more kindly, he added: 'Don't lie beside the exit hatch then.' There was a pause. 'Do you want me to go up a bit?' 'Please,' said Craig, faintly. The Lancaster gained a little height and Craig, grumbling to himself, splashed about the nose thankful that his electric flying suit had not been switched on otherwise he might have received another kind of shock.

Others in the cockpit had mentioned that water was being sprayed into the aircraft, but only the bomb aimer got a soaking.

They got back to Langar at 5.40 next morning where, after over eight hours of sitting and tension, they found their legs temporarily inflicted by the trembles and the Lancaster's four silent engines continued to roar in their ears.

They returned to Duisburg on 26 April then, the next night, they went on a gardening trip to La Rochelle at the vast mouth of the Gironde river, even further south than St Nazaire. It was the biggest mining operation of the war so far, involving 160 aircraft. One Lancaster did not return after 458 mines were laid in the Frisian Islands and off ports in Brittany and the Bay of Biscay. McIntosh recalls a searchlight fastening on to them after the last mine dropped into the water:

'This op called for absolutely accurate navigation with a time and distance run from the mouth of the estuary. We dropped our mines from 200ft, turned to leave and a bloody searchlight came straight on to us. I fired and it went out. Fred played bloody hell saying that I had given our position away, but nothing fired back, we flew out into the Bay of Biscay and went home.'

There was something satisfyingly sneaky about laying mines. They could be left squatting with sinister intent in the sea or at a harbour entrance for days, weeks even, waiting for victims to come slinking in only to be seriously crippled or blown to bits by an enemy who had paid a fleeting and forgotten visit to the area.

McIntosh's twentieth sortie, on 30 April, was to Essen, the sort of prospect which turned strong men's stomachs when their destination was revealed at briefing. No target was more staunchly defended than Essen where the huge Krupp armaments factory sprawled over several acres.

'There used to be an old saying, that the flak was so bloody thick over Essen you could have put your wheels down and taxied on it. Essen was in the heart of the Ruhr and you were flying through heavy flak for half-an-hour to get to it, and another half-hour to get out. There were so many towns to fly over, there was no way to get round them and it made no difference which way you approached the target. It was a hell of a target, a terrible place. It had these great guns which could pump flak up to twenty thousand feet, the height from which we usually bombed. On this occasion we came away unscathed.' Less fortunate were six Lancaster and six Halifax crews, among the 305 aircraft sent to Essen, who did not return.

McIntosh's most vivid memory of the trip on 13 May to Pilsen, Czechoslovakia, was an optical illusion. The moonlit raid was on the Skoda armaments factory. This was the second raid in a month sent to crush the factory. The first had totally missed Skoda but lost thirty-six bombers in hammering a big asylum seven miles away. This time the factory was still difficult to find, most of the bombs falling in open countryside and nine aircraft were lost. McIntosh says:

'I had a great view of the bombs bursting on what appeared to be acres and acres of glass, like the roofs of vast greenhouses. They were either steel roofs or wet slates shining in the brilliant moonlight. It was a long haul and the highest we'd flown, 24,000ft. At one point I told Fred we were leaving con trails and he came down like a shot to our normal height, 20,000ft, because they were a dead give-away. As soon as you started leaving con trails the fighters would vector on to your aircraft and come straight at you. There was a lot of flak over the target, but nothing going in or out. No fighters. Every time I see a Skoda car I think of that place.

Ten nights later Richardson's Lancaster, ED550, was one of 826 aircraft sent to attack Dortmund, the biggest raid in the Battle of the Ruhr. Thirty-eight aircraft were lost, large areas of the city were obliterated and 599 people died.

They were coming up to their bombing run over Wuppertal on 29 May when Richardson's starboard inner engine caught fire. Flames leapt back to the tail, but the pilot continued straight and steady until Craig released the bombs. Flight engineer Ralph Fairhead feathered the engine and extinguished the fire.

'There was no nervousness aboard when we lost the engine. The other three engines were fine and the Lanc was perfectly capable of flying straight and level on three unless there was some other problem. If you lost an engine you just stepped up the revs a wee bit on the others.'

Much of the town was badly damaged and 3,400 people were believed to have died. Thirty-three aircraft were lost.

In June 1943, McIntosh and his skipper both heard they were to be commissioned. In the thirties a poor boy with no background and his feet rooted deeply in the Scottish soil could only dream of making the leap from common man to someone of importance and status. When he joined the RAF being an officer was not even a remote possibility and he never thought of it. Ambition was something else, a man should always have ambitions but miracles, in his experience, did not happen. And yet in a very short time he had made that impossible leap to join the RAF's privileged classes. He had become an officer and a gentleman and would be the talk of Errol. McIntosh himself was a little more stoic:

'You got a bob or two extra, let's put it that way. I went from around seven shillings a day to about twenty-one shillings. I preferred being an officer and thought I was in a privileged position doing the same job as I did as a sergeant. If you had the intellect and were prepared to work hard, being an officer was better. There were perks; I got a first-class seat on a train and shared a batman with seven or eight officers. Mind you, when I joined the RAF, never in my wildest dreams did I think I could ever be an officer.'

Richardson had not wanted to be commissioned, fearing that he would be faced with impossible expenses. He explains:

'I'd heard that you had to buy your own uniform and mess kits, including a sword, at a time when my father was on ten bob (50p) a week. Then I was told I wouldn't have any of these problems because it was wartime. But an edict had come through from Bomber Command saying all captains of aircraft had to be commissioned. I was told if I was not, the only officer in my crew, at the time, Ken Gray, would be made captain. I said there was no way that was going to happen, so I had to go through all the rigmarole of being commissioned.'

McIntosh and Richardson had both been briefly interviewed by 5 Group chief Air Vice-Marshal the Hon Sir Ralph Cochrane at his headquarters in the grand spired house of St Vincent's, Grantham.

Langar was a satellite of nearby Bottesford where the group captain, with a reputation for disliking volunteers, did not care for Richardson, who had been summoned back from leave for this interview. He did not think the quiet young pilot was officer material and said so bluntly in his report to Cochrane.

The AOC, who might have been aware of the group captain's blinkered opinions, glowered as he read his junior officer's comments and asked: 'How many trips have you done?' Richardson said: 'Nineteen, Sir.'

Cochrane snapped: 'Anybody who has done nineteen trips and is still alive! – the group captain is a fool. Your commission is granted.'

Richardson left Cochrane's office wearing a broad grin. There is no record of whether Cochrane delivered a verbal rocket to the Bottesford CO.

McIntosh, who had been recommended for a commission by the squadron, had encountered no local animosity in the weeks preceding his interview with the AOC. He says:

'About a dozen of us went from Langar to Grantham that day. Cochrane already had the data on me and asked me one or two sharp questions about air gunnery, including what action would I take in certain hairy situations. He was very knowledgeable about each crew member's job. Then he said:

'You fly with Richardson?'

'Yes, Sir.'

'Right, you will be as sharp as possible as an officer. Back you go and do well. I wish you luck.'

The paperwork took an age to be processed and McIntosh had completed his first tour and left Langar before his commission came through. Because the clerical work took so long to complete he went straight from sergeant to flying officer, bypassing the rank of pilot officer. He was then at Skellingthorpe, Lincolnshire, attached to 1485 Gunnery Flight. His transfer into the officers' mess there was achieved without difficulties.

'I wasn't nervous going into the officers' mess for the first time because I knew everybody there. I rather enjoyed it and it certainly didn't change me, but going home and telling my grandparents that I had got a commission was my proudest moment in the RAF. They were elated because this was something they had never expected. Officers and farm labourers were a breed apart.'

Later, during five days' leave, McIntosh went to Perth to be measured for his new uniform which he put on later to show his grandparents. He felt very smart, but uncomfortable sitting in a first-class carriage going south as 149980 Flying Officer W. McIntosh. McIntosh was still thinking about his meeting with Cochrane as their bombing operations continued from Langar.

They aborted a raid to Düsseldorf on 11 June after a bad fire in the starboard outer engine, which again left McIntosh without guns to fire, and the next night after being badly hit by flak approaching Bochum, the port outer was feathered. The mid-upper turret was hit, shattering some perspex, deafening McIntosh and tearing off one of his gloves. He felt the heat from a piece of twisted shrapnel and said, astounded: 'I've been hit.'

Richardson asked, anxiously: 'Are you bleeding?' McIntosh, replied gruffly: 'Yes, but I'm staying here.' Richardson, getting briskly back to the matter in hand, exclaimed: 'We're bombing.' McIntosh recalls:

'I had been cut and deafened in one ear. I stayed in the turret until we got over England. It was painful but I got treatment, and I refused to go sick because I didn't want to lose my crew. My ear got better and it was not a problem on the aircraft, although it was never the same again.

'It was a Saturday afternoon when the Tannoy made an announcement ordering five crews to report to the operations room. We were included in the five. We were told that we were to start intensive training, including time and distance runs, for a special operation on a priority target. Night and day for the next week we flew at all odd hours with much thought as to what our objective would be. It was all leading up to one of the big raids. This was Friedrichshafen in southern Germany. The day before we had been issued with tropical kit, which confused everyone slightly and led to a good deal of speculation in the mess, but this was explained to us on 20 June during the briefing when we were also spoken to by the AOC.'

The raid involved sixty Lancasters from 5 Group attacking the Zeppelin works at Friedrichshafen, on the shores of Lake Constance. The factory was now turning out gun-laying and searchlight-directing Würzburg radar sets. Five of the attacking force came from 207 Squadron.

The time and distance bombing run involved a technique being developed by 5 Group. It was made from a point on the edge of the lake to an estimated position of the factory. Reconnaissance pictures taken after the raid proved that ten per cent of the bombs had struck the target.

'There was a lot of flak at Friedrichshafen, but we bombed at 10,000ft and flew on across the Mediterranean because we were not going straight home. I remember rattling across the top of an Italian seaport at great speed because we were losing height to cross the Med.

'Then Fred said: "You can come out of the turrets now boys and put on your Sunday best". I climbed down, put my shorts on and returned to the turret, which was warming up. It felt odd to be sitting there in shorts instead of being muffled up to the eyeballs in flying gear.

'We'd been airborne 10hr 10min when we landed on an American airfield at Blida, Algeria, and were put in tents which stood in a school yard. The food, which included a lot of tomatoes, wasn't great but we got plenty of cigarettes. They were dishing out big cartons of Navy Woodbines, fifty in a tin. It was a pretty dismal place. I wasn't taken with Blida at all, although it was quite exciting to do that trip because not only were we flying away from Britain we were flying out of Europe to Africa. It was quite something walking freely in the streets of Algiers, to have a drink at a roadside café, a bit different to going to the Flying Horse in Nottingham or the Nag's Head in Lincoln.

'Some soldiers had been out in Africa fighting the Germans for three years, we were there for a three-day break. Just a taste of Africa, then home. We were briefed to bomb La Spezia on the way back to England.

'We were now edging towards the end of our tour and feeling slightly apprehensive for a lot of men had died on their last handful of sorties. Three crews: ours, John McIntosh's and John Stephens' were flying neck and neck at the top end.'

These were tense and nervous times, for there were no easy ops. They were so close, surely they would get through now? But these doubts were never expressed to each other. Such doubts were contagious and expressed by veterans, as these twenty-one men now undoubtedly were, could spread through the squadron like a plague, screwing up morale and self-belief.

In July 1943 Richardson went to Cologne and Gelsenkirchen and there was a ten-hour trip to Turin when his gunners shot out two searchlights on the outskirts of the city. As they crossed the Alps a Ju-88 was spotted flying aimlessly among the peaks as if he were looking for a bomber to play with. They hurried into the mountains and lost it.

The summer was drifting along without any major upheavals then, on 16 July they were sent to Cislago in northern Italy. Again they were issued with tropical gear. Two targets, both power stations, were to be shared between eighteen Lancasters from 5 Group. Five were detailed to go from 207 Squadron, four took off, including LM334, piloted by Fred Richardson, who left Langar at 10pm. Their brief, with an Allied landing expected soon, was to destroy the stations and disrupt the supply of power to railway trains carrying German troops and supplies. This operation was quite different to anything they had been told to do before.

Eleven bombers were unable to find one power station and bombed an alternative target. The other Lancasters, including LM334, did find their station, but it was not without difficulties.

'This was a special operation, with special ammunition. All the tracer had been taken out of the armour-piercing bullets we were given. We knew when the ammunition was changed that something queer was going on, then we were told that we would be shooting up the target. It was the first time that air gunners had been briefed to open fire on a target. We didn't have tracer because using it would have given away our positions. We also carried delayed-action bombs.

'We had a problem after crossing the Alps. We had to go down and find a small lake from which we had to do a time and distance run that would take us to this power station. When we got down we found no lake and it just shows how bloody awful the intelligence was that we received in those days. A reconnaissance Spitfire could have been sent high over Italy that morning and would have easily seen that the lake had dried up. We wasted time farting about until we found the target, which was a marvellous piece of navigation. It was a massive building in clear view so we went down, had a look at it, went back up and bombed it from about 1,200ft.'

When their bomb bays were empty the Lancasters came down to below 500ft and began circling the stricken building, whirling round and round until it was within fifty yards of their wing tips, like monster chair-o'-planes, the old-fashioned fairground attraction. But there was nothing entertaining about this sortie as they pumped bullets into it and as their fingers were on the triggers they watched terrified people running away.

'Some of the station burst into flames. While circling the target a Ju-88 fighter came down to join in the fun, going round and round with us, we could see him quite plainly. Then he suddenly turned on one of 207 Squadron's Lancasters. We saw it go down and skitter across the ground with flames spreading for about a quarter-of-a-mile and thought nobody could get out of that. The German might have had a pot at someone else, but after knocking down that bomber he pulled away. Some gunners may have shot at the fighter but without tracer they would not have known where their bullets were going. Shooting at the power station from almost point-blank range we didn't need tracer. But it was dangerous because we were concentrating on that whilst knowing fighters were active in the area which you also had to watch for. The bombs started going off as we were leaving.'

One man did escape from the burning Lancaster, which had been piloted by thirty-one-year-old Pilot Officer Len Stubbs. The wireless operator, Sergeant Eric Morris, twenty-three, became a prisoner of war.

'Cislago was a very important raid because it was later revealed that by knocking out that station we paralysed the electric railways in the north of Italy to inconvenience the Germans. We battered the hell out of the buildings. It was a complete knockout and very little was made of it, perhaps because the wrong people had done it. If 617 Squadron had done that we would never have heard the bloody end of it.'

The previous night twelve Lancasters of 617 Squadron had carried out their first bombing operation since the Dams raid in May. Called in for a precision bombing raid they were joined by another twelve 5 Group Lancasters in attacks on two similar power plants in northern Italy, which were partially hidden by mist. The raid was unsuccessful and two of the supporting bombers were lost. Some agreed that if flares had been available their results might have been more favourable. Afterwards the attacking force flew on to Blida, as did Richardson and the other surviving Lancasters from the following night's raid.

They were among thirty-three 5 Group Lancasters to leave Algeria on 24 July, bombing docks at the Italian port of Leghorn en route to England, touching down at Langar at midnight after an eight-hour flight. 'There was little opposition, just a few poops of flak, but no fighters. I remember seeing a ship sunk in the harbour.'

Their main worry as Leghorn receded into the distance was slumped miserably in the rear turret. Grant Booth had become seriously ill in Algeria with dysentery and while they never contemplated leaving him behind it was clear he needed urgent hospital treatment.

'He sat in the rear turret until we were clear of Leghorn then came out to lie on the rest bed. I went into his turret and Sammy Craig moved into the mid-upper position,' says McIntosh. 'I think Grant's condition was caused by some food he had eaten. He was taken to hospital after we got back to Langar.'

What became known as the start of the Battle of Hamburg opened with a devastating raid on the city on the night of 24/25 July. It was the first time Window (strips of aluminium foil dropped by Allied bombers to confuse German radar) was used, and five nights later Richardson and his crew were among 777 aircraft sent on the third in this series of attacks against the north German port. This operation would complete the end of their first tour.

Now Booth was in hospital nursing his stomach they needed another gunner and they were given Les Mitchell, the rear gunner for the flight commander, Squadron Leader David Balme. Mitchell went into the dorsal position allowing McIntosh to remain in the rear turret, to which he had become rather attached.

They carried a second dickey in ED550 that night: twenty-one-year-old Pilot Officer Gordon Moulton-Barrett, from Andover, Hampshire, on his first sortie. Taking off at 10.15pm flight engineer Ralph Fairhead was employed to drop Window over Germany.

'We had not used Window before and did not, at that time, have a dispenser,' says McIntosh. 'We had all these packages of Window which had to be dropped through the flare chute. Ralph went aft wearing an oxygen mask and flung it out, but half the bloody things were blown back into the aircraft. Ralph went back to his position, totally black. The Window was silver on one side and black on the other and all the black had come off.'

They could see Hamburg burning from halfway across the North Sea and went in to add their bombs to the devastation. Two nights before around 40,000 people had died when a fire storm swept the city after a heavy raid and over a million residents, terrified of what might follow, fled into the countryside. On this third night another 370 people died and twenty-eight aircraft would not return.

As they entered their bombing run Moulton-Barrett saw searchlights target another Lancaster. He says:

'It was coned by a master blue and then white searchlights, creating an unpleasant situation for the pilot who chose to go into a vertical dive. As he picked up speed the searchlights followed him down, but their reaction was not fast enough and the Lancaster escaped, pulling out at 10,000ft. I felt like clapping my hands to applaud the pilot's skills.'

Richardson might have been excused for leaving the target area with more alacrity than usual when they saw a Lancaster on the port side being attacked by a fighter. McIntosh recalls:

'It would have been no more than 1,000 yards away, slightly above us being set about by a Messerschmitt Bf-109. The Lancaster was blazing like hell, destined for oblivion and we saw five parachutes come very quickly out from the front. The rear gunner was firing at the fighter even though his aircraft was going straight down. I have never seen such bravery. The poor bugger was still sitting there firing away and the fighter went back in to have another blast at him with the gunner, still defiant, and the Lancaster blew up. No other 'chutes came out.

'It is possible that the gunner didn't know they were going down because communication to his turret had been severed by fire or a cannon shell. At that rate of descent there was no way that poor bloke could have got out, the G-force would have beaten him. Ever since that night I have wondered who that gunner was. It's likely that his mate in the mid-upper turret was also trapped. But I had completed thirty-three ops and had that to think about too.'

McIntosh heard later of aircrews who had baled out safely during the Hamburg raids only to be flung alive into raging fires.

'After all,' he says grimly, 'the fire raids on Hamburg were terrible. I could just imagine the raging women who had lost their families and homes. It is something I would not have liked to endure, and yet fifty-five times I courted such situations.'

Moulton-Barrett was shot down on his seventeenth operation, his seventh against Berlin, early on the morning of Christmas Eve. He and five of his crew became prisoners of war. His rear gunner, Sergeant David Davies, aged twenty, was killed. He had been drafted into the crew as a spare bod because the pilot's regular gunner was suffering from a bad cold.

The end of the tour was a strange anti-climax for Richardson and his crew. They went to Nottingham with their ground crew for a few celebratory beers, an exchange of the latest anti-Hitler jokes, and mild observations of the state of the war, but did not think to exchange addresses. Seven men, who had been closer than brothers, all cheerfully went their separate ways removed, at least temporarily, from the strictures of flying over Germany and close encounters with death. The future was all-important, even if it was clouded with uncertainties. The most recent past, which they had all shared, had been filled with death and mayhem. Perhaps that was best forgotten while looking forward to less traumatic lives, but taking nothing for granted. John McIntosh and John Stephens also completed their first tours.

Wallace McIntosh was awarded a Distinguished Flying Medal at the end of his tour. Fred Richardson, Grant Booth and Ken Gray each got the Distinguished Flying Cross. McIntosh's excited grandmother went into Errol post office to send the first telegram in her life, congratulating her grandson, who also received a warm letter from the Rev Fyfe Scott in Rhynd. The minister wrote:

'I congratulate you most warmly, and feel very proud of the distinction you have so magnificently earned. You have a ribbon now which brings you into a distinguished company, and one you can wear with honourable pride.'

McIntosh's award, dated 19 October 1943, was promulgated in the *London Gazette*. It read:

> *Sergeant McIntosh has completed twenty-eight successful operational sorties out of a total of thirty-two. His tour was particularly marked by the coolness of his co-operation with his Captain and other members of his crew. His skill in working with his rear gunner and in providing a commentary on attacks by enemy fighters, together with the accuracy of his return fire in the face of many attacks resulted in the probable destruction of at least two fighters, and have on all occasions enabled his Captain to avoid serious damage to his aircraft, thus furthering the confidence of his crew and the success of their missions. His great sense of responsibility, keenness and determination to improve his own efficiency have set an admirable example to the rest of the Squadron.*

For various reasons McIntosh would not receive his DFM until the war in Europe had finished, but he could sew on the ribbon. It looked good.

CHAPTER SEVEN

PART OF THE FURNISHINGS

It was awkward and curiously sad saying goodbye for these seven men, fortunate survivors of the bomber war, whose lives had been so intertwined since the beginning of 1943. They had depended one upon the other for their survival during unbelievable times of stress and now they were to be split up. They might easily have died together like so many of their friends at Langar, instead they lived and were elated for it, but this parting business was an unfamiliar situation none of them really knew how to handle. Having become a respected team, learning through hectic and traumatic months to work and live together, they must now learn to exist without each other. The sense of loss would start fading even during those early days of leave, yet like so many other closely-knit aircrews most would not forget even if the urge to make contact with old wartime buddies did not start stirring until each was approaching retirement. Some chaps though, having suffered enough, simply allowed themselves to disappear, in an attempt to erase the war from their minds.

They packed their kit, shook hands and went on their way. Fred Richardson became an instructor at Gamston, leaving when the airfield became a Canadian training unit, spending the rest of the war at Wymeswold and Castle Donington.

Vince Cairney, one of Richardson's navigators, was killed in an accident at an OTU. Booth was whisked off to an OTU to instruct and pass on useful tips for survival.

Flight engineer Ralph Fairhead was an instructor at 1661 Heavy Conversion Unit, Winthorpe, near Newark, when during a training flight about midnight on 28 October 1944 his Stirling iced up, lost its engines one by one, crash-landed and broke in half. Fairhead, the pilot and both gunners survived. The engineer, with a smashed right leg and foot, dragged himself away from the burning aircraft and was haunted for years by the screams of men trapped inside. In hospital for months, his foot, lucky to escape amputation, was rebuilt with bone grafts. He did not fly again.

Despite never losing his fear of heights Sammy Craig became an instructor before joining 570 Squadron on Stirlings and completing a second tour. Mentioned in despatches in June 1944 for distinguished service, he did not fly after the war, even turning down opportunities to visit his married sister, Queenie Didonato, at her home in Florida. At the end of hostilities he returned to Queen's University to complete his studies and qualify as a dentist. He had busy practices, first in Grimsby, then Skegness.

Wallace McIntosh had been told towards the end of his first tour by squadron gunnery leader Jimmy Moore that he would not be posted off 5 Group. McIntosh suspected the influence of Cochrane here and was flattered to think he had been singled out for special attention.

'Jimmy was only my age, but he considered that I'd gone through the tour with a bit of credibility. Even if there was no flying I would always be up at the flights, probably in the gunnery room. He sometimes asked me to take a new fellow out to a turret and I walked round the Lancaster with them. I made myself useful because I was interested and wanted to know as much as I could.'

A gunnery leader did not have a regular pilot. With luck, he had an extended life on a squadron, running the gunnery room, organising the other gunners, being regarded as an elite spare bod who could decide for himself when he went on an op, occasionally picking out an experienced skipper whose regular gunner might have gone sick or been injured.

The luck of the popular Flight Lieutenant Jimmy Moore DFM ran out on 10 March 1944 when he was killed in the target area of the Michelin tyre works at Clermont-Ferrand. There were no survivors in the shot-up Lancaster which was piloted by thirty-two-year-old Squadron Leader Dudley Pike, officer commanding B Flight. Moore was twenty-two. McIntosh says:

'Poor Jimmy, he was a great lad, but he picked the wrong trip that night. They carried three air gunners, we don't know if he went into a turret, he may have just wanted to get another op in as an observer with an experienced skipper.'

Flight Lieutenant Jimmy Wardle, who had been with the squadron on his first tour when he was awarded the DFM, returned to 207 as gunnery leader. A Yorkshireman, he came from Sherburn in Elmet, near Leeds.

In August 1943 McIntosh was posted as an instructor to Fulbeck, where 5 Group had set up its own gunnery unit, 1485 (Bomber) Gunnery Flight.

'These air gunners had spent six weeks at an OTU where they'd been skittering about in Wimpeys and thought they knew everything until they arrived at 1485 where they found out they were pretty basic. We laid into them.'

Tour-expired pilots flew clapped-out Wellington Xs and Manchesters which were put up against fighters in heartily-fought battles of wits known as fighter affiliation, mainly during mornings over the Lincolnshire countryside. The exercises simulated real traumas over enemy territory with the British fighter – usually a Martinet, occasionally a Spitfire or Hurricane – diving in to attack the bomber which desperately tried to outwit its aggressor. One of the four Browning machine guns in the Wellington's rear turret had been replaced by a camera which was used by the gunner for testing his reactions which became revealed when the films were developed. A camera was also fixed inside the fighter.

McIntosh went up three times in a Wellington to fire the camera at a bustling fighter before getting into a routine as an instructor. Gunners, usually four at a time, were taken up and treated to generous helpings of fighter affiliation, with gut-squirming diving turns and corkscrews.

By now McIntosh had become self-confident and easy in most situations, while remaining an uncomplicated man with a tendency to call a spade a spade. He was never comfortable in the company of fools, wafflers or time wasters, particularly when there was an urgent job to be done, like saving the world from the Nazis. His voice was an impressively guttural mixture of bulldozer, scythe and battering ram, mercilessly honed in the green glens and hills of rural north-east Scotland.

McIntosh was with the gunnery unit until February 1944. In that time it moved to Skellingthorpe, where his commission came through, then Syerston, eight miles north of Langar. McIntosh remembers Fulbeck as a lovely station, but Skellingthorpe, three miles from Lincoln, was unbeatable for food. The messing officer came from the family owning the chain of MacFisheries' shops: 'He saw that we had good rations. We had wonderful food there and I'd never seen such a selection of fresh fruit.'

McIntosh enjoyed his six months as an instructor even though some work could be a little boring. He had a few days off when sent to a special unit at Southport where he came top of an advanced aircraft recognition course of twenty air gunners and was told to give the final lecture about the aircraft of his choice.

'Other chaps wanted to talk about the Lancaster or Spitfire. I wanted to do something which was different, without repeating what they were saying. I gave a twenty-five minute talk on the single-engine Lysander because it had a lot of odd features. Looking at the Lysander you can introduce it as being like a bug, or a beetle, or a dragonfly, because of its shape. It had spats on the wheels, a high wing and long fuselage. And I told them the story about the Lysander that shot down one of the first Me-110s during the war.

'I wouldn't say I had felt safe on ops, anything but. You didn't know what was round the corner taking off on an NFT, never mind anything else, because a lot of aircraft that never flew on ops were lost. I felt settled when I was on my rest period and instructing. I really felt that I was part of the furnishings. It was the time that I could pass on my experience to the younger chaps. I and two other instructors, Ginger Bale and Tommy Cook spent a lot of extra hours helping people.

'Besides gunnery, I took two classes on sighting and aircraft recognition every morning. Some of the lads were so bloody hopeless at aircraft recognition that we brought them back at night. They would only have been at the bar drinking pints so we saved them money. We hoped we might also help save their lives.

'I met a few characters in that period. Micky Mills was a small dark-haired fellow, very industrious, who rose to be a wing commander. He not only instructed in gunnery he also hung a sign outside his room advertising his haircutting service. A great lover of music, he collected records and was in charge of the big radiogram in the mess. We called him The Record Man. All records played had to go through his hands and those which weren't his had little labels stuck on to say who they belonged to.'

After one or two instruction flights aboard creaking Wellingtons, McIntosh recalled the boredom endured by Polish pilots on the Blackburn Bothas at

Morpeth. Although the Wellington pilots did not resort to daredevilry to tear away the monotony of the occasion, those who had been on operational tours now viewed the repetitive training as rather tedious.

'The Wellington pilots were not keen on careering all over the bloody sky in these old kites. They just wanted to get up, have a nice gentle exercise, get down, away to the mess, or into Lincoln. Maybe one flight in the morning and another in the afternoon, each taking about an hour. The pilots and the instructors didn't want to be stooging about with these guys all day. We'd done all our stooges some time ago. Since then we'd been all over Germany.'

The Vickers Wellington was of geodetic design featuring a lattice work of thin steel, covered by a taut doped fabric, which created a very robust aeroplane. One August day a Wellington piloted by Flying Officer Smith was subjected to more than the normal amount of buffeting that should be expected by an old lady who was coming to the end of her useful life.

'There was the pilot and me and four sergeants who were taking turns to go into the rear turret. They had been taken from their crews and brought here for three or four days of intensive training. Three sat behind the main spar waiting for one of them to replace the chap who was in the turret. You didn't want any obstructions and the aircraft had been stripped bare, but the fuselage was very narrow and the chap leaving the turret and the one replacing him had to pass each other. There was just a small plywood catwalk, with a bit of support underneath, which went from the main spar to the rear turret. I always stood in the astrodome so I could look down the fuselage and see them. I could also see the fighter which was on our tail. If the aircraft was rocking about and some chaps might not be feeling too well they had to be careful how they moved past each other in the fuselage, otherwise they might end up putting a fist through the fabric of the aeroplane. As soon as the new man was in the turret we called up to the fighter: "Attack us!"

'On that day we were flying at around 1,500ft and about to get the last bod into the turret. It used to be a case of: "Fingers out! Get moving!" For the last attack we were going into the funnel, so the quicker we got down the better.

'These two lads had to pass quickly for one to get in, fire off his magazine at the fighter and get the hell out of it. The last one got into the turret but the fellow who was coming out staggered off the catwalk, his foot went through the bloody fabric and out into the sky, rapidly followed by his leg. His other leg slid down so both legs dangled from the bottom of the aircraft.'

The terrified gunner thrashed about but his cries of alarm were lost in the roar of the Wellington's two Bristol Hercules engines as the bomber plunged, chased by a scurrying fighter, cameras whirring. The three gunners who had completed their uncomplicated stints in the turret tried unsuccessfully to yank their companion to safety. McIntosh lent a hand but the man was stuck, with the great weight of air pulling strongly on his legs. The gunner was on the edge of panic, afraid of being dragged out of the aircraft or having his legs smashed when they landed. The design of the Wellington would have prevented this from happening but the gunner, whipped by the slipstream, did not know that.

'We were approaching the funnel and the fighter was still going at us with the gunner in the rear turret shooting away with the camera. Then flying control comes on and there's this plummy voice announcing: "You have a protrusion." Smith came through on the intercom.

'What the hell's going on, Wallace?' he asked. McIntosh explained. Smith said: 'With the tail wheel and the height he'll be okay. We can land with him dangling there.'

The 'protrusion' message was repeated several times until Smith replied with a sharp wisecrack which silenced control while inducing slight concern: 'That's okay, if he keeps in step we'll make a good landing.'

'We landed at Fulbeck, got him out and he received a wee bollocking from Smithy and me,' says McIntosh. 'He would be extra careful next time, but there was no way he could have been hurt, unless the undercarriage had collapsed, in which case he would have been rubbed out.'

Senior officers from other groups, who had heard of 5 Group's important work at the gunnery unit, were keen to see it for themselves. They were particularly interested in a type of corkscrewing which seemed to be unique to Cochrane's group. On 9 September McIntosh and the pilot, Pilot Officer Dashper, were briefed to take the officers up and demonstrate a series of diving turns and make it as realistic as possible. On no account were they to ease up on the corkscrewing.

McIntosh's pupils were two group captains and a squadron leader who were all keen to experience the stresses experienced by a rear gunner in battle. As they drifted out to the aircraft, Dashper, who might have belonged to the breed of young fellows who took pleasure from creating maximum turbulence among the internal workings of senior officers, murmured cheerfully to McIntosh:

'Jesus Christ, Mac! Really give the buggers the works and they won't be able to last out in the arse end. When we get the bloody wings flexed they'll fill their pants.' Dashper followed up his advice with a violent display of flying which more than adequately demonstrated the barrel corkscrew.

Because he was the masterful instructor and had been told to treat this as a normal training exercise McIntosh did not hold back after steering the first group captain into the turret and explaining what was expected of him. McIntosh thrust his face forward, glared at the groupie and snarled:

'Right, when it's done get your arse out of here and let somebody else in. We don't want to be up here all day.' The group captain appeared startled but did not argue and afterwards all three said they had been intrigued by their experience, and the unit, hoping the visitors would relay their newly-acquired knowledge to their own squadrons, decided to hold more demonstrations.

'The senior group captain congratulated Dashper on the work we were doing to increase air gunners' efficiency. I was delighted to see them take part and experience the cramped position gunners had to endure on long trips.'

One exercise, on 17 September, was less successful when a wing commander became very ill with air sickness and the exercise was terminated early. His vomit, sprayed copiously around the rear turret, was cleared up by a long-suffering ground crew.

In March 1944, McIntosh, now instructing at Syerston, was posted to 5 Lancaster Finishing School, which was based at the same airfield. This meant he simply moved across the road to the school and remained in the mess.

The school had evolved from 1668 Heavy Conversion Unit two months earlier. Before leaving the gunnery unit he was called to one side by its leader Squadron Leader Underey.

Underey, who was regarded by McIntosh as a bit of a tough character, said: 'I've just been informed that there's a Squadron Leader Grey arriving here and he's looking for a very experienced rear gunner.'

McIntosh replied, prickly with suspicion: 'Who is he to make such a demand?'

Underey shrugged and said, cannily: 'The thing is, Wallace, if you don't go with Grey you might be put back on operations with an inexperienced pilot.'

That was enough for McIntosh, even though he had expected to spend longer as an instructor before returning to operational flying. He met John Grey, liked him, the feeling was mutual, and McIntosh agreed to join him and flew with the squadron leader for the first time on 10 March. They had two sessions of circuits and bumps that day with pilot Flight Lieutenant Chopping and Grey flying second dickey. The first trip lasted 2hr 25min. The second, with Grey in charge was for half-an-hour. McIntosh was impressed with his new skipper. He says:

'Grey was a very experienced pilot, having flown over eighty operations in a lot of different aircraft, most of the twin-engine bombers, including Blenheims and Wellingtons, but this was the first time he had piloted a Lancaster.'

John Francis Grey had come from 1660 HCU, Swinderby where he became familiar with four-engine aircraft flying Stirlings.

From being the tallest man on Fred Richardson's crew McIntosh suddenly found himself almost the smallest. Most stood about six feet, but this did not bother McIntosh. He was with another group of men in whose company he was comfortable and they soon blended together well as a team. Besides, giants were not at ease in the crushed conditions of the rear turret where McIntosh could only operate his Brownings in what he describes as a three-quarter crouch.

Grey was a big strong thirty-one-year-old six-footer, red-haired, with a neat moustache. The second of five children, he lived on an estate which had been in the family since 1720 at Milfield, near Wooler, Northumberland, where the Greys became one of the more influential families in the Borders. They were involved in most of the wars with Scotland but their allegiance might have been different had the family seat been eight miles to the north-west and the pilot and his new rear gunner would have been fellow Scots.

John Grey, who was educated at Royal Grammar School, Newcastle, had already crammed a lot into his life before arriving at Spilsby. He had gained his second mate's ticket in the Merchant Navy, and served in the City of London police until joining the RAF before the war. Based in India he later escaped from Singapore which had been invaded by the Japanese.

McIntosh thought he had a determined streak which bordered on ruthlessness:

'He was a straightforward man who never minced his words and did not tell jokes. He had tremendous presence and commanded attention when he walked into the mess. He was a man's man, enthusing everybody around him. He raised your hopes because he had that great air of confidence, but he didn't stand for any nonsense and was very strict in the air. He had been around a bit and was a fine pilot. He had a public school sort of accent, normally calling me "Mec" on the station and usually "Tail" in the air. The others called me "Mac".

'Grey was some chap, I'll tell you. He had a good crew, regarded them highly and was excellent at congratulating anybody who did anything that was beyond the norm. He was absolutely dedicated and a stickler for things being right, but he was fair. He was also a man in a hurry. He didn't hesitate about going on ops. A lot of wing commanders took a year to go through a tour. Grey didn't hang about after his promotion, he was off, bang! bang! bang!

'He knew about the rear turret and knew what the navigator did. He made himself busy and I liked him. We all got on marvellously together. It may have been slightly different for these five guys who were here with a squadron leader and someone who had already done a tour, but I found them wonderful chaps and we went out a lot together.

'On 11 March we went up with Grey for more circuits and bumps, corkscrewing on three engines and, Jesus, with his limited experience on heavy bombers, we landed on three. On the morning of the thirteenth we had a daylight cross country and late that night circuit and bumps for over an hour. We got back down and Grey said: "Right, let's go up again." And we had another half-hour at it. He was a workaholic. He wanted to get out of here and back on operations.'

Next night they took off for a bull's eye exercise, returning to Syerston to drop off the mid-upper gunner who had been badly sick, then back up for a bombing test. It was the last flying they did at Syerston.

To McIntosh's delight they were posted to 207 Squadron on 19 March 1944, where Grey, now on his third tour, was to take over as officer commanding B Flight following the demise of Dudley Pike. The squadron had moved the previous October to a big brand-new airfield, RAF Spilsby, on the southern edge of the Lincolnshire Wolds, two miles from the small market town after which it had been named.

Several minor roads had been closed to accommodate the new bomber station on 630 acres, where its three concrete runways were above average length, the main one stretching to 7,590ft. Accommodation was in Nissen huts. In winter Spilsby was not the ideal posting. Icy winds belted in from the North Sea five miles away and personnel felt a discomforting affinity with Siberia. Spilsby became a two-squadron station when 44 (Rhodesia) Squadron – the first unit to fly the Lancaster operationally – joined 207 in September.

Grey had fortuitously put together a fine team. Unlike the unfortunate Fred Richardson he did not have any drones to deal with although, like the Yorkshireman, Grey had selected most of his crew from the heap of bodies milling about at OTU. Everyone knew their job and was good at it, any pilot would be happy with that. They included the navigator, Sergeant 'Happy' Hall, an unassuming but confident Londoner, whose ability McIntosh equated to that of the slick Ken Newby from his first tour.

Bob Jack, the bespectacled wireless operator, came from Edinburgh.

'He was very studious. Grey always said that Bob was a typically dedicated wireless operator. He was a bit scruffy with a spare piece of wire and some string sticking out of his pocket. Not exactly eccentric, he was a genuine down-to-earth lad. We talked football a lot and argued about it good-naturedly, I was a big Dundee United supporter, Bob followed Heart of Midlothian. Some of us kicked a ball about on the station occasionally in our spare time.

'Our bomb aimer was a Canadian, Bob Casey, who was about thirty, a marvellous chap, full of fun who told great jokes, enjoyed going out for a drink and had a great singing voice.'

Flying Officer Casey was smaller than the others, slim, sandy-haired with a bristly moustache, but he had a sparkling personality that made him appear to stand tall. Before joining the Air Force he had wandered about Canada, singing with his guitar. In the mess he brought alive the wild beauty of Canada through his songs and stories.

Sergeant Tommy Young was from Chester-le-Street, where his family ran a garage. The flight engineer was tough and swarthy, standing about 5ft 9in. He could sing and tell compelling stories like Frigging in the Rigging, and Eskimo Nell with its innumerable verses. They occasionally took a train from Firsby to Boston and on to Skegness or Mablethorpe and found a pub where Young and Casey soon got the building shaking with good humour.

The mid-upper gunner was Sergeant Reg 'Johnny' Johnstone, a young Londoner.

They left Spilsby at 7.05pm on 22 March for a heavy raid on Frankfurt, in a massive force of 816 aircraft: 620 Lancasters, 184 Halifaxes and 12 Mosquitoes.

McIntosh had forgotten to pick up one of the new microphones which contained a heated element, and also prevented the top of the oxygen mask from freezing up.

'That was my fault and I paid for it,' he says. 'The microphones came out just prior to me coming back on operations. I should have checked. I didn't become unconscious when the oxygen hose froze, but I felt groggy and was sick. I pulled the mask off and let blast. After that I was as fit as a fiddle and told them up front what had happened. Grey was going to send the engineer back but I gave him the all clear. A couple of good snorts and I stayed where I was.

'We spotted a Focke-Wulf-190 fighter shooting past our rear. He wasn't attacking us but Johnstone and I gave him a half-second burst just as we were going into the target to let him know he had been seen.'

Frankfurt suffered widespread damage but thirty-three aircraft would not come back, including the Lancaster piloted by the popular officer commanding 207 Squadron, Wing Commander Vashon Wheeler, who had taken off from Spilsby four minutes before Grey. Wheeler was a forty-six-year-old veteran of the Royal Flying Corps in which he had flown fighters.

As an Army officer in the First World War, he had earned two Military Crosses and lost part of one hand and some fingers fighting in the trenches against a German soldier armed with a spade. He had also been awarded the Russian Order of St Stanislaus and, from the present conflict, two

Distinguished Flying Crosses. Few men could have served their country with more credit. Wheeler and three of his crew were among 186 men who were killed or fatally injured that night. Fifty-six were prisoners of war, including Wheeler's two gunners and navigator. Two others, from 514 Squadron, became evaders.

Grey learned after they got back that Wheeler was missing and they hung about the debriefing room and in the mess for news. When a batman came in and said there was still no word Grey said, disconsolately: 'Oh God, it looks as if he's gone. We'd better go to bed.' Much later they learned that Wheeler had been given a full military funeral by the Germans.

Next morning Grey was promoted to wing commander to take over the squadron and Squadron Leader Norman Jones was posted in to assume command of B Flight. Grey called McIntosh into his office and said:

'Right, Wallace, I have added responsibilities. From now on you will be responsible for my crew; to know where they are and gather them together when I need them.'

Every morning McIntosh had breakfast in the mess with Grey who often asked:

'What are you doing today, Mec?'

'I'm not sure yet.'

'Take the whole crew and give them a bit of aircraft recognition in the gunnery section.'

Grey knew of his rear gunner's obsession with this discipline and how important it was. McIntosh recalls, smiling:

'He always had me doing something with them. In the afternoon I might take the lads for a run or clay pigeon shooting on our range at the back of the airfield. We had an allocation at Spilsby of 13,000 twelve-bore cartridges a month. At other times I would take a few gunners with me, sometimes with my crew. Jimmy Wardle was happy for me to take gunners off to the range, he knew Grey was chasing me the whole time. They enjoyed doing it because they were fully occupied and the gunners' accuracy was improving all the time. I couldn't afford to miss because I was regarded as a crack shot.

'If Grey wanted them, say for an NFT, he just phoned or Tannoyed me and told us to get out to the aircraft. He arrived later in his Hillman car when we'd have everything checked and he'd press the button for the run up.

'Grey took a drink or two with us in the mess, but didn't come into Skegness to a pub or for a fish and chip supper, although he often came on the clays with me and was an outstanding shot. When he went home on leave he was always well laden with twelve-bore cartridges. We had an Airspeed Oxford at Spilsby and he used it to fly home.'

The new CO and the others had not been introduced to the pleasures of Essen and when they were briefed to go there on 26 March, McIntosh regaled them with horrifying tales of the vast barrage of flak they could expect going out to this deathtrap of a target and when they were attempting to return: 'Mention Essen in pubs and aircrews dropped their pints, it was the roughest of targets.'

They had an NFT before lunch, were bombed up in the afternoon and took off at 7.50pm for the Ruhr. The rear gunner was not disappointed that the trip was more straightforward than the gory picture he had painted, but there was a reason for this: 'Many of the big guns had been moved to the Russian front and although there was plenty of flak it was not as fierce as it had been in 1943. But there seemed to be more fighter activity.'

Nine of the 705 aircraft sent on the raid were shot down, about 1.3 per cent of the force, a lower percentage than normal.

It soon became clear that Johnstone, the mid-upper gunner, had a problem settling into a crew skippered by such a high-ranking officer. The youngster was shy, a non-drinker, and uneasy in the company of men who were more mature.

'He was an unfortunate lad. I used to take him out, give him instruction, chatting, trying to lift him. He got friendly with a chap in the mess, a pilot whose gunner had gone off sick. Johnny asked if he could fill in for him and Grey let him go. After he'd done a couple of ops with us he asked if he could go with the other pilot permanently, his heart was set on it. I knew I could get a replacement so he transferred to the other crew. They got hit by a Ju-88 coming back over the Dutch coast on 23 May after attacking Brunswick and he was so badly injured he died two days later in Rauceby hospital. It was very sad.' He was twenty-one.

The new gunner found by McIntosh was Flight Sergeant Bill 'Ginger' Charlesworth, who was only nineteen but he had already been to Berlin eleven times and only needed a handful of trips to finish his first tour. A Sheffield lad, Charlesworth was short, but stockily built. He was awarded a DFM at Spilsby.

'He had been posted from 3 Group where he had lost his crew. He had plenty of experience so we bagged him and he was a gem. Ginger was young but oh my God, he was always searching and checked everything.'

Moving from the top to rear turret had been accomplished smoothly, although McIntosh had to adjust to a more crumpled posture in the new berth.

'I stood nearly all the time in the tail turret, as Grant Booth used to do, crouched up so I could get my eyes down. I sometimes sat on my tin helmet which gave me an extra two or three inches, and I could lean back on it slightly.' The helmet also had the advantage of giving modest protection to his genitals.

It was much colder in the rear turret, which had a clear vision panel. This was a euphemistic description for a perspex panel which was no longer there. It had been removed earlier in the war, leaving a rectangular gap about six inches wide from the top to the bottom of the turret through which freezing air flowed unimpeded, although this gave the gunner better vision, without any tiny smears which might persuade him to think a night fighter was swooping into the attack. Some rear gunners made it even wider. An attempt was made to fit a panel which slid up and down, but it could not be kept clean and was abandoned.

It was impossible to have a panel removed from the mid-upper turret which, unlike the tail, could turn right round. Facing front, with the wind screaming in, would have provided the gunner with insurmountable problems.

'Some tail gunners felt cut off from the rest of the aircraft, but I didn't. I was confident there cocooned up in my own little war chest; my tank defending the aircraft and the fellows I flew with. This was my territory. As long as I knew I had a top gunner who was watching everything above I looked after the level and below. Most attacks came from below.'

Many rear gunners died after their turrets had been ripped off by flak or fighter but McIntosh did not think about that.

'If that happened I would have known nothing about it. But I did wonder how easy it might be to bale out from this turret if the aircraft was on fire and I had to get out quickly. My parachute was in the main structure of the Lancaster, which meant opening my doors and grabbing the 'chute. I would then need to step back into the turret, rotate it and fall out backwards. But I had heard of people getting caught up by something. Not many baled out of the turret, there was no time, everything happened so quickly, and there was the problem of the terrible G-force – if the aircraft went into a dive or a spin I wouldn't have been able to reach the doors.

'A lot of gunners were killed. I have seen turrets that were really minced up, what we called a wash out. By that I mean they had to be hose-piped out.'

CHAPTER EIGHT

TRICKLING ON

Dropping bombs on a city 20,000ft below was a cold and impersonal act by men who were fighting a long bitter war, many of whom believed the only good German was a dead one. It was not the aircrews' job to think too deeply about the civilians down there who had been killed, injured or lost their homes. The Germans had started it, after all, and the more of them that were killed would surely bring the end of the war closer so those who were left could get back to normal lives. Britain, especially London, had been unmercifully bombed, now it was pay-back time with a bit of interest.

Wallace McIntosh did not disagree with the policy of area bombing although he did not necessarily think it would cut short the war.

'It was a battle. You were fighting an enemy and you were fighting to win. The loser was a loser in a big way. But I thought the war would trickle on for years.' And it was difficult to visualise a time when he would not be part of it. 'The end of the war never entered my mind. I never thought of the future. When you think of it there wasn't a hell of a lot of future dropping bombs and being shot at every night. You didn't go shopping for early Christmas presents.

'I never had any plans. I had nothing to go back to anyway. I was going to be starting from scratch whatever and wherever it was. My only aim then was to stay in the Air Force and to be given a permanent commission, that was my great hope.'

From 1 April 1944 the Allies were preparing for the invasion of Normandy. Certain targets, including military camps, munitions factories, railways and ammunition depots needed to be wiped out before attention was turned towards coastal gun batteries, together with radio and radar stations.

An aircraft repair factory near Toulouse was the target for a force of 144 Lancasters from 5 Group on 5 April. Wing Commander Leonard Cheshire, in the first low-level Mosquito marking of the war, dropped red markers over the factory which was bombed with astonishing accuracy and severely damaged.

Grey's ME681 T-Tommy was among the Lancasters to hit the target and McIntosh recalls: 'For us it was quite a soft trip, but it was long, 7hr 55min, and on our return bad weather at Spilsby led to us being diverted to Little Horwood, Buckinghamshire, where we landed at 4.15am. We flew back to Spilsby next day.'

One Lancaster, from 207 Squadron, hit by flak, exploded near Toulouse, killing all aboard, including a second dickey pilot, leaving empty places at the breakfast table and the kit belonging to eight dead men to be moved as soon as possible.

There was another different kind of obscenity attached to the death of aircrews. The gathering up of dead men's possessions was not always the quiet and dignified affair it was meant to be. It could be foul, degrading and upsetting when it was not only the Germans who made a killing. McIntosh can still feel the anger of the day when he and his crew, asleep in their hut at Langar after a night op, were suddenly wakened by the door bursting open.

'It was fairly late in the morning. There was a hell of a noise. Two or three chaps ran in without speaking. Ignoring us, they went straight to several beds, grabbed uniforms and some of the other stuff that was there, maybe watches and money, then out of the door and away. You knew then that the crew, our hut mates, were not coming back. The thieves might even have been on the same raid as the men who were killed. Later the provost came round and took what was left for the next-of-kin. I only saw it happen once, but pilfering like that was not unusual, I can assure you.'

McIntosh still remembers the men he was closest to who did not come back.

'You couldn't think too deeply about them otherwise you would have gone nuts. You gave them some thought in your subconscious mind, especially when it was a crew who were nearly finished, who you'd known a long time and you couldn't see why the hell it should be them. At Langar, when we were a smaller squadron, we got to know one another and when you lost somebody you felt you had lost a friend. Later, in 1944, that seemed to matter less. They came and went like knives and forks into a drawer. Some people took the losses hard but it was something you never discussed.'

To speak about the dead might have put a jinx on the living. Aircrews needed to be cheerful, positive, pumping up their self-belief that they would always come back and death only happened to other people. But death was indiscriminate in war. Much depended on luck and where you were at a given moment. Bullets and shells did not have anyone's name on them, most scorched through the air until, energy spent, they fell harmlessly to the ground. Yet because so many thousands of bullets and shells were blasted into the sky during a single raid some, inevitably, brought down an aircraft and ended lives. No one would be spared the brutality of death because they were nearing the end of their tour, went to church on Sundays or someone aboard wore a lucky rabbit's foot. War was not like that, and luck only held until it ran out.

It helped to have an outstanding pilot and an alert and conscientious crew to deal with fighters. Anti-aircraft fire was another matter. Ack-ack was the grimmest reaper. Not aimed at a particular aircraft it was fired from the ground thousands of feet below, into an area of sky at the predicted height of the bombers in the hope that it might hit something.

'I was very lucky with my pilots, but even with a skipper who had all the skill in the world you still needed luck because nobody could divert an 88mm cannon shell if it was heading up through the sky and you happened to get in the way of it. There was nothing you could do to stop it. You could possibly evade a fighter, but flak was my enemy. And sitting in the rear turret I was also very afraid of fire, because obviously any fire was always directed to the back of the aircraft.'

Lucky charms were important for men who faced sudden death every time they went off to work. Some were openly superstitious, making sure they always took on a bombing raid the special scarf knitted by their mother or girlfriend, a child's doll, or a reeking pair of socks which would not be washed until the end of their tour. These talismans were thought by the owners to carry special even awesome powers which would keep them safe, failing miserably when many were killed. But this did not prevent other men from clinging to their own charms which they considered were endowed with more luck than those which had not lived up to the expectancy of other chaps.

McIntosh, who still wore Grandma's scarf and a number eleven flying suit, and another air gunner, Larry Sutherland, who would later join Grey's crew, went to Skegness for a night. McIntosh says:

'We met some middle-aged women; they could have been our mothers. They'd been to a meeting where knitting was done for the Forces. They gave us a knitted koala bear and I remember somebody saying later: "Every bloody crew that has a bear from those women gets the chop." I told him: "We'll hang on to it and see if it's true."

'We had this bear fully decorated with medals, and he had his own parachute. I hung him up just inside the back door. Oh, by God, he was important. If I'd left him at home they would have sent me back to get him. Before leaving for an op Grey would say: "Have we got that thing with us, Mec?"

'That bear got us through our tour but, after I'd been home on leave, I left him in my wardrobe at Errol. After the war my sister Flossie came and took him away. My grandmother had not known of his significance. I never saw him again.'

One of the least envied and rarely lauded jobs on a wartime RAF station was that of the armourers, without whom no bombers could have left the ground. These men worked busily and stoically, often in filthy weather, transferring bombs from the dump, near the village of Candlesby, at the far northern side of the airfield on trolleys towed by tractors to the fusing sheds over 200 yards away, and then to the dispersal points, spread around the station perimeter. Here they were winched cautiously into the Lancaster bomb bays. It was dangerous work and occasionally led to tragic accidents.

On the evening of Easter Monday, 10 April, when McIntosh and his crewmates were away on leave, most of the Lancasters due out that night on a sortie from Spilsby had been bombed up. The last delayed-action 1,000lb bombs, each fitted with an anti-handling device pistol, were being dealt with by armourers in a fusing shed. The armourers were very tired, having bombed-up and de-bombed the bombers twice before that day with different types of bomb for sorties which did not take place.

Less than a quarter-mile away farmer Len Bark stood outside his house at Monksthorpe, happily sniffing the fine spring air. The calm was suddenly shattered at 8pm by an enormous explosion, the vibration of which nearly threw him off his feet as a great mushroom cloud of smoke and debris ripped into the sky above the airfield. The shock wave lifted the roofs of his outbuildings, stripping off all the pantiles, while windows shattered behind him in the house. Detritus from the explosion began clattering around him like a ferocious hail storm, and a heavy steel bomb trolley soared over his house like a Heath Robinson shell, crashing into the road 100 yards away. Nearby communities were shaken, including Firsby where a concert was in full swing at the village hall. Glass was shattered and roofs damaged at several farmhouses which stood beside the airfield and extensive repairs needed to be carried out at the nearby Baptist church.

At the fusing shed, a fire raged around the edge of a deep smoking cavity, a scene of horrific carnage. Ten men were dead or fatally injured, others were seriously hurt. Three bodies were never found. The dead men ranged in age from twenty to forty, armourers and general duty aircraft hands. Several bombs, which had been fused, still lay on their trolleys.

Leading aircraftwoman Vera Tomlinson, a twenty-year-old MT driver, recalling the horror of that night, says:

'I had the window wide open in my little green garry and was within spitting distance of the bomb store when there was a great whoof! Bits of metal, uniforms and bodies were flying all over the place and, for a moment, I was awfully dizzy and disorientated, the sort of situation in which your hands do things that your brain doesn't understand. Men covered in blood staggered out of the smoke and I took some to station sick quarters where those covered in shrapnel were screaming. I helped there for two hours. It was not a pretty sight.'

The theory among the station's shocked armourers was that either the fuse being used was defective, sheer exhaustion had led to a mistake, or one of the anti-handling device pistols had crossed a thread while being screwed into the detonator inside a bomb, and instead of calling for help the armourer had tried to unscrew it, releasing the firing pin.

After debris had been cleared from the runway that night's attack on the railway yards at Tours went ahead. Early next morning another blast rocked the airfield as the remaining fused bombs detonated. No one was hurt.

The men killed at the fusing shed, together with an entire crew from 207 Squadron lost over the North Sea the previous night on a gardening trip, made this a black Easter for RAF Spilsby and the surrounding villages and hamlets.

Over the next few days and nights John Grey took his crew on tests and exercises. On the afternoon of 13 April 1944 they practised high-level bombing, dropping six dummy bombs over Wainfleet Sands. The exercise was treated as if they were over Germany, with a proper bombing run to the target and the bomb aimer, Bob Casey, crying: 'Bombs gone!'

Grey then said, crisply: 'Okay, now we're going round again, Mec has one to put out.'

'Practice bombs were not difficult to get hold of,' says McIntosh. 'I'd got one, weighing about 16lb, and put it between the guns when we took off. It wasn't easy to handle in the turret where there was very little room, but it was a bit of fun and one or two other chaps did it. We went round, got on the bombing run and Bob said: "Ready!" I pulled out the ring which armed it so the bomb would smoke off, and flung it out through the clear-vision panel.'

They left Spilsby at 8.45pm on 18 April, returning to France, part of a successful attack against the railway marshalling yards at Juvisy, south of Paris, bombing from a precise 8,900ft against little opposition.

'It was a clear night and we had a good look at the town. I saw quite a few aircraft coming up from behind us to bomb. I peeped down at the town and saw a mass of smoke and flames rising from the marshalling yards. Another job well done.'

A total number of 1,125 sorties, mainly on targets in France, were carried out that night, a new Bomber Command record.

Two nights later they hit the marshalling yards at La Chapelle, just north of Paris, and on 22 April, they were briefed to attack Brunswick. The raid was not successful but it was the first time that 5 Group's new method of low-level marking was used over a heavily-defended German city.

Although 617 Squadron dropped accurate markers visibility was obscured by cloud and communication between the bombing controllers was faulty.

'It was another 20,000ft job,' says McIntosh, almost salivating at the distant memory of temporary release from low level ops over France. 'The height was a psychological thing. The Lanc performed tremendously at 20,000ft, they were very economical at twenty and it was about the highest you could get with a full load. If you tried to go higher you were wasting fuel. So everybody aimed to get to the magic twenty, which we felt was safer than at eighteeen.

'Bob Casey liked Grey to go straight and level for about a minute-and-a-half on the bombing run. He'd say: "Okay, we've reached the target. Steady. Bomb doors open."

'After the bombs had gone we had to continue flying straight and level for ten seconds for the photoflash to go. They used to tell you that but it could take less than ten seconds. You did that to try to get a good photograph, but if a fighter was up your backside you'd get the hell out of it. Or you might have your photo run ruined with a burst of flak which made the aircraft shudder and instead of the photoflash going straight down you're maybe sitting at forty-five degrees and saying: "Jesus, that bloody bomb's landed six or seven miles away."

The bombing run was a critical time for all the aircrews in an aeroplane which had been described earlier in the war as a bomb bay with wings.

'It was terrible. The time seemed to have stretched to twenty minutes. We were so exposed. The bomb doors were open and the bombs were hanging there, vulnerable to a piece of flak. There was a good deal of relief when the bombs had gone because there was always a possibility of something unpleasant happening with them aboard. Going home there was less chance of you exploding if you were hit by flak or fighter. You knew, with experience, that you were more likely to be attacked after the target than before, because many a fighter hit a fully-loaded Lanc underneath and was blown out of the sky with the bomber. Many also flew into the debris of an exploding bomber which, if still carrying its bombs, became a deathtrap for any loitering fighter.'

Stepping into the restless stirrings and murmurings of a typical spring morning, while heading briskly for his breakfast, he hardly thought of the vulnerability of a man perched inside the rear turret of a Lancaster. Listening to the song of a blackbird, he was for a moment transported back to one of his favourite locations near the river Tay, until the image was erased by the increasing clatter of a busy airfield.

'At the back of nine o'clock I naturally wandered up to the gunnery section to have a blether with Jimmy Wardle, the gunnery leader. He might have some gen about new training methods or what happened to so-and-so the night before. I might just sit there chatting until 11am came and went and we'd say it didn't look as if there would be ops. A phone call was made to each department and a Tannoy call to the billets if there was a stand down: 'We'd wander back to the mess and have lunch, and I'd glance through the *News Chronicle*. I occasionally played snooker, although I was no good at it.

'It was impossible to switch off from the war completely, even if you had wanted to. There was always something different every day about the war to talk about. Somebody had heard of a chap who had been taken prisoner or they had heard something on the radio. What you didn't talk about was people dying.

'If there was nothing to be done I might go back to the billet for a snooze. We often needed to lie down to catch up on our sleep because you worked such erratic hours and each operation was physically and emotionally draining.'

If the brutality of war could not be banished entirely from a man's thoughts, it could be diminished for an hour or two by the frivolity and high spirits of youth and the mild craving for a pint of beer.

When McIntosh was on his first tour he and his crewmates occasionally 'bombed' the villages of Harby or Stathern on bicycles in the evenings as they hurtled in from the airfield at Langar.

'Six or seven of us cycled like the clappers down the lane, going into single file as we approached the pub. Putting our foot down on to the front mudguard we pressed it against the wheel and it went: "Zzzzzhrrrrm!" And they'd say: "Here are the boys".'

The "Zzzzzhrrrrm!" was a satisfactory imitation of a squadron of baby Lancasters turning in over the target, while upsetting some of the locals who had lingered for an hour over their half-pint of bitter, drowsing pleasantly at a half-hearted game of dominoes. They were less exuberant on the return flip to Langar.

'We normally pushed the bloody bikes back to Langar and spent a bit of time falling down with them. There was a lot of that. Some found themselves crawling about in ditches. None of the crew drank heavily – I'd never been inside a pub until I joined the RAF – but we were not used to drink, had taken a pint or two and were quite jovial. We didn't go to many pubs while I was at Langar. I didn't drink a lot at that time. At Spilsby I didn't need much prompting. I got a taste for it. I also smoked, a habit I learned in the RAF. I got through twenty Capstans a day, they were very cheap. A packet of fags was about a shilling (5p). Beer was rationed at that time. Sometimes the pubs only opened three nights a week. Other nights they might be open maybe from eight till nine. It was pleasant relaxing in a village pub chatting to people.'

One of the more memorable characters at Langar was the ebullient Squadron

Leader Peter Field-Richards, chief wartime test pilot for A V Roe which reconditioned and carried out major repairs on Lancasters there during the war. He mixed easily with everyone, but had a tongue which could be as abrasive as the harshest sandpaper, delighting his friends. But his fruity invective and icy glare demolished many arrogant senior officers who thought they knew more than him about his job.

The pilot also had the sharpest eyes in a beer drought when returning to Langar with the fiercest of thirsts. Field-Richards and his flight engineer, Paddy Armstrong, often did low-level trawls of pubs in the Vale of Belvoir, tracking down one with a brewer's dray drawn up outside, reporting the good news to their parched pals at the airfield.

As the war trickled on pubs also had an important part to play in the lives of airmen even when they were not really off duty. When bad weather forced an extended stand down at Spilsby frowning senior officers observed the cigarette smoke-choked messes through critically narrowed eyes. They saw men who, briefly relieved from the trauma of bombing operations, were beginning to romp like children let off early for an unexpected holiday. They chatted exuberantly at the bar, downing more beer than was good for them, losing money playing cards or snooker, or merely gossiping loudly and at length, sometimes about the war and how they could finish it by the end of the month. If rain was not actually pelting down groups of aircrews were outside playing football in the murk. This might be all right for the odd day or so, agreed the officers, but it was a rotten example to the erks who were getting on with the war behind their desks, in the hangars, and in any number of warm buildings dotted about the airfield. They decided, rather unsportingly, that the men were restless, it was a bad show and something had to be done about it.

Next evening, with the weather still closed in, six or seven coaches appeared. Their windows had been blacked out and aircrews were told to get aboard. Some displayed the sort of drooping expressions that could be loosely associated with being hung over. Most were cheerful enough later, comparing the day with the mystery tour they might be persuaded to join many years later with their local branch of the Darby and Joan club.

They had been comprehensively briefed, but boiled down the message was simple: they were being driven out into some corner of the Lincolnshire countryside and dumped. Each coach was heading for a different location. The aircrews had to find their way back to Spilsby. They were to show initiative and behave like gentlemen. It would be good practice in case they were shot down over enemy territory. There was one stern condition: they were to leave all their money behind.

Wing Commander Grey, whose lofty rank did not excuse him – and he might even have been one of the perpetrators of the unwelcome coach trip – was left with his crew by the coach in the dark on an anonymous damp road which offered no clues to their whereabouts. Road signs were removed during the war, a ploy designed to confuse any Germans who might be parachuted in. Their absence also perplexed and inconvenienced the British people, but this was considered a small price to pay for confounding the enemy. Navigator Happy Hall was consulted but pointed out that they might have been driven in circles and they decided to follow the direction the coach had taken.

They soon arrived at the small market town of Louth and made their way smartly through the dank fog to the nearest pub where they were welcomed by the locals. McIntosh recalls their relief: 'We had a few beers and enjoyed talking to people. We had cheated by keeping a pound or two in our pockets, but that didn't hurt anybody.'

When they began thinking about making a move Happy Hall told them gloomily that they faced a fifteen-mile walk back to the airfield. It was late at night and the thought of a long hike did not stimulate anyone's enthusiasm. Hall had a compass, but no one fancied cutting across soggy fields for short cuts. The landlord brought the bloom back into their faces with the fortuitous offer of a lift. They crammed cheerfully into his van and he took them to within a mile or two of the airfield.

On other stand downs they might go to Skegness for a bracing afternoon by the sea.

'There was a good bus service into Spilsby and we had our liberty buses. There wasn't a lot in Skeggy in those days, just pubs and one or two little dance halls. There was a war memorial right on the front. The Canadians used to climb it and piddle from the top.'

Many Australians served with distinction in Bomber Command. Not all lived up to their unfortunate reputation of being brash, or even objectionable. Although coming right across the world from such a large country to help save a small one from its tormentors, their perceived attitude could perhaps, after careful and prolonged analysis, be understood, if not so easily tolerated. Numerous Aussies, however, who flew bombers were less brash, more high-spirited, and certainly very likeable friendly young men, who fitted in well at Spilsby with 207 Squadron.

One of these was Pilot Officer Vic Glann, from Queensland's Sunshine Coast. Intelligent, good looking, likeable and impetuous, the pilot enjoyed having fun on nights off, but occasionally his pranks caused a little unease.

'I remember Vic and me and some others went cycling one night to go to a pub. Some, including Vic, carried their revolvers on their bicycles, I can't imagine why. At that time we were issued with revolvers. We were each entitled to have a revolver with six rounds, although I didn't have one, nor did anyone in Grey's or Fred Richardson's crews. Can you imagine me baling out and waving a revolver about after I'd landed? Some of those German women would have lynched me.

'Vic planned to shoot at some Aylesbury ducks that he had seen on a farm pond. He got off his bike, carefully laid it down, walked a few paces to the pond where the ducks were milling around quacking, took out his revolver and began taking aim.'

One or two of Glann's companions hastily pointed out that not only was there an element of foolishness in what he was planning but relations between the airfield and the farming community might be further strained. Not every civilian in Lincolnshire shared the drollness of airmen, especially those with an Australian accent who toted loaded firearms near duck ponds. Not only that, but the farmer who owned the pond might have hated airmen and Australians in equal measure while being totally devoid of a sense of humour. Farmers also owned twelve-bore shotguns which could put a bigger hole through a man than Glann's revolver could inflict on a duck. Glann was convinced and got back on his bike with the mild observation that the bloody duck would be lucky to live beyond Christmas.

Some men signed for and collected their revolver and bullets from the armoury, took them back to the billet, lay on the bed and thoughtfully fired the six rounds through the roof, then handed the gun back in next day. Although they had not wanted to take them on an op they did not want to miss the fun of firing them. They or their successors in the hut might be reminded of that the next time it rained.

'Wandering about Germany with a loaded gun was not a good idea unless you wanted to commit suicide. I suppose there was at least one fool who baled out with one in his pocket and I would be very interested to hear what happened to him.'

Vic Glann and his crew went to Spilsby one market day and found a farmer who was selling pigs. They appeared to be intelligent creatures displaying a sense of fun and inquisitiveness, which appealed to the young men. So they bought a young black and white pig, took it back to the airfield and showed McIntosh.

'It's a pig,' they said, beaming a little oafishly after indulging in what had become a merry intake of beer. 'It's a pig, all right,' said McIntosh, with the authority of a countryman who knew what he was talking about. 'It's a Wessex saddleback weaner. What are you going to do with it?'

They were not sure, then somebody thought the other officers might like to see it and it was carried off to the mess for formal introductions to be made, but the visit was complicated by the squealing pig running at high speed all over the place. This caused hoots of laughter from men who followed it at a crouch, hands outstretched, some offering the animal tempting glasses of beer, but the frightened pig eluded them all until a senior officer appeared, like a clap of thunder, wearing an aggrieved smile. He glared sternly at the rampaging creature and bellowed: 'Right boys, you've got a minute to get that out of here. And,' he roared, pointing a quivering finger at the offending steaming heaps and puddles, 'you can tidy that up.'

'I can always remember that little pig careering among the chairs,' says McIntosh, grinning. 'That was the devilment they got up to. They took it to a pillbox near the mess, maybe intending to turn it into the squadron's mascot. They put in some straw, barricaded the pig in and were planning to feed it from the mess, but this was going to be unsatisfactory and they were told to get rid of it. They gave it to a farmer and that was the last we heard about Vic's pig.'

Vic Glann was not always letting off the steam of exuberance. He occasionally explored the countryside with Wallace, who recalls:

'On fine evenings we used to go for walks or on our bikes looking for birds eggs. There were a lot of hedges near the airfield and we looked around the lanes a bit and I gave him a few tips about wildlife. Vic didn't know a lot about the countryside. He thought Aylesbury ducks were wild and should be shot on the farmer's pond.'

Grey and his crew went back to France on 29 April, taking off in ME667 X-X-ray at 10.10pm. The target was the Michelin tyre factory at Clermont-Ferrand, west of Lyon, which was attacked by fifty-four Lancasters and five Mosquitoes, which all returned safely: 'It was a fairly long and uneventful stooge, an easy target which we bombed from 6,900ft.'

They were all tired after being in the air for six hours and forty-five minutes, while maintaining the usual high level of concentration. McIntosh sat down as they were coming in to land.

'I had just relaxed a little and was resting my eyes. I leaned forward over the top of the guns, looking down for the flare path. We landed with a slight bump, which was unusual for Grey, and as I always sat with my fingers on the triggers my arms were nudged forward and "brrrrp!" I inadvertently pressed the triggers, firing off a short burst. It would have been too bloody bad if there had been somebody behind us. Normally if Grey had a wee bump on landing I would say: "Scratching the bottoms off the tyres eh, Skipper?" I said nothing this time. Grey didn't mention it but at debriefing someone did say they had seen my tracer going into the air. I wasn't bollocked, Control closed their eyes to these things, but I made sure I didn't do it again.

'We had an argument in the gunnery section about this when chaps were saying it shouldn't have happened because everyone's guns were switched off when coming into land. But that was the worst thing you could have done because the odd intruding German fighter was still following bombers through the runway at airfields near the east coast.'

This comparatively peaceful trip did nothing to prepare them for the nightmare which followed four nights later.

CHAPTER NINE

THE TRAGEDY OF MAILLY-LE-CAMP

'And tonight, gentlemen, your target is –'. The aircrews stared warily at the large map being uncovered at the end of the briefing room. '– Mailly-le-Camp.'

There was a nervous clearing of throats and scraping of chairs as the same question, accompanied by faint sighs of relief, was passed up and down the frowning rows of young men who, while being rather pleased that they had not copped another shitty target in the Ruhr, wondered why this place with such a high-faluting name was so important.

They filed outside having learned that Mailly-le-Camp was a small village some forty miles south of the French cathedral city of Reims. Their task that night, 3 May 1944, was to bomb a Panzer training and tank repair base near the village. The 21st Panzer Division was believed to be here, together with a large accumulation of military stores and equipment. This dot on the map was of significant importance to the enemy.

It was likely to be a fine clear night but the crews were told that if they were forced to bomb after their allotted time they must wait to allow the Mosquitoes to re-mark the target. It sounded routine without much sweat.

The general opinion was that targets in France were, on the whole, preferred to anything they had found over Germany and the ritual pissing on the rear wheel would be a light-hearted affair. Most agreed that Mailly-le-Camp would be just that: a piece of piss. Grey's crew later chewed more thoughtfully over their skipper's belief that they should expect fierce resistance on such a bright moonlit night.

Another raid, with eighty-four Lancasters and eight Mosquitoes, was planned the same night to hit the Luftwaffe airfield at Montdidier which lay near the route to be taken by the invading bombers. Hopefully the attack would shake up the airfield sufficiently to reduce the number of fighters it might employ to interfere with Bomber Command's main operation. Fourteen Mosquitoes were briefed to attack an ammunition dump at Châteaudun, while thirty-seven Halifaxes were to lay mines off the French coast and in the Frisian Islands. Several other minor raids were planned for that night.

The 346 Lancasters and sixteen Mosquitoes briefed to attack Mailly-le-Camp included eighteen bombers from 207 Squadron, with ME667 X-X-ray piloted by Wing Commander John Grey. Each of 207 Squadron's Lancasters carried a 4,000lb Cookie and from eleven to sixteen 500lb bombs.

In Grey's rear turret, as usual, was Flying Officer Wallace McIntosh who much later would say: 'This was the most deadly raid I was ever on, and the most frightening night of my life.'

It had been a pleasant balmy day and that night was dry and clear, as expected. After running up the engines and making the usual checks, crews, seemingly relaxed and happy, sat beside their aircraft smoking and talking about anything to take their minds off what might happen during the next few hours. To a stranger they would have looked as calm as if they were waiting for the pubs to open, but their insides were knotted with apprehension, although they did not talk about that night's op.

'You might look across another crew doing their run up, and watch the bowsers coming past. Everybody had his specific job and knew it and you'd be casting doubt if you spoke about what might happen. Nor did we talk about what we hoped we would do tomorrow or next week. There was none of that. I knew the pilot and navigator would get us to the target.'

The dispersals eventually became little pockets of quiet, broken only by a few murmurings as chaps were looking nervously at their watches.

Grey's new mid-upper gunner, Bill Charlesworth was to fly his first sortie with them that night. He was a pleasant likeable lad, and although it was not easy being transferred to an established crew the Yorkshireman had settled in well.

Everything seemed normal as X-X-ray sat calmly at the head of the runway, sniffing the wind, waiting for the green light. When it came McIntosh, crouched confidently behind his Brownings, and exchanged cheery waves with onlookers as the Lancaster sped past, building up a good head of speed to around 110mph. What happened next was alarming. McIntosh recalls the moment.

'It seemed to be a normal takeoff and then a quarter of the way down the runway there was a bang and the starboard outer engine caught fire. Flames started coming past the tail turret and at the same time I could hear our engineer, Tommy Young, cry: "Fire! Feather! Full power!" It was a critical moment because we were going hell for leather with a full bomb load and wouldn't have been the first crew to crash and explode at the end of a runway. There was no means of stopping, we had gone through the barrier for lift off. But I had complete faith in the chaps up front. I knew they would make something happen.'

The sudden kerumphing explosion of the disabled engine was heard and felt all over the dark airfield and resounded awesomely into the countryside. In the same instant the tortured Merlin, with an apoplectic cough, released a fierce surging torrent of flame which streamed terrifyingly past Wallace McIntosh in the rear turret. The gunner felt less secure than he had a moment before and worse, there was nothing he could do to help save himself or his crewmates. He could only sit tight, mumble a hasty prayer and rely on the skills of his skipper.

The great vibrating boom and intimidating shudder passed convulsively through X-X-ray as if it had been caught in the fist of a monstrous yowling giant, squeezed then shaken angrily in punishment for some terrible misdemeanour. The bomber continued to tremble and McIntosh, with his immense experience of near disasters and widespread knowledge of the sudden demise of other unfortunate crews in similar circumstances, knew they might only be a microsecond away from spectacular obliteration. If the fire sneaked into a petrol tank it would, instantaneously, rip through the aeroplane transforming it and them into a gigantic fireball leaving little evidence that they had ever existed.

He stared down at the unravelling concrete, but was tuned into positive thinking. Rather than dwelling on the moment he looked ahead to the target for that night. A small French village would soon play reluctant host to a large unfriendly party from Bomber Command. Increasingly, he wanted to be part of that party.

At the front the pilot, with cool discipline, heaved desperately on the control column and his engineer feverishly worked the extinguisher inside the burning engine. They were doing everything they could. Four other men in X-X-ray, equally as helpless as the rear gunner, forced into reluctant idleness, could do nothing but wait. And hope.

In the Lancaster's long cavernous belly one of the 500lb bombs with an early death wish, dropped loose from its mountings with a fearful thud and began rolling sinisterly back and forth. Its moment would come.

They had already run out of options. There was no time for John Grey to slow down the stampeding Lancaster in time to seek the security of the perimeter track and it would be suicide to veer off the runway on to the grass. This was a manoeuvre which others had tried with disastrous results, for fully-loaded Lancasters needed to be handled with paranoid care shortly before the point of takeoff. To give themselves a chance they had to keep going. The rest of the squadron would then have the opportunity to lift off in safety instead of being forced to fly over their funeral pyre at the end of the runway.

Meanwhile, the runway was shrinking, three engines were screaming and the fourth still burned fiercely when, incredibly, McIntosh felt his turret float off the ground like a soap bubble. Seconds before he might have risked dropping out on to the runway in a rash attempt to save himself, but now twenty feet off the ground and the aircraft pushing towards 100mph he stayed put, a little more confident and risking a thin smile.

Then, with a minimum of fuss, the bomber slipped into the air, the boundary hedge rushed by beneath the huge wheels, and McIntosh, with immense relief, heard them clattering obediently into their stowage position and locking shut.

They were in the air and painstakingly climbing, but the restless rogue bomb continued to prolong the agony and McIntosh, who anxiously watched the flames blazing a funereal trail for the rest to follow, says: 'Grey hit full power and we took off with flames still tearing past me.'

The Lancaster limped roaring into the air at two minutes to ten, dragging a great gout of billowing flame high over the hedge, accompanied by a terrible noise, which suggested the end was nigh. The horrified spectators held their breath and prayed for the aircraft not to explode. Meanwhile normal business proceeded as other Lancasters shuffled on to the runway and took their turn to charge down it and lift off, their crews half-expecting to see the wreckage of

Grey's kite burning fiercely in some field between Spilsby and the North Sea. They saw nothing. Young had extinguished the fire and they climbed slowly and thankfully over the green edge of Lincolnshire and the restless cold black water of the sea.

The fire in Grey's engine and the loud noise caused considerable anxiety at the airfield and no one was surprised to learn later that one bomber was obliged to return early. When the control tower discovered that it was not Grey's aircraft the concern deepened. What had happened to the squadron's commanding officer?

The second Lancaster in trouble was piloted by Warrant Officer W R Birdling in ND871 P-Peter, which was making its maiden sortie. Birdling later told debriefing officers he had used the whole length of the runway to get airborne. After that nothing he could do would persuade his aircraft to climb above 3,000ft, even with full power, although there was no apparent defect and the engines were all running smoothly.

He had decided to turn back but as the instructions were not to jettison bombs in the Channel he kept his full bomb load until just over the Wash when he jettisoned all fifteen 500lb bombs. With the loss of weight the aircraft climbed a little, allowing him to go out into the North Sea and get rid of the 4,000lb Cookie. Even without the bombs the Lancaster was not flying properly and it was a struggle to make a proper landing. The aircraft would be repaired but was lost over Brunswick later that month.

Meanwhile, X-X-ray had its own difficulties, but was coping well. McIntosh recalls:

'Grey would not have broken radio silence to let Spilsby know what had happened. The Germans would have heard and known that he was part of a group taking off. We went out over the sea for safety until we had sorted ourselves out.'

Grey switched on his intercom and said, with cheerful briskness: 'Right chaps.' Then: 'What are we like, Engineer?'

Young replied: 'The fire's out, Skipper, the other three engines are okay. We've lost the top turret.'

Grey, relieved that the fire had not bitten into a fuel line, said they would jettison a few bombs to help gain height and speed. They had become a straggler the moment they left the airfield and stragglers were not a protected species in war. A solitary Lancaster in trouble, beautifully profiled in a clear sky would attract German night fighters eager to add to their 'kills'.

Discipline was paramount at such a time. The minds of seven ordinary men might have been screaming their way towards hysterics, but these were no ordinary men. Any sweaty fear of death was brushed aside by the discipline that had been drilled into them over months of training and subsequent sorties. They knew it would only be cool heads and an instant assessment of the situation that could pull them out of this crisis. Panic would guarantee their doom. A Lancaster could fly well on three engines, but was not normally expected to do an entire sortie on three from takeoff. Nevertheless, having escaped calamity the crew soon experienced a curious euphoria, which had the effect of tightening their vigilance and determination.

'There's only one thing you can do in that situation, and that is go direct to the target. While the rest of the mob went south to Beachy Head we set a course on a straight line to Mailly and began crossing the North Sea. Grey had asked Happy Hall, the navigator, to give him a direct course, regardless of whatever we were forced to go over, we just wanted to get there. The other aircraft were following dog legs, but we headed for the target in a straight line. We didn't follow the proscribed route because we no longer had the speed.'

They jettisoned the loose 500lb bomb into the sea, followed by a further twelve as Grey knew the loss of weight would allow them to reach a greater height and help save fuel for, perversely, three roaring engines were now gulping down more than was normally used by four. They hung on to the 4,000lb Cookie and two 500lb bombs which they intended to deliver, as briefed. McIntosh remembers the tenseness of that night:

'Grey had done a marvellous job lifting her off the deck and getting us out over the sea. It was a decision which had to be made automatically, one which confirms the difference between the men and the boys. He said: "Right, we've deposited the bombs, the engines are okay, but we've lost a turret. Are you happy in the back, Tail?" I said: "Go, Skipper!" And we went.

'Despite what a lot of people think, a Lanc on three engines was fairly manoeuvrable. Grey just increased the revs to get the speed he wanted, although this meant, of course, that he was harder on the engines. The aircraft could have weaved too, but nobody was going to pop underneath us at the low altitude we were about to drop down to. The only thing that would have given us any concern was another engine failure. That would have meant us jettisoning, turning round and coming home.'

The main force had turned across the Channel from Beachy Head and would make landfall north-east of Dieppe before flying straight to a point around twenty-five kilometres north of the target. A yellow marker would be dropped near the village of Germinon, indicating the final run in to the target. Grey, who had already scrapped this route, crossed the French coast at around 2,000 to 3,000ft, bearing in mind that German gunners might be interested in the movement of a solitary low-flying bomber.

'We then came down very low, sometimes no more than about fifty feet because we were on our own and wanted to get below German radar and, hopefully, avoid fighters. We flew on in quite a bit of excitement because we were only on three engines. We had a new gunner, poor chap, who was sitting there quite exposed with no guns to fire because his turret had been worked by the dead engine. He was now just a lookout, but he wasn't complaining. We also knew that the territory between the French coast and Mailly-le-Camp contained around ten German fighter squadrons, which gave us something else to think about. We weren't bothered by anything on the way, although we did see the odd little combat in the distance with bits of tracer pooping off here and there.

'I remember the strange feeling I had that we were battling along on our own. I knew there would be fighter activity ahead. We were trying to make up time and as we got nearer the target we had made up quite a bit.

'We were about twenty or thirty miles from Mailly-le-Camp and climbing, when Grey said he could see a lot of combats going on ahead. There was considerable fighter activity and we soon saw aircraft being shot down. We could all sense the difficult situation ahead. We were going into that lot with only one turret.'

No one in the attacking force that night could have imagined what chaos they were flying into. The chaos had been caused by an odd, even ludicrous combination of foul ups. Marking for the raid had been co-ordinated by Wing Commander Leonard Cheshire, directing the main force to bomb. The markers had been dropped properly at the right time, but Cheshire's orders to bomb could not be sent to the waiting Lancasters by the 5 Group Controller, Wing Commander L C Deane, of 83 Squadron.

Only a few sharp-eared wireless operators were able to pick out Deane's faint orders, relayed through his VHF radio set, which had been virtually drowned by a loud confusing babble of voices coming from a powerful American forces broadcast. When Deane tried to back up his message in morse code he failed because his wireless transmitter had not been properly tuned. Angry voices were heard urging the Controller to get his finger out, a clear breach of radio discipline, but understandable for most of the first wave of bombers were left helplessly circling the target in moonlight, like great lumps of bait being whirled round and round on a cord by a falconer for hovering birds of prey, not knowing what to do. When the bewildered second wave appeared elated German fighters pounced.

The Lancasters which always appeared so big and fierce on the ground now seemed flimsy, plodding along death row, terribly vulnerable to the attentions of these small darting predators which carried such a destructive arsenal of weapons.

It was like flying into their worst nightmare and the hushed words from the rear turret summed up what they were all thinking: 'Jesus, fighters everywhere.'

'The main force had arrived over the target at the different times they had been given at briefing. Since then several bombers had been going round and round for some minutes because of the balls-up in communications. It must have been absolutely terrifying for the people who had arrived early. Some had to go round six or seven times, which was bloody disgraceful. The other Lancasters from 207 Squadron were circling at 5,000ft, 6,000ft and 7,000ft. There was nobody above that. We had climbed to 4,000ft. The fighters were very active as we arrived, tearing into the bombers. You could see combats, tracer flying, Lancs firing and fires burning below. It was a moonlit night made even brighter by the flames of bombers exploding and going down everywhere. Our wireless operator, Bob Jack, was helpless. He was waiting for the instructions that did not come. Intermittent messages came on and off on the r/t, but they were unintelligible.

'I murmured to Charlesworth: "All eyes open here. Complete search, level and above." Everybody was on visual. Grey, knowing we had one turret out, made sure everyone up front was on search as well. We were great guys for search. Our whole success was based on seeing without being seen. Our main concern was fighters, looking for fighters. Our lives depended on seeing them before they got to us.

'It was very nerve-wracking going into all that. Everybody was on their toes, but it was one of those ops where you felt so naked, so exposed. One pilot was clearly fed up and thought: "To hell with this." He just flew in to drop his bombs and get out of it. This had a snowballing effect with a few others following to release their bomb load.

'We veered left to join the other bombers which were circling the target in an anticlockwise direction. A Lancaster was sitting just below us and Charlesworth was giving a running commentary on it from his useless turret, watching to make sure it didn't get any nearer. Suddenly, a Messerschmitt Bf-110 came shooting right along below our tail, ignoring us but opening up on the Lanc, which didn't return his fire.

'I said to the pilot: "There's a fighter. Steady, I'm going to open up on him." The fighter dipped, came back and was sitting no more than 100ft below me. I even had a glimpse of the pilot when he fired another burst at the Lancaster. The fighter was still banging shells into the Lanc when I depressed my guns and fired at him at virtually point-blank range, full blast, straight into the top, it couldn't have been easier. He was just sitting there taking no notice of us.'

The fusillade of bullets from McIntosh's rear turret smashed into the fighter, its nose went up in agonised supplication, before turning over on to its back, one engine catching fire. Tommy Young and Bob Casey watched it go straight down and explode as it hit the deck. The crippled Lancaster, which could not have seen its assailant, had also fallen, engulfed in flames from the second attack. No one saw parachutes coming out.

Seven men who had left their airfield in Lincolnshire on what should have been no more than a routine sortie to knock out a few tanks had been blasted into eternity by a German who had followed them down less than a minute later, himself eliminated because he had not been more careful. Back at Spilsby the armourers discovered that McIntosh had fired 1,000 of the turret's available 10,000 rounds at the doomed German fighter.

'It must have been a terrible ordeal for young Charlesworth who was a very experienced gunner, but he was not in a position with his dead guns to help me. He couldn't get a good view from the top, because the fighter was right below us, until it went away in flames.

'Once we had got rid of the fighter Grey gave a waggle of the wings to make sure no other fighter was trailing us then it was full search again and continuing to circle the target although we did not make a complete circuit. It was absolutely bloody chaos. Other Lancasters were coming in to bomb from all angles and collisions were difficult to avoid. Here you were sitting in your Lanc on a moonlit night, fighters all over the place and some guy is sitting there broadcasting on the wrong wave length. It was a monstrous cock-up that should not have happened. We had become uneasy when we got within forty miles of the place and, of course, we were now in the worst situation because we were late arrivals and tearing along on three engines, using up more fuel than the others with four. Nor did we have the same power to get out of trouble.

'The Germans never seemed to display any reluctance in attacking bombers over their target, whether it was a big city teeming with people or a military camp. They wouldn't bother. Towards the end they were desperate. In 1944 they waited for you on the outskirts of a target then followed you through. You would be silhouetted by the fires and markers and they waited their chance. If a Lancaster was on its bombing run they'd go straight in at them. If the Lanc fired at them they might veer off to find another one. Over Mailly they had plenty to choose from.'

The order to bomb – which came too late for some – was eventually sent successfully to the circling bombers by the Deputy Controller, Squadron Leader E N M Sparks, also from 83 Squadron. Shortly afterwards his Lancaster, JB402, was shot down, but he and his crew all survived and Sparks, helped by the Resistance, got back to England.

'When we got the message to bomb, Grey just said: "Right, here goes." We went in, Bob Casey opened the bomb doors and we bombed on the flames. We had not seen a marker.

'After waiting for the photoflash to go off, Grey just turned hard starboard down into a dive and away. He said: "Okay navigator, a course for home." The word "home" had never seemed so sweet.

'That was us. Get those bloody lights behind us. We didn't muck about. We were so glad to be out of it because it had been such a balls-up. We went down to 1,000ft until we had steadied up and got a course. We had left behind a lot of combats going on. There was a load of fighters up that night. It was absolute bloody carnage.

'The only thing we were worried about now was the possibility of being attacked by a fighter before we got to the coast. That's why we went back down on the deck. Nothing came after us and we saw nothing as we went back across France at fifty feet. We speeded up a little, doing about 180 to 190mph. I loved it when we were very low because I knew we would not get anyone attacking us underneath. I was just sitting and watching. We were trying to keep below the radar all the time. The fighters had easier pickings well above us, without risking making an attack on something very low which might end up with them going into the deck. They had those sitters above cruising around as if nothing was going to happen as many of our bombers did through lack of discipline.

'We were worried about fuel, that's why we cut off the corners and returned virtually on the route we came in on. Grey asked Happy for a direct bearing then he and the flight engineer discussed the fuel situation. Happy also gave Grey an ETA for this course and they discussed this at different times during the return flight.'

The toll among the bombers attacking Mailly-le-Camp was high. Forty-two Lancasters were lost, and another, ME703 UL-S2, from 576 Squadron, badly shot up by a Ju-88, limped back to its base at Elsham Wolds, its rear gunner dead. The aircraft was so badly damaged it was written off. A total of 253 men had been killed, eighteen became prisoners of war, while thirty-three were evaders.

Two Lancasters from 207 Squadron were shot down. There were no survivors in ND575, piloted by twenty-two-year-old Pilot Officer Cyril Bell. In the other, ND556, rear gunner Sergeant Ron Ellis, twenty-five, was killed. His pilot, Warrant Officer Les 'Lizzie' Lissette, twenty-six, a teamster from New Zealand, died in hospital from his injuries. Another crew member became a prisoner of war, while four slipped away from the Germans and got back to England. 'Back From The Dead', the story of McIntosh's friend twenty-year-old mid-upper gunner Sergeant Ron Emeny's remarkable survival and escape over the Pyrenees back to England after being badly burned, is told in Mel Rolfe's *Flying Into Hell* (Grub Street).

Considerable damage was inflicted on the Germans' camp in which barrack blocks, workshops and other buildings were flattened or badly damaged and 102 vehicles, including thirty-seven tanks, destroyed. Most of the 218 soldiers killed were Panzer NCOs, some of whom had been sheltering in splinter-proof trenches. Another 156 were injured. A French family – a couple and their two children – died in the small village of Trouans, three miles from the camp, when their house was crushed by falling aircraft wreckage or a wayward bomb. Another small community near Mailly-le-Camp, Poivres, was a victim of crashing Lancasters and short bombing which caused the deaths of several villagers.

Four Lancasters were lost in the attack against the Luftwaffe airfield at Montdidier where severe damage was inflicted among buildings and installations.

When it was safe to do so Grey brought his Lancaster down low until they were again touching around fifty feet. McIntosh, his eyes darting restlessly about the sky, loved the moonlight and believed that, aided by Charlesworth, he would be able to give plenty of warning of approaching fighters who might be less interested in attacking a bomber at such a low level: 'Grey was flying from the arse of his pants, but after we left Mailly we saw nothing. We came back very low, climbing only to cross the French and English coasts.'

Luck had dried up for many men over Mailly, but Grey and his crew at last found a morsel of good fortune. They were not spotted by fighters or anti-aircraft positions on the ground. They were alone, the three engines were still turning sweetly, but they remained prepared for the unexpected.

Grey's three engines did not let them down, they climbed to around 3,500ft to cross the English coast and when they landed at nearly 4am they had plenty of fuel left in the tanks. Their aircraft was the last to land at Spilsby where everybody was pleased to see back a crew they thought had gone for a burton.

They climbed exhausted out of their Lancaster and reached for their cigarettes. Grey said grimly: 'There'll be high losses tonight, boys.' He reckoned as many as fifty aircraft would not return.

They were welcomed home by their faithful ground crew, who were always interested in where they had been and what kind of trip they had had, but there was not enough time to give a full report of the awfulness of Mailly. Grey told them of the problem with the duff engine and that the others had been on high revs for nearly six hours. McIntosh adds:

'It was the time to report any problems. The pilot would tell them of anything else that was faulty on the aircraft. There might have been coolant leaks, for instance. My guns had been fired and there might have been a bit of oil on the perspex or some damned thing like that. It hadn't happened that night, but I sometimes had a leak in the RSG (rotating service joint). The RSG took the hydraulics through to rotate the turret. The electrics also went through

Top left: Wallace McIntosh, aged fourteen, dressed for church, had already been working full-time for a year.

Top right: Grandpa and Grandma Hendry, the two most important people in McIntosh's young life.

Bottom: McIntosh at eighteen, with Grandma and sister Frances at Errol.

Top: France, 1914. McIntosh's father, Wallace Snr, second from left, fired a bigger gun than his eldest son, but did not match his successes.

Bottom left: 1939: McIntosh will soon be off to war but for now he is coming out fighting from the bothy where he lived at Rhynd.

Bottom centre: The Rev J L Fyfe Scott, minister at Rhynd, helped McIntosh fulfil a dream.

Bottom right: 1939: The sprog, with shiny boots but no thoughts above his station of flying in bombers.

Top left: Cockburnspath, 1941. Happy languid days. McIntosh is between two MT drivers.

Top right: Little remains of the radar station at RAF Cockburnspath now.

Middle: September 1942, 4 Air Gunnery School, Morpeth. It was here that McIntosh learned his trade. He is in the second row, fifth from right, circled.

Bottom right: The underpowered Blackburn Botha had a bad safety record.

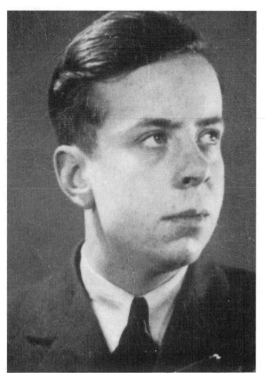

Top left: Fred Richardson, a pilot at nineteen.

Top right: December 1941, Sammy Craig is nineteen. Terrified of heights, Craig, a bomb aimer, went on to complete a second tour with 570 Squadron. *(Jean Craig)*

Bottom: Bombing up. Armourers load bombs into the great belly of a 207 Squadron Lancaster. *(Glynne-Owen)*

Top left: The smiles of these pretty MT drivers cheered up scores of aircrews. From left: Joyce Summerscales, unknown, Peggy Meeks (now Priestley). *(Peggy Priestley)*

Top right: Intelligence officer Joyce Brotherton was awarded an MBE for her work with the Red Cross after the war.

Middle: Lancaster LM326 Z-Zebra carried Fred Richardson and his crew to Friedrichshafen and on to Blida.
(Jan Verhagen)

Bottom left: Wing Commander John Grey, a larger-than-life character, whose crew would have followed him anywhere. *(Ivar Grey)*

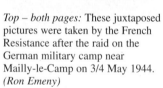

Top – both pages: These juxtaposed pictures were taken by the French Resistance after the raid on the German military camp near Mailly-le-Camp on 3/4 May 1944. *(Ron Emeny)*

Middle left: Flying Officer Wallace McIntosh – Grey's dedicated tail-end Charlie.

Middle right: Skegness, 29 May 1944. Dinghy drill. The first three from left are: John Grey, McIntosh and Harry Orchard, a flying control officer at Spilsby. *(Harry Orchard)*

Bottom right: The squadron commander and his crew. From left: John Cook, Bob Jack, Happy Hall, John Grey, Larry Sutherland and Wallace McIntosh. Flight engineer Tommy Young was away on a course with Rolls-Royce at Derby.

Middle left: Sharpshooters Larry Sutherland and Wallace McIntosh.

Middle right: John Cook's aiming point photograph of the raid on the railway junction at Culmont-Chalindrey in July 1944. Dark smoke rises from exploding bombs. White puffs in midair indicate photoflashes. The white light in the centre is a Pathfinder's ground marker. *(John Cook)*

Bottom right: At ease, gentlemen. Happy Hall (left) and Larry Sutherland.

Top left: 5 August 1944: bombs hit St-Leu d'Esserent. *(John Cook)*

Top right: Dutch pilot Johnny Overgaauw died within a few miles of his home. *(Jan Verhagen)*

Bottom: A quartet of air gunners. In the centre gunnery leader Jimmy Wardle stands next to Wallace McIntosh (hands folded), now the squadron's gunnery analysis officer.

SPILSBY 1946

207 SQDN. AIR GUNNERS.
MAY 1945.

Top: In 1946 the Lancasters were only a distant memory at Spilsby, but the runways, dispersals and perimeter track are clear in this fine aerial shot of the airfield. John Grey's dispersal point was second down on the right.

Bottom: McIntosh was on leave when this photograph was taken.

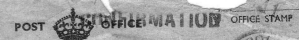

Charges to pay
s.   d.

RECEIVED

POST OFFICE CONFIRMATION **OFFICE STAMP**

TELEGRAM

Prefix.   Time handed in.   Office of Origin and Service Instructions.   Words.

15

m   115 10.42 ERROL 20   To   m

From

PO MACINTOSH W OFFICERS MESS RAF STATION

SKELLINGTHORPE NR LINCOLN =

= HEARTIEST CONGRATULATIONS ON YOUR DECORATIONS

= FROM ALL AT THE CROSS + PO +

For free repetition of doubtful words telephone "TELEGRAMS ENQUIRY" or call, with this form
at office of delivery. Other enquiries should be accompanied by this form, and, if possible, the envelope.   B or C

Top: Congratulations from Errol, 15 October 1944.   *Bottom:* Catfoss, Yorkshire. Not the happiest of times.
McIntosh is in middle row, third from right.

CENTRAL CHANCERY OF
THE ORDERS OF KNIGHTHOOD,
ST JAMES'S PALACE, S.W.1.

21st June 1945.

CONFIDENTIAL.

Sir,

The King will hold an Investiture at Buckingham Palace on Tuesday, the 3rd July, 1945, at which your attendance is requested.

It is requested that you should be at the Palace not later than 10.15 o'clock a.m. (Doors open at 9.45 a.m.)

DRESS:—Service Dress; Morning Dress; Civil Defence Uniform or Dark Lounge Suit.

This letter should be produced by you on entering the Palace, as no further card of admission will be issued.

I am desired to inform you that you may be accompanied by two relations or friends to witness the Investiture, but I regret that owing to the limited accommodation available for spectators, it is not possible for this number to be increased. The spectators' tickets may be obtained on application to this Office and I have to ask you, therefore, to complete the enclosed form and return it to me immediately.

I am, Sir,
Your obedient Servant,

Cockley.
Secretary.

Flying Officer Wallace McIntosh,
D.F.C., D.F.M., R.A.F.V.R.

Top left: By order of the King.

Top right: 1945: Flight Lieutenant Fred Richardson on his wedding day. *(Richardson)*

Bottom left: Linton-on-Ouse. Baggage and freight officer McIntosh (second from right), with some of his staff.

Top: A concert party from Linton-on-Ouse is ready to entertain at Crosby-on-Eden, near Carlisle. McIntosh, who organised these trips, is third from right. Pilot Wg Cdr Warner holds his parachute harness.

Bottom: Syerston, 1947. Outside station headquarters. All smiles as the stirrup cups are drained after the CO has led the local hunt into the Nottinghamshire countryside. McIntosh is second from left, back row.

Top left: Wg Cdr Warner piloted this Dakota from Syerston on a hay drop to stranded race horses.

Top right: Lindholme, 1948. Civvy Street beckons. McIntosh and Mosquito after a fighter affiliation exercise.

Bottom left: Two weeks after their wedding day in 1957: Wallace and Christina McIntosh.

Bottom right: Lizzie McIntosh in happy retirement at her comfortable Aberdeen flat.

Top left: A 207 Squadron reunion. From left: Ralph Fairhead, Wallace McIntosh and Fred Richardson.

Top right: Wallace McIntosh leaves a moving Battle of Britain memorial service in Edinburgh.

Middle left: The body of former air gunner Robert Banks is laid to rest in Cambridge.

Middle right: McIntosh was in his eighties when he returned to this bothy where he slept as a lad and the yard where he broke his leg, at Flock House, near Kinross.

Bottom right: Return to the runway at Deelen. From left: Peter Verrals and his father, Bill Verrals, Wallace McIntosh, Ken Williams and Alec White.

Top: Return to Mailly-le-Camp. Wallace McIntosh beside the memorial to those who died.

Bottom: Wallace McIntosh has achieved a good deal since walking along this drover's road as a boy. His Mercedes' number plate tells its own story.

Top: With pals from Grampian Aircrew Association. McIntosh, front row, is holding a pamphlet. *(Rolfe)*

Bottom: RAF Buchan, 2002. Still talking to people interested in the bomber war. *(Crown copyright)*

to this little service joint which was like a little revolving ball and carried all the services, and the oxygen. Anything which needed seeing to would be dealt with later that morning.

'We were picked up fairly quickly by a truck. They were pretty good at Spilsby, they didn't keep you hanging about. As we went round the perimeter track we looked over it to see if there were any spaces. It only took a few minutes to be driven to the debriefing room where it was nice to get rid of the parachute and the Taylor suit. An anteroom bloke took my Taylor suit and hung it up. A girl collected the parachutes. Normally we had a chat to chaps inside while we were waiting for a table to sit down. We were also given cups of tea and fags.'

They were debriefed by Joyce Brotherton and in the middle of it were joined by the station commander, Group Captain G Cheshire, who brought over his cup of tea and asked pertinent questions about the raid.

Afterwards, they waited patiently for the truck, driven by a WAAF, that would take them to the mess for a bacon and egg breakfast, one of the aircrews' little perks in a country plunged into austerity where there was strict food rationing. Here the casual chattering to people was refreshing, helping revive them a little from the long awful night, then they wandered back to the billet, a long walk, but less of a drag than it would be in winter. There were worse places than Spilsby just before dawn on a fine spring day.

McIntosh did not lie in bed reliving the tragedy of Mailly-le-Camp:

'It was gone as far as I was concerned. Sleep was more important than dwelling on something that was already history, however disturbing it had been a few hours ago. I was physically and mentally drained, but I knew it was one op less I had to do. At this time I was looking forward to the end of another tour. But I got into bed, got my head down and slept, hoping that I was not awakened too soon.'

He awoke refreshed later that day.

'I still wasn't dwelling on Mailly. I was just looking forward to the next op and I walked over to the intelligence department to look at the report on the night before and see the aiming point photographs. I liked to see what kind of picture we'd got and we had a great photograph of Mailly. Bob Casey was really pleased. The place must have been devastated.

'We were on the spot more often than not. Early in the war, of course, when we were saturation bombing cities it didn't matter where you bombed as long as they were dropped on buildings with people in them. There was more precision in the second tour although some from Langar, including those which went to Friedrichshafen and Cislago were extremely accurate. The Pathfinders helped a bit if they got their markers on the spot. Occasionally clangers were dropped; take Mailly-le-Camp for instance.

'Yet despite the chaos I think, without any doubt, that Mailly-le-Camp was one of the sharpest raids of the war. It was certainly one of the toughest raids ever carried out by 207 Squadron. It epitomised everything that was good with accurate bombing, but had the darker side with the terrible blunder that cost so many lives.

'Many books and articles have been written about the attack on Mailly by people who have made excuses and by others who have seen the mistakes that were made due to bad communications. Personally, it was the most devastating night of my life and I would like to think that those who took part will think of it as one of the great turning points of the war because the crews who came back after Mailly knew what was lying ahead and that they had to make it better.'

While McIntosh was walking from the gunnery section to see Grey he met the station commander with the station adjutant: 'I saluted them and the adjutant stopped and came across to speak to me as the group captain walked off. He said: "You had a hairy do last night. An award will be coming to the crew."'

The award was an immediate Distinguished Flying Cross which went to John Grey for his sterling work that night.

'I was absolutely delighted for him,' says McIntosh. 'I couldn't imagine that his effort would go unrewarded. By now Grey was the kind of guy you would have followed anywhere. He was a man and a half, a man who did not take chances, because he was always prepared. This was the great thing. I'm sure that many people were never as prepared as us nor had our strict discipline. Discipline was the key to winning the war, without it Britain's fighting machine would have fallen apart. Grey tried to be a perfectionist and was always in command. There was no bullshit from him, he always gave it to you straight from the shoulder.

'He liked to know everybody's job. He was pretty good at that. We used to sit and talk about turrets and one thing and another. As a crew we discussed situations that might arise and what we would do. We thought of all the things that might happen. The only thing that we never discussed was being shot down. That was never an option. That would have been defeatist in his eyes. He wanted us all to be so bloody super confident and by the time we went to Mailly I think that is what we were.'

A Distinguished Service Order was also awarded to John Grey at the end of his tour.

CHAPTER TEN

TERROR IN THE TREETOPS

John Grey and his crew went home for leave shortly after the raid on Mailly-le-Camp. The break could not have come at a better time. They were drained, needing time to relax and build up their emotional and physical strength after a particularly gruelling sortie. Currents of exhaustion generated by many hours of fierce concentration flowed down from the dull ache lingering stubbornly behind their eyes to lay heavily in their limbs. It was the fatigue of men who needed a break before they began making mistakes, for theirs was not a business in which mistakes could be tolerated.

The express steam train snorted majestically into the crowded platform at Grantham station, and drew to a halt, releasing a hissing torrent of steam. Wallace McIntosh was not the only serviceman heading north from Lincolnshire with a six-day pass safely in his pocket that night, but officers were in the minority. There were even fewer civilians to be seen. He picked up his bag and pushed slowly through the packed fag-fumed corridors, past crumpled erks and tommies sitting on kitbags, into a first-class carriage. He found a seat and fell into it with a relieved sigh. There was something to be said for being a cosseted RAF officer, although even first-class seats were invariably taken on this train.

Usually one or two men were prepared to talk to the affable young air gunner on a long train journey, but few spent much time discussing the war. Leave was the most important topic. What they planned to do on leave, how long it had been since they last got leave, how much they were looking forward to seeing their home and family, and wondering how much taller their children had grown.

He slept a lot that trundling and clattering night, but was awake and alert well before Dundee where next morning he changed to the Perth line. The slower train bumbled through a familiar landscape beside the river Tay to Errol, near the road on which he had ridden his bicycle another lifetime ago. He sifted idly through the memories of that first disheartening ride to Dundee before the war when, unable to afford the bus, he was desperate to get into the RAF. If a fairy godmother had then granted him three wishes McIntosh could not have imagined how much he would achieve and how much farther he had got than his most fanciful dreams. Gazing out bleakly upon fields and hills which had broken many poor but conscientious men and where he had once toiled for a pittance and little thanks, he knew he would never work on the land again.

In Errol, reunited with his family, he also saw men of his own age he had known pre-war. Most were dressed in Army khaki, privates, with glistening black boots and forage caps squatting on their heads at impossibly rakish angles. They stared at him not knowing whether to snap to a smart salute, or grin and hold out their hand in greeting. Some had fought in the Desert Army. Each had his own dark memories of war. None spoke of them.

Nor did McIntosh talk about his job as a Lancaster air gunner to anyone at home. He thought no one was interested, that they were more concerned to see him alive and well than speculating on what horrors might suddenly wrench him from them. His grandmother might have been tempted to ask how a man occupied himself in the rear turret of a bomber, but she feared the truth might keep her awake at night. Had she asked he would not have told her. Some things should not be shared with one's family. Gentle chatter about Dundee United and the price of beer were safer topics than relating with a shrug and a stoic grin how death came more easily to a man in a bomber than it did to a rabbit in a poacher's snare.

His grandparents had spoken of their one tenuous brush with Hitler earlier in the war when they took a rare train journey to attend a funeral in Aberdeen. That afternoon, on the way back, near Montrose, the train shuddered to a halt on the long viaduct over Montrose Basin after air-raid warnings had wailed chillingly across the town. The couple never found out whether the signalman had thought it would be safer for the passengers to be sitting above this large expanse of water for half-an-hour, or if the train had been offered as a tempting titbit to the Germans to steer them away from Montrose. Staring nervously out of the carriage window they spotted a farm, Old Montrose, where McIntosh's father had worked for the Fleming family before the war.

No bombs fell on the town or the viaduct, but it was a sickening experience which had frightened Elizabeth and Sandy Hendry, making them even more concerned for the safety of their favourite grandson.

One Sunday he cycled to Glenfarg where he met his old pals, Bill and Bunt Deas. Bill was a soldier, but Bunt had failed his service medical because of a chest weakness. The brothers were expecting him. They stood a long line of bottles beside a burn, handed McIntosh an air rifle and told him to deal with them. The lead slug of the rifle did not pack the punch of four Brownings, but the bottles were smashed explosively and the friends wandered the fields, chuckling over escapades of years ago.

McIntosh returned to Spilsby with a photograph of his baby daughter. He would often turn to it with pride in the weeks to come.

It was about this time that Tommy Young asked McIntosh if he would go with him one fine evening to see the parents of his best pal, another flight engineer, who had recently been reported missing. The man had flown with 207 Squadron and Young wanted to offer them a few morsels of comfort and hope. He had visited them with their son in happier times and although he remembered the parents as a kind friendly couple there was a pressing need to be backed up by chaps who would help him soften the blow of any anguish that might follow.

They squeezed into a tiny car driven by another flight engineer and headed for Derby. For McIntosh, who had completed over forty bombing operations in a big four-engine Lancaster, this was a curiously exciting experience. A passenger in a car no more than two or three times before the war, he enjoyed the thrill of chugging through the English countryside, having a while to look at the scenery, without needing to be totally focused on searching for incoming fighters.

The couple lived in a long row of terraced houses and as the car pulled up, the front door opened. Cups of tea were pressed on the three visitors who urged the anxious parents to cling to hope, earnestly explaining that the lad might have been shot down and was being processed at a prisoner of war camp. He could be in hospital. Or he might be walking at night, evading the Germans, hoping to make contact with the Resistance. He was a popular lad, missed on the squadron. The parents seemed cheered by these more acceptable alternatives to death and that their son had so many friends, which in itself offered some welcome solace.

'It was a sombre sort of twenty minutes. You didn't need to see them but felt it was your duty to go. His parents did not know if he was alive or dead, but they were both quite composed. I found it very difficult and it was worse for Tommy who had done his training with their son and was very close to him. They thanked us at the door where the father gave us two pounds each for a drink. I will never forget that. We heard later that their son had been killed.'

On 19 May they were among 112 Lancasters and nine Mosquitoes of 5 and 8 Groups sent to bomb railway yards at Amiens. It was a night which turned with brutal swiftness for Grey and his crew from smooth uneventful routine into calamity, and McIntosh believes it was the closest so far he had come to getting the chop.

Other railway targets in France that night were at Boulogne, Le Mans, Orléans and Tours, which were attacked with the loss of four Lancasters. The yards at Amiens were covered by cloud and after thirty-seven Lancasters had released their bombs the Master Bomber stopped the attack. One Lancaster failed to return.

'We were just approaching the target when Bob Jack received by code the order to abandon bombing, so we locked the bomb doors and came home. It was normal, after recall, to land back at base with the bombs still aboard. The bombs, after all, were very valuable, but while Spilsby was always prepared for any emergency there would be a little bit of a flutter at the thought of all the Lancasters coming home with full loads. We took our reciprocal course back and crossed the east coast of England where the weather had deteriorated. But our flight had been normal and nothing was said as we headed for base.'

They crossed the coast between Mablethorpe and Skegness and, losing height in clouds, approached the small market town of Alford, just below Lincolnshire Wolds, before turning south for the eight-mile doddle to the airfield. The flight engineer, on command, would soon be lowering the undercarriage before going into the funnel at Spilsby.

People in Alford and outlying villages had got used to the bellow of Lancasters taking off and coming in to land at RAF Spilsby, having given up complaining to the airfield and police station of exuberant young pilots in charge of hedge-hopping bombers. But early on the morning of 20 May, folk asleep in their Georgian houses and thatched cottages were shaken awake by the thunderous roar of an aeroplane skimming their rooftops. Some threw open their bedroom windows in alarm, expecting to hear the bomber plunge into the ground, but after a loud unidentifiable sound of a crunching and grinding the aircraft rumbled mysteriously off into the gloom.

'We had been cruising at about 200mph when everything happened so suddenly,' McIntosh explains. 'It was fairly dark but to my alarm I thought I saw leaves flying past my turret. They were leaves, but I had no time to think before there was a great crunching crash, the aircraft lurched and reared into the air. We had gone through the tops of some trees and the four propellers were cutting through them like great chain saws. Everything in our path was sliced down, the nose was torn right away from the aircraft and branches, four or five inches thick, ripped inside, slamming through the fuselage right up against the rear turret. Other branches struck the bottom of the mid-upper turret. The navigator was lucky not to have been killed as they swept past his table. Everyone aboard was shaken rigid, realising it was a miracle that we were still flying, but wondering what the hell was going to happen next.'

The words: 'Goodness me!' gasped by the appalled John Grey filtered through to each position as he and Tommy Young defied the odds by hauling the stick back to persuade the screaming engines to drag the shuddering aircraft off its bruised belly, unsteadily back into the sky, while a torrent of cold air surged through the ruptured nose. It was a supreme effort of strength and skill. Just before Grey had spoken the flight engineer had darted to the controls where he had been virtually in charge of the faltering bomber for a short time because the pilot had been taken ill. Grey had suffered from dysentery since his posting to India and occasionally it flared up to remind him of that country and its more unpleasant bugs. They had been clawing through his turbulent insides since their return from France, although he had probably been too embarrassed to mention his discomfort to the crew.

By this time they had probably spared a thought about the full bomb load they were carrying. Only a few feet from smashing into the ground they were lucky not to have blown up.

The Lancaster staggered into the air, flinging shreds of wood and greenery in its wake. Grey eventually got it stabilised and climbing and said: 'Okay, we're going out to sea to jettison.' He told the crew that he had misread the altimeter by 1,000ft.

It was at this point that the skipper thought of Bob Casey, who had been lying on his stomach in the nose. Young and the wireless operator, Bob Jack, slipped cautiously down the steps into the bomb aimer's compartment and found a horrifying sight. What was left of the Lancaster's nose was crammed with mashed-up branches, some of which had hit Casey. One slim branch had penetrated Casey's left eye, spearing right into the back of his head, bursting out through the leather flying helmet. The impact had flung him to the back of the nose, otherwise he would have been dragged out of the aircraft. Now lying unconscious and bloody, his screams of agony had not been heard.

Before Casey could be moved the branch pinning him through the eye had to be broken off. No suitable tool was available and Bob Jack was as careful as he could be in taxing circumstances. As the Lancaster headed steadily out to the North Sea, Young reached down and slowly dragged the injured bomb aimer up two steps into the cockpit. Jack helped ease Casey along the dark branch-choked fuselage, past the navigator's jutting table, which had been swept clean of charts and instruments, through the armoured doors behind the wireless operator's position, over the towering main spar, to the rest bed, where they tried to make him comfortable. Jack gave Casey a shot of morphine and McIntosh fought his way through from the rear turret to lend a hand. He was staggered by what he saw.

'The bulge in the nose of the Lancaster underneath the front turret was gone. The front turret with both its guns was still there but the nose from below the turret right back to the escape hatch had been torn out. There was quite a wind rattling through the aircraft, circulating the navigator's papers. It was absolute bedlam. Here we were with a load of bombs, an injured bomb aimer, a smashed-up aircraft, and a pilot who wasn't feeling too clever.

'There was no question that Tommy Young had saved us all. He had jumped in when he saw Grey was in trouble. He deserved an award of some kind but got nothing. We were very fortunate to only have one chap injured because many other aircraft in similar circumstances might have gone straight into the side of a hill or bumped into something more solid than the branches of trees. It would have been a bloody terrible way to end a second tour.

'During this period everything was going: "Bang! bang! bang!" and the aircraft was rearing up into the air as they pulled the stick back, kept it up and got her climbing. Everything was then under control.

'Grey had told me within two or three days of meeting him at Syerston that he suffered from dysentery. He took medication but the disease had been working on him during the return flight. He hadn't said anything that night and nothing like this had happened to him before on an op from Spilsby. He must have been praying that he could get back to the airfield and find a toilet as soon as possible.

'I was the designated first-aid man for the crew and came to see what I could do. It was one of the qualifications I had but until now I had never needed to use it. Bob, covered in blood, was unconscious with the branch, with leaves still on it, sticking through his head. His flying helmet had been eased off and was hanging round the side of his neck. Bob Jack and Tommy were sitting next to him and explained what had happened. I said: "Okay boys, the skipper's got dysentery, it'll be all right".'

The squadron's operations record book for that night reports that '. . . the rear gunner rendered first aid to the injured bomb aimer. This he did most efficiently.'

'Striking the trees had really brought Grey round and Tommy was helping the skipper because we knew he had big problems. He stood beside Grey, watching him closely, but it was difficult to stay on his feet because of the gale blowing through. There was a fear that, because of his condition, the skipper might collapse and present us with another difficulty. No one else aboard could have landed the aircraft.

'Grey climbed up to about 4,000ft over the sea. There was no time to find the designated area for jettisoning bombs. You don't bugger about with that in an emergency. Besides, some of the bombs had broken loose and were rolling about in the bomb bay and we were a bit worried about the Cookie, the 4,000lb bomb, which had a thin outer skin. It looked rather like several big dustbins welded together. We just went straight out and "Bop!" just off Skegness. There were no hang-ups, they all skittered out and we felt better for that. The bomb doors had been buckled by the trees so again we were lucky that the bombs had not gone off aboard.

'Grey sent off a May Day and received a QDM for Spilsby, we were given a priority clearance to land and full emergency services were activated. Some of the others were in crash positions when we touched down because we didn't know what damage had been done to the undercarriage. The wireless operator stayed with Bob Casey as we went down. I actually went back into my turret because I always felt safer in there while we were landing. I used to land with the turret on the beam, so if there was a crash I could open the doors and fall backwards. It was a self-preservation thing.

'Grey made a good landing at 3.15am, with Tommy holding the throttles back. Coming along the runway the ambulance and fire brigade were haring after us. We didn't go to dispersal. The aircraft stopped at the end of the runway for poor Bob to be carried out and taken to Rauceby hospital. We taxied round the perimeter and then the fun started.'

John Grey was taken to station sick quarters after the medics wondered if the rest of the crew should jump into the ambulance with him but although shaken up nobody was hurt. They were taken quickly by truck to debriefing and told to give their version of what had happened.

Visibility was poor over Spilsby with mist creeping across the airfield which was one of the few 5 Group stations open that night. A large volume of aircraft were circling patiently, waiting for a call to come in. Two 207 Squadron Lancasters, returning from Amiens, narrowly avoided colliding as they were about to come in to land. They were piloted by Pilot Officer Vic Glann, and Flight Lieutenant Albert Hollings DFC, who was on the last trip of his first tour.

Grey was next day transferred to Rauceby hospital, near Sleaford, for a complete check up and at 11am the others were summoned by Tannoy to report to the flight office. McIntosh says:

'I can remember the navigator saying: "We'll let Tommy and Wallace handle this." They felt they had nothing to add to what had already been said. I suppose I was the senior guy, and they knew of my relationship with Grey, who accepted that what happened was his fault. I would like to think they appointed me as their spokesman, although it was Tommy who explained what had happened after we had hit the trees and the pandemonium that followed.

'We met two senior officers from 5 Group at the flight office. They were carrying out a little post-mortem and were not terribly complimentary about John Grey. I told them that if he had been a lesser man we may not even have got up off the bloody trees and said he had done wonderfully well to get us back into the sky considering the condition he was in.

'They asked if I would be afraid of flying with him again and I told them straight that he was one of the finest people I knew and I'd be happy to fly with him next day if need be.

'Just me and a couple of the others were called in to be interrogated later at the court of inquiry which was held in a room at station headquarters. Grey was still in hospital and was spoken to later. We were only there five or ten minutes. None of the senior officers involved tried to impress us in any way or attempt to force us into saying anything. We just told them the truth and Grey was later exonerated because he had admitted mis-reading the altimeter. The fact that he was sick at the time must have helped him.

'I think if he had been a lesser pilot he would have got the sack, but the worst they could have given him with his seniority and record would be to retire him to a desk job. He was back with us less than a week later, flying an op without even doing an NFT. Everybody was glad to see him fit and well. He was a good CO and none of us had any reservations about flying with him again.

'Grey talked to us individually and was full of apologies for what had happened, said how sorry he was for Bob, and told us a new bomb aimer would be found straightaway and we'd carry on as usual.'

Some weeks later a familiar grinning figure appeared in the officers' mess, sporting a new left eye. Bob Casey's shorn hair had grown back after the operation to remove the intrusion and patch up his facial and head injuries. Luckily his brain had escaped injury and his spirits appeared undiminished. McIntosh recalls the moment when he saw Casey approach the bar.

'Bob was looking quite normal until I saw that false eye – it was pure white – and then he looked strange, although he said it was only a temporary one. He was complimentary to us all, even Grey. He looked on the entire incident quite philosophically. He was a great guy and stayed with us for two or three weeks because he was going backwards and forwards to Rauceby getting fittings for a permanent false eye. He wanted to fly with us again, but was eventually sent back to Canada.'

Although Bob Casey could no longer fly he still had the spirit to cause a stir. He was at his happiest and most mischievous sitting on one of the high stools at the mess bar, raising his pint, talking amiably to anyone who cared to listen, reaching into a pocket and casually exchanging the white eyeball for a blue one. Or black. Or red. He carried a selection and they were all displayed in turn to the watching officers. Business was always brisk when Casey was holding forth, although young inexperienced crews did not know how to deal with a man who could blink all the colours of the rainbow while supping his beer.

'Even at Skegness in the pubs Bob used to flick the eyeballs about. He had nothing but good to say to Grey because if the pilot had not got that aircraft back into the sky the aircraft would have had seven dead bodies inside it.'

A spare bod, Flight Lieutenant Wenham, was Casey's temporary replacement. Wenham caused a few ripples of envy when he first appeared in the mess where size most definitely mattered. Wenham claimed his enormous red handlebar moustache was eight inches long from end to end. Fitting the moustache neatly into the confining space of his oxygen mask, with a flurry of twists and twirls, working on one side at a time, was a masterly feat which was much envied by aircrew who had cultivated rather less imposing little festoons of hair on their upper lips.

Anyone born after the war and knowing little about it might imagine that men who flew in bombers must all have been gung-ho, beer-swilling, womanising, card-sharping tough fellows, who spent most of their nights off displaying their prowess as fornicators or drinking pubs dry because they never knew if they would see tomorrow. A few indeed displayed these admirable characteristics, but they did not always last their full tour.

Most aircrews enjoyed having fun and bending the occasional rules without going off the rails. Yet many were quiet self-effacing men who shared everyone's grim purpose but in civilian life would shrink from squashing a fly. Now they were being asked to kill, maim and destroy on a massive scale, and yet it had to be done.

One of the quiet men was twenty-two-year-old Flying Officer John Cook, a Scot, who followed Wenham into the nose in July. Born at Findochty, on the north-east coast, near Buckie, Banffshire, he had been brought up in Dundee. He had no qualms about the job he had to do.

Cook's father was an insurance agent, although many of his family were seafaring or fisher folk, but his ambition to join the Royal Navy was foiled by an accident. He joined the RAF on his eighteenth birthday.

After completing eight operations from Syerston, Cook was off flying for six weeks after breaking a leg. Another spell of ten sorties ended when his second crew finished their tour and he was posted to 207 Squadron on 9 June. On Sunday stand downs Cook, a devout Christian, cycled several miles to Boston or Wainfleet to play the tuba for a Salvation Army band.

McIntosh thought highly of the softly-spoken Cook, who had previously flown with 61 Squadron:

'John was a friendly, sincere and excellent chap, efficient at his job, and he got some good aiming points. He came out to the pubs with us and although he didn't drink he never spoiled anyone else's fun.'

They set off on 25 May to attack Stuttgart but again were recalled and came back nursing their full bomb load, delivering it safely back to Spilsby after a flight of 1hr 20min. Grey seemed on top form, none the worse for his debilitating experience after Amiens.

He took them back to France two nights later. They lifted off from the airfield in NE678 at twenty minutes to midnight to attack the big German guns across the Channel on the coast at St-Valéry-en-Caux, just east of Dieppe. This, his forty-fourth sortie, was the sort of op that made McIntosh almost purr with pleasure.

'We bombed gun emplacements fairly low at around 7,000ft. There was a lot of flak, but it was a nice short trip, a beauty. Just in over the coast, bombing with our armour-piercing 1,000-pounders and back again in time for a good early breakfast.'

On 29 May John Grey took his crew and a few others to Skegness where the agonies of war were brushed aside for a few hours. A little gentle dinghy drill was a very useful balm to men who had had little to laugh about in recent weeks. There was one anxious moment, as the tide was going out, when Grey began drifting out to sea without a paddle, but he had not gone far before the stronger swimmers of 207 Squadron plunged to his rescue and instantly jokes were born about the Lancaster pilot who had lost all his engines.

At this time senior German commanders were getting jittery, knowing an invasion was imminent, but not entirely sure where the full thrust of the Allied attack would be directed. On 4/5 June the Germans were thrown into even more confusion when three gun batteries, all deception targets, were attacked in the Pas de Calais. A fourth gun position, bombed at Maisy, Normandy, stood between what in thirty-six hours would be swarming with American troops on what became Omaha and Utah Beaches.

John Grey's Lancaster was briefed to bomb Maisy. He had a new mid-upper gunner for this trip: Pilot Officer Clarence 'Larry' Sutherland, a Canadian. Bill Charlesworth, who had completed his tour, was posted to 84 OTU at Desborough, Northants on 8 June 1944.

Sutherland had already flown twenty-two operations with six different pilots when McIntosh, who had been impressed by the Canadian while instructing him on fighter affiliation and aircraft recognition at Skellingthorpe, asked if he would like to fly with the squadron commander. Sutherland joined Grey on 30 May.

Four years before, aged eighteen, Sutherland, a well-built six-footer, with fair wavy hair, had been toiling with his older brother, Harold, in a 5,500ft-deep gold mine at East Malartic near the border of Ontario, earning forty cents an hour, eighty-four hours a week. He had been brought up near Truro, Nova Scotia, where his father, who ran a small dairy farm, could only make ends meet by also working as a superintendent on highway construction. Although the family, with four boys and four daughters, had little money, they did not starve. Sutherland snared rabbits and shot porcupines, squirrels, ground hogs and deer to help put food on the table. Shooting was a way of life. In winter they breakfasted on moose steaks which helped prepare the youngster for the job he most loathed: pulling turnips on frosty mornings with his bare hands.

After twice being rejected because of an eye problem – non-binocular vision – he joined the Royal Canadian Air Force in June 1942. Sutherland says:

'On the third occasion, when I tried to join as an air gunner, they let me in after I'd been told that I really only had one eye. But I told the recruiting officer I could shoot a sparrow easily enough off our barn roof from fifty feet. After the war I saw my papers in which the doctor's report had said that I was "Not aggressive enough for aircrew".

'I was the mid-upper gunner with Grey and realised I could see so much better from that position than in the rear turret. At night I could also see better as it was best to look to the side of a German fighter rather than straight at it. But I was virtually a one-eyed gunner.'

Curiously, Sutherland and John Cook discovered that they were distantly related and that their great-grandfathers had known each other, leaving Scotland on the same ship in 1856 during the Highland Clearances, sailing to Cape Breton island, Canada. One stayed in Canada, the other went on to New Zealand.

Maisy was covered by cloud and had to be marked by Oboe markers and Grey's aircraft was one of fifty-two from 5 Group to bomb the gun battery.

McIntosh says:

'What amazes me is that there we were on 4 June, totally operational, and we had no hint that we were coming up to D-Day. It was kept as an amazing secret. We knew the big push was coming, but didn't know if it would be in a day or two or a month. When it came we thought it would go straight across the Channel to Calais. But these other chaps on the ground only had one invasion, we had our own invasion every other night and Maisy, of course, was just one of them, part of the softening-up process.'

The following night they took off from Spilsby at 1.35am to attack the coastal battery at La Pernelle. McIntosh recalls the astonishing sight on their return:

'Coming back from this one at about four or five in the morning I looked down on a very busy Channel, full of ships and we suddenly realised that there was more to life than Bomber Command, but we had cleaned up the place ready for them to go in. We knew it was the start of the awaited invasion and told each other that we would soon be retired.'

CHAPTER ELEVEN

THREE KILLS IN A NIGHT

Although all aircrews regarded lurking Luftwaffe fighters with a deep burning hatred they did not share the same technique in dealing with them. Some adopted a passive role after spotting a fighter, the theory being that it was unwise to draw attention to themselves by firing their guns. Far better to give the German the opportunity to drift arrogantly by and find a more convenient victim. Fire only if it was clear that you had been seen. This was a philosophy that did not always lead to a positive result.

Other bomber crews were more constructive, combining daring with decisiveness and a press-on spirit. Both Wallace McIntosh's skippers, Fred Richardson and John Grey, were forthright, unflinching characters, preferring to make a fighter pilot aware he had been seen by letting him have a quick unnerving burst that might scare him off. McIntosh was convinced that cold-blooded aggression was the best way to survive.

'You had to show them immediately that they had been seen. I would have a pop at them and nine times out of ten the fighters would steer away and look for easier pickings, which is what they did at Mailly-le-Camp. They didn't want to be hit any more than we did. To sit back and wait was not the answer. Too many people were caught and put away by doing nothing.'

German fighter pilots much preferred running amok among a field of sheep than a pack of wolves. It was human nature to prey on the weak or the crippled. And having successfully attacked a bomber the fighter melted smugly into the murky darkness.

McIntosh, who knows of air gunners who never needed to fire their guns during an entire tour of operations, had no misgivings about trying to shoot down a German fighter.

'It was them or us. I always looked on it as a job. If I didn't get him and he got us he was going to get six of my mates as well. Our incentive was slightly better than his. I never gave it two thoughts. If we saw a fighter at slightly over 600 yards away and closing fast we opened up on it because it would be on top of us in a fraction of a second. Let him know you're there. I had a 22ft 6in square spread of bullets at 400 yards if the guns were harmonised.

'We knew the Germans were as fly as a bunch of monkeys, but their favourite trick was to get underneath a bomber, to get you silhouetted against the sky or the fires on the ground. He trailed about underneath you until the moment when he thought he was not being seen.'

McIntosh believes the Luftwaffe fighter crews were fearless during an attack and yet, perversely, could be just as frightened as the men trapped inside a crippled bomber if their lives were threatened.

While the Ju-88s, Bf-109s and company inflicted a horrifying toll on bombers and their crews, British air gunners did not always get the full credit for the damage they had caused their tormentors. A fighter which fell through the sky, trailing flames and smoke, hitting the deck or the sea, was an obvious kill. But many, which pulled away after a brief skirmish, did not always return to the prowl for an easier victim. Some struggled back to base with faltering engines or an injured pilot. Other men were forced to bale out many miles away, while there were those unaware that their airfield had been bombed, and taxied helplessly into a crater.

In a scrap between bomber and fighter, much depended on whose finger was first to press the firing button. Some air gunners squandered any possible advantage they might have trained hard for by being so surprised by a sudden fighter attack that their fingers were momentarily paralysed before they could apply pressure to the button. The advantage was then passed swiftly to their adversary, often with tragic consequences. A gunner really needed six pairs of eyes to have a reasonable chance of covering his area of the sky, and even then it might have been a struggle.

McIntosh did not waste time when it came to killing Germans. He was a crack shot, which helped considerably in a Lancaster which, compared to a German fighter, was inadequately armed. With only a split second available to react to a sudden attack he knew that if he did not get in the first burst the fighter would probably rake them with bullets and cannon shells, with a good chance of causing terminal damage. His position in the tail turret was not an agreeable place for anyone contemplating living long enough to draw his pension. But given the advantage of a microsecond the Scotsman could drill holes into a vital part of an aircraft with a minimum expenditure of .303in bullets.

'The toughest German fighter to deal with was the Junkers-88. It had tremendous fire power and could trail you for much longer than anything else because it had the range.'

The Ju-88 was indeed a prolific killing machine. Powered by twin 1,340hp Junkers Jumo 211J-1, or J-2 engines, with a crew of two or three, it had a top speed of 307mph, and a maximum range of 1,230 miles. It was equipped with three 20mm cannon and three 7.9mm machine guns in the nose, and one 13mm machine gun at the rear of the cockpit. Some night fighters, including the Ju-88, were also fitted with a pair of deadly upward-firing machine guns or cannon in the fuselage. They became known as Schräge Musik – jazz music – and were responsible for shooting down many RAF bombers. Bomber Command did not know of their existence until after the war.

'German fighter pilots were fairly daring guys to go up the backside of a Lancaster full of bombs and have a go at it. They were very confident, knocking down twenty or thirty of our aircraft every other night and thought nothing was ever going to happen to them. A bit like the bomber boys, I suppose.'

Early in the war gunners were not as highly regarded as the more technical members of a bomber crew. Being an air gunner was generally thought to be less prestigious than having a pilot's wings, or the half wings of the navigator or wireless operator. Times changed when brass hats realised there was more to a bomber crew than setting a course, listening in for coded wireless messages, or even flying the aircraft. Gunners could save lives.

Not surprisingly air gunners regarded themselves as a special breed who spent hours talking tactics and swapping stories in the mess or the large gunnery room at Spilsby where eighty or ninety often gathered, absorbed in their own particular skills, always eager to sharpen their reflexes and consider ways they could outthink night fighters and blast more of them across the sky.

Having completed over forty sorties Wallace McIntosh was regarded by the younger men as an icon for survival, a rock to cling to in this terrible war. And when McIntosh talked about aircraft recognition and searching they listened, because they were attracted by the unlikely notion of living long lives. Many a lad shyly approached McIntosh for guidance.

The gunners taking part in these sessions were not all sprogs, some were experienced gunners with maybe fifteen or twenty trips behind them. McIntosh's aim was to give everyone confidence in their ability while sharpening their reflexes.

'We often projected pictures on to a big screen by an epidiascope. We always used tricky ones, trying to fool them. The silhouettes were only there for a fraction of a second because that's all the time they would normally have in the air. We showed them the 109 and Spitfire, fairly close together, a Focke-Wulf and a Thunderbolt, and the Dornier 217 coming in at different angles.

'I involved Larry Sutherland too because it was good for him. Larry pulled the handle and one day he put his false teeth in the epidiascope and flashed them up on the screen. They were identified as the new Gnasher night fighter.

'We had a bit of fun and it was good for chaps to have a laugh. I think all this helped give them confidence. I spent a lot of time with gunners, often just chatting, knowing bloody well that seven out of ten of them weren't going to be running around in a few months. Experience was a great thing and I was cajoling and nurturing them every day they were in for lectures between ops. I always encouraged them. There was nothing better than a bit of praise when they did something good. But I kicked their arse if they did something wrong.'

Tom Rogers, a rear gunner who had shot down two German aircraft, remembers being instructed by McIntosh. Fulham-born Rogers says:

'I was extremely good at aircraft recognition, but Wallace tore me off a strip something diabolical for wrongly identifying a wing tip that came up in a split-second flash on the screen. I thought it was a Bf-109, but it was a Hurricane. If I'd been in the air I might have shot down a Hurricane and that was frowned on. Wallace was the driving force for me in the gunnery section and I'm very grateful to him.'

Grey took off at thirty minutes before midnight on 7 June 1944, heading once more for France. His aircraft, LL973 M-Mother, was among 112 Lancasters and ten Mosquitoes which had been sent to attack the enemy who were lurking in great numbers in extensive woods to the west of Caen at Forêt de Cerisy, between Bayeux and St-Lô. McIntosh well remembers their briefing:

'We were told that the woods, covering many acres, were concealing fuel dumps, a heavy concentration of tanks, mobile guns, and a lot of armoury which was to be used to repel the Allied invasion and back up the stuff which was at the front. It was our job to pattern bomb the woods and destroy as many tanks with their crews and back-up equipment as possible. There was also a lot of transport, repair people and hundreds of troops. We were sent in groups to attack different parts of the woods which were fairly-well defended because this was the Germans' main armoury to fight off the invasion.

'We went in at around 7,000ft and bombed heavily. It was quite a good night, reasonably light and we could feel it was the sort of target that would demand a little bit of defending from the air. The woods were back from the coast, and there were a lot of German fighter 'dromes in the area. We sensed fighters would be about and we were right.

'As we were leaving the target, flying above a piece of nice white cloud, we spotted a Ju-88 about 1,000 yards out on our starboard wing keeping pace with us. The German made no attempt to do anything except occasionally put on his lights, then flick them off.

'While I was searching around another Ju-88 suddenly came right up at the back of us. I could see his props twirling as he came up to less than 300 yards behind us and slightly below. He was too bloody close, I thought, very negligent. It was almost as if he was trying to ram us. Larry Sutherland and I immediately opened fire and I shouted: "Corkscrew!" and we went into this nice shallow corkscrew, not a full-blooded dive, which put him above us and meant we could utilise all our guns. At the same time we had to keep an eye on the other fighter. The one behind was so close, Larry Sutherland and I easily dealt with him and he was on fire when he went down very quickly. The funny thing was, he had never once opened up and never fired back at us. But if he had his bullets and shells would have passed over the top of us anyway.

'The first Ju-88 was still lying off us in the same position, waiting to come in. The two had obviously been working together. After seeing his mate go down he immediately came tearing straight in from the starboard side. We nailed him, too. We went towards the fighter with the corkscrew, diving into him to increase his angle and get him superimposed against the sky. We blazed away from about 750 yards, and Sutherland was getting great shots in off the beam as he came in and the fighter exploded almost beneath us, lifting our aircraft which shuddered as the Ju-88 went down in flames.'

There was no question of either Ju-88 hobbling back to their base in France. Both fighters had clearly plunged straight down, giving the crews no chance to bale out. The first Ju-88 was shot down at 1.56am. The second splashed into the sea one minute later.

In that single minute the odds had been weighed heavily against anyone surviving in the Lancaster. They lived because their skills – and probably their experience – were superior to that of the Germans who lost the fights because they hesitated.

Grey was an expert at getting out of trouble with a quick carefully-executed corkscrew:

'A lot of pilots made the mistake of just sticking the bloody nose down for a corkscrew. That threw the arse of the aircraft into the air and the gunner lost control. If you suddenly go: "Bffff!" you're not going to have the same control of your guns. It should not be done violently. We had practised the corkscrew so much with cameras and all sorts that we knew exactly how our pilot was going to go into it.'

Grey asked, cautiously: 'How much ammunition have you got left in the back, Mec?'

His rear gunner replied, with confidence: 'We're okay, Skipper.'

The crew settled down quickly after the excitement of two fighter attacks and the navigator crept anxiously through the dark fuselage trying to recover some of his equipment which had been scattered by the corkscrews. Grey was back on track, skating perkily along a bank of white cloud at 6,000ft, approaching England, conscious that British ships and coastal defences might open up at any second, even though they had been warned that ops were on that night. Such nervousness among ship and land-based gunners suggested a not unreasonable overwhelming desire for self-preservation, although such action directed at the crews of bombers who had just escaped a particularly shaky do usually caused a certain amount of alarm and irritation.

They were approaching the English coast and other Lancasters were switching on their navigation lights prematurely to reassure gunners on the coast that friendly bombers were overhead and that they should relax. Having been attacked twice in rapid succession everyone on Grey's aircraft was on full-scale lookout and scornful of the other bombers' careless attitude. Tommy Young was staring out of the side and even Happy Hall, the navigator, was looking out of the astrodome, but he was aware that the pilot now knew his way home. Almost without realising it the skipper's eyes also flickered speculatively out into the gloom.

Suddenly wireless operator Bob Jack's troubled voice crackled over the intercom. McIntosh recalls the moment when hearts sank and they wondered if this was a case of being the third time unlucky.

'Bob said he had picked up on his monitor an unusual movement of an aircraft down underneath on our port side. He explained that the aircraft was acting very suspiciously coming in, then drawing back. None of the Lancs were doing that, they were going straight home.

'I was really in control in these situations and said quickly: "For God's sake lads, keep your bloody eyes open. What distance, Bob?" He said: "About 600 to 700 yards." I replied: "All right." It might have been another Lancaster or a Mosquito because Bob now said it was holding its position. Sutherland was watching the port side and I was looking below and beyond the tail. Even Grey said he was looking.'

Seconds seemed to stretch worryingly into minutes. They would soon be crossing Beachy Head and then home. But would they make it? The tension inside the aircraft seemed almost tangible. It was one thing being shot down over enemy territory, but to be nailed over your own country after the jubilation of bagging two night fighters would be a real pain in the backside. Bob Jack's voice exploded with excitement: 'It's disappeared.' Then, urgently: 'It's coming in fast behind, now!'

'And looking down on the port side there it was, settling right underneath us, his props whirling,' says McIntosh. 'It was big and shiny and had a glassy look about it. I said abruptly that it was a Messerschmitt 210. It had clearly been vectored on to us and was just hanging there, but we were ready for him. Grey put the nose down slightly and there was the fighter, fully exposed. I had a great view as we edged down to get him up. The German moved up and Larry and I blasted him with all six guns. He didn't have a chance and we gave him no opportunity to get in a shot at us. He wasn't very clever, a sitting duck. The fighter turned over, caught fire, and went spiralling down, crashing into the sea quite close to the beach at Beachy Head. It was 2.33am. The two German crewmen were killed and we carried on back to Spilsby. It had been quite a night, but if it had not been for Bob Jack we would have been in a lot of trouble. Another four Lancasters nearby with their recognition lights on suddenly switched them off pretty quickly.'

They landed with some relief at 3.40am and climbed groggily out of the aircraft. Wenham, their temporary bomb aimer, fell dramatically to his knees on the ground and exclaimed: 'Jesus, is it always like this for you chaps?'

Grey and his crew were not exactly afforded VIP treatment that morning, but their activity near Beachy Head had been seen by other 207 Squadron crews and they spent more time than usual in the debriefing hut with the intelligence officers. McIntosh remembers the increasing interest when it was known that there was more to their story.

'Back at Spilsby our trip caused bloody panic, a lot of flap. It was unusual for one bomber to shoot down three German fighters in one night. Chaps began asking: "Is this what we have to look forward to?" Because at that time the German fighters were increasing tremendously in numbers. More night fighters were being seen, there were more attacks on our bombers and more were being shot down. There was a sort of peak time for the number of Luftwaffe fighters around April to July in 1944.

'People were becoming more nervous and what happened to us made pilots think that their gunners were more than just sitting on their arses at the back. This was where the extra training came into it and aircraft recognition.

'Credit should also be given to the armourers because when I checked with Larry he said he hadn't had one stoppage on his guns. I had one stoppage after the second combat. I had four guns blazing away and didn't know which one had stopped. After we had levelled out I pulled the cocking toggle which drew the breech back of that particular gun, loading it ready to fire again. I fired a quick burst to make sure. The armourers' maintenance of the guns was marvellous. For us it was like driving 200,000 miles in a car and only having one carburettor failing. I fired over 8,000 rounds in those three combats and Larry had just about emptied the cases on top. The first thing I did after getting some sleep was to go out to the aircraft and congratulate the armourers on the way my turret had been maintained.'

There were no cheers or speeches after their return, just a few quiet sincere well dones. One or two chaps said laconically they had heard the Grey crew had enjoyed a quiet night.

They were given an extended briefing and later that day a stopper was put on their Lancaster to check the amount of ammunition that had been used and the condition of the guns. They slipped into the mess for breakfast, then bed, the bedlam of battle behind them, their weary brains closing down.

After a few hours' sleep McIntosh and Grey met in the mess. The pilot, who wore an unfathomable grin, said:

'That aircraft we shot down at Beachy Head was an Me-410, Mec. You clever fellows said it was a 210.' McIntosh, bristling, growled: 'Can you tell the difference, Skipper?'

'Yes, the 410 has got more aerials.'

McIntosh remembers the exchange with relish:

'I said: "Oh shit!" But it became a bit of a joke. He liked to have one over on us, especially knowing how keen I was on aircraft recognition. In fact, externally the 210 and 410 looked exactly the same.'

When Grey read through McIntosh's logbook entries for June 1944 before signing it as squadron commander on 1 July he pressed a quizzical forefinger against the remarks column for the Forêt de Cerisy raid, where McIntosh had written: 'Quiet trip.' Grey said:

'That's a really sharp witticism.' He paused, then added, in mock severity: 'You're being rather cocky with that.'

'It was something to be cocky about,' replied McIntosh, grinning.

Nearly sixty years later, he says:

'We were told that the fighter wreckage had been recovered, then heard it had been washed out to sea. A Lancaster popping off three fighters in a night was virtually unheard of and the phones were hot between Spilsby and Group and Bomber Command. Cochrane, the AOC for 5 Group, rang our station commander, then the great man himself, Air Chief Marshal Sir Arthur Harris, Bomber Command's commander-in-chief, got on the phone to Cochrane and said: "Who are these fellows?" It was a busy sort of a day.'

McIntosh and Sutherland were called to station headquarters with Grey, where the two gunners learned that they had each been awarded immediate DFCs.

'This was a great honour for the gunnery section and the boys there were very happy for us. The group captain also told us that Cochrane had ordered Larry and I to go to 5 Lancaster Finishing School at Syerston to give the chaps under training a pep talk and tell them about our experiences on the night we went to Forêt de Cerisy.'

Ten days later McIntosh was delighted to receive a postagram, signed by Sir Arthur Harris: 'My warmest congratulations on the award of your Distinguished Flying Cross.'

The air gunners' award, promulgated in the *London Gazette*, read:

> *One night in June 1944 these officers were rear and mid-upper*
> *gunners respectively of an aircraft detailed to attack Cerisy. Just*
> *after crossing the enemy coast Flying Officer McIntosh sighted a*
> *Junkers-88 coming in to attack. He promptly warned his pilot*
> *who took the necessary combat manoeuvre. Both gunners then*

*opened fire, hitting the enemy aircraft with well-placed bursts,
causing it to spin towards the ground with both its engines on fire.
Almost immediately another Junkers-88 was sighted. As the
enemy aircraft came into close range Flying Officer McIntosh
and his co-gunner met the attacker with devastating bursts of fire
which caused it to explode in the air. Half-an-hour later, these
gunners engaged yet a third enemy aircraft. Following their
accurately-placed bursts of fire the enemy fighter fell away and
was seen to catch fire before it hit the sea. Flying Officer
McIntosh and Pilot Officer Sutherland defended their aircraft
with great skill and resolution and undoubtedly played a large
part in its safe return. Their achievement was worthy of high
praise.*

Their three kills featured prominently in the next issue of *5 Group News* with
a foreword by Cochrane who praised Grey's crew for going on the offensive
against night fighters.

McIntosh was still thinking about what he could tell the aircrews at Syerston
when they were sent on another sortie. Bomber Command were still pounding
German positions in France and an attack was planned in great haste on 14
June after the British Army reported large numbers of German troops and
vehicles at Aunay-sur-Odon and Évrecy, near Caen.

New guns had been fitted in the mid-upper and rear turrets and McIntosh
and Sutherland each fired a quick burst into the ground at dispersal to test them
before leaving.

Still preoccupied with the traumas of Forêt de Cerisy they were all more
nervous than usual. McIntosh recalls the flight to and from Aunay-sur-Odon:

'We left Spilsby at 10.15pm quite bothered about this trip. Our eyes were
popping out of our heads twice what they would have been normally, we were
certainly on our toes. And so were all the squadron because they knew those
fighters were lying about out there. But it turned out to be a run-of-the-mill op.'

Certainly, if the Luftwaffe had been sent to deal with the bomber stream they
did not molest Grey's Lancaster which landed comfortably at Spilsby after a
4hr 30min flight.

On 17 June Wallace McIntosh and Larry Sutherland really did become VIPs
for the day. They also became willing propaganda tools of Bomber Command
which, at last, had credibility for a theory that the Lancaster could not only be
defended with great vigour and panache, but could also be used offensively
with some success against persistent German night fighters.

A Lancaster laid on for them at Spilsby late that morning was piloted by
Flight Lieutenant Cullinane, who also held the DFC. During the thirty-minute
flight across Lincolnshire to Syerston McIntosh, who in a few years had risen
to the status of a decorated sharpshooter, scanned the scrap of paper on which
he had written a list of headings, and thought through what he would say.

'This had been sprung on us. I hadn't spoken to so many people at one time
before, but Grey had told me: "You've got to do it. This is important." I wasn't
nervous but, as always, it was something I wanted to do properly.'

By this time the two gunners had become legends on 207 Squadron, and were among Bomber Command's top scoring air gunners. They were pointed out to new arrivals as the squadron's sharpshooters, whose ability had been brought to the attention of Butch Harris.

They were taken into a hangar where their audience of around 250 men had been told that they were to meet a pair of air gunners who had shot down three night fighters on a single sortie, an exceptional effort even in this bloody war. Expecting a pair of super heroes they watched their group captain introducing two men who looked no different from themselves. Two or three years older, perhaps, and a bit more weary about the eyes. But it was the unremarkable appearance of the visitors combined with their undoubted experience that compelled the predominantly raw young crews to listen attentively. Although, in their minds, death still only happened to the other fellows these gunners might have something to offer, for they had been to the other side of hell many times to tangle with the enemy and had survived. They might even have real tips for outwitting the Hun that they could discuss later in the mess, together with the sort of good positive news they could send home in letters to cheer up families, wives and sweethearts. Suddenly it seemed that this was not going to be another bog-standard rallying call.

McIntosh climbed on to a trestle table, turned, shoulders erect, and faced his seated audience, all aircrews in training, and others who were coming through for their second tours. They saw a proud 'honest' self-confident man whose stern intelligent face quickly crinkled into a warm friendly smile. He was a man they immediately knew would not give them any irritating waffle or egotistical bullshit. The more diffident Sutherland settled into a fold-up chair next to the table with the flight lieutenant who had been given the task of looking after them.

The rear gunner had no microphone, only his voice with its own built-in megaphone, made in Scotland, which turned up the volume as he rapidly gained in confidence. The operation was fresh in his mind, his words describing it succinctly, chilling when necessary, capturing the sudden violence of the three encounters and how the emotions of seven men could be tumbled, screwed up and magically restored to robustness after the last echo of the Brownings had juddered through the Lancaster. The men were spellbound. McIntosh says:

'It was what I had always wanted to do. I was giving them actual facts and an idea of what they could be up against. At the same time I hoped I gave them the confidence to deal with any attacks which might come their way. You see, a lot of these fellows had a very light-hearted opinion of what going on bombing operations was all about. Some would go through the motions of going out to the aircraft, sitting in the turret and taking off for an op.'

Some youngsters did not do everything they should to prepare for a sortie because they felt it was inconvenient. Others were in the RAF mainly for what they could get out of it. Pretty women of all ages were attracted to fresh-faced uniformed men who flew in bombers on dangerous missions and whose heads were easily turned by floozies and booze. Consequently, they might take less care with their work on the aircraft which could lead to fatal mistakes. Few jobs were available in the 1940s which came complete with death warrants for men who failed to take the war seriously.

'I told the lads to get into the bomber and check everything. Then double check it and make sure their clothing was all right. Be correctly prepared. Have their guns cocked and properly harmonised, and look after them. Make sure their perspex was clean. Wear the heavy equipment so if it did get cold and they had an electrical failure they were not going to be frozen. Switch on the oxygen at ground level to stay fresh and alert and discuss with the pilot anything that was not right. Search was the greatest thing because I maintain today that nine out of every ten bombers shot down by a fighter never saw what attacked them. I also reinforced the importance of never relaxing their concentration, even when they seemed to be near their base.

'A lot of chaps switched their guns to safe while coming back in over the airfield. That was deadly. German intruders occasionally followed bombers in through the funnel. One bomb aimer, based in Lincolnshire, told me his Lancaster was forty feet off the runway, coming in to land, when they got knocked out by a German fighter and several of his crewmates were killed.

'I was very proud to be asked to give this talk which was a highlight of my career in the RAF. It was also a nice little break at the time having recently had two particularly scary jobs.'

After McIntosh's thirty-minute talk he and Sutherland answered questions and they returned to Spilsby that afternoon agreed that if what they had said saved one man's life their trip had been worthwhile.

CHAPTER TWELVE

FIGHTER ALLEY

Scattered through Wallace McIntosh's flying logbook are brief entries of non-operational flights he made in England while on 207 Squadron during the war. These do not include airfields where his Lancaster crept down in fog or those where it landed in difficult circumstances after another dodgy do. They were short flips from Langar or Spilsby to places like Wellesbourne Mountford, Bottesford, Wittering, Upper Heyford, Gamston and Market Harborough.

The time his aircraft left the station for each trip is written boldly in ink into his logbook as is the time it spent in the air, the aircraft's code letter, the pilot's name and the target. McIntosh took as much trouble in faithfully recording these apparently unimportant trips as he did when he went to Hamburg, Essen or Mailly-le-Camp in a Lancaster packed with bombs. He was – and still is – a precise and meticulous man who took care in everything he did. Even before he joined the RAF no one could ever accuse him of being careless or failing to do the best possible job at whatever task he was involved.

The difference between a trip to Hamburg and another, say to Upper Heyford, is that he has little or no recollection of these local flights. Yet he has an amazing recall for most of his fifty-five bombing operations, including actual conversations aboard the aircraft, his feelings when seeing the devastation of the targets they were attacking, and gut-contorting moments when he came close to being killed. The reason, of course, is that the drama from these sorties is burned deeply into his memory, which is also bolstered by the recall of the routine of wartime bomber stations where he felt most at home, and what it was like to be an air gunner, the job which he loved and will never forget. Flips to other airfields were minor affairs, most of which have been banished from his memory.

There is, however, one short trip which McIntosh does remember more clearly, although he knows no more now about the reason for it than he did on 20 June 1944.

It was clear that this was not going to be an ordinary flight from the start after the station commander, Group Captain G Cheshire, stumped cheerfully up the metal ladder at the rear door and through the fuselage to sit beside the pilot. He sat on the flight engineer's tip-up seat, which would be occupied by a second pilot, if they ever had one, or someone going second dickey on his first operation. Tommy Young might have sniffed in mild irritation to see the

CO sitting there without an inquiring glance in his direction, but the engineer had not really had his seat stolen. Young never had a chance to sit down on a sortie. John Grey's attitude was that his engineer was there to work, and this should not involve sitting. The pilot would not let him use the seat, insisting that he spent the flight checking instruments or, at certain times, looking through the astrodome to watch out for prowling night fighters.

They took off from Spilsby at 1.10pm for a forty-minute flight to RAF Hethel. McIntosh recalls his surprise when they landed at the airfield, south of Norwich.

'There were Lancasters, Liberators, Fortresses, Halifaxes and Stirlings all pulled up into this one corner. Grey told us to find the mess and have a drink before he went off with Groupie. It was just a jolly for us but for them it was some sort of high-powered conference, I think, to discuss tactics for the bombing of the V-weapon sites in France. There were numerous high-ranking RAF officers here and others from the Royal Navy and a lot of Americans. They all disappeared into a building with guards at the door.

'We found the mess, had a drink, then Larry and I went to look at the Flying Fortress sitting beside our Lancaster. It was the first time we had been close to one of these kites. We looked at the turrets and spoke to the crew. It was a tremendous-looking aircraft with bloody big point-five guns, but it had awful little wee wheels and we were not impressed by the size of its bomb bay. The Lancaster had a tremendous gaping bomb bay. It also had big nacelles which closed after the wheels had gone up into them. These nacelles only seemed a foot or two shorter than the Fortress bomb bay. We were glad to be flying in the Lanc.

'But the Americans were having a rougher war than us. They went out in daylight, exposed to everything and once their fighter escorts pulled away they were at the mercy of the Focke-Wulf-190s. They flew in formation, but after German fighters had broken through and shot down one or two out on the periphery they ripped right through them. It was the Americans' choice to fly during the day. They thought that flying in tight formation with so many gun turrets and all this armoury pointing out, including wing and beam guns, they would be impregnable. But they were not. They caught a lot of shit and took a terrible beating. Many of their aircraft were shot down and high numbers of bombers returned with two or three dead crew.'

The conference broke up in less than two hours and they left at 3.50pm for Spilsby where they had time for a drink before settling down for dinner. It had been a pleasant relaxing break.

A week later they left Spilsby at 11.25pm to attack the V-weapon site and stores at Mimoyecques near Calais. The Germans had a huge concrete structure here which was planned to contain fifty 416ft-long barrels that could, in total, fire ten 300lb finned projectiles a minute at London. Even before it was heavily bombed the site had encountered technical problems which prevented it being used.

'It was just over the French coast. We bombed at around 7,000ft and came straight back. It wasn't far, taking us two-and-a-half hours, but these could be deadly targets. They were tremendously well defended and we went into a lot of light flak which came hose-piping up, although we didn't encounter any real problems.'

Training continued. They went on a bombing exercise on 4 July which was a waste of time when John Cook discovered that his bomb sight was u/s. Two days later pilot Flight Lieutenant Cullinane came round the mess during a stand down looking for volunteers to fly with him to Woodbridge that afternoon to pick up a crew from 207 Squadron which had landed there after encountering a spot of trouble. McIntosh said he would go with him for the ride.

'Woodbridge was a big emergency landing airfield in Suffolk. There seemed to be hundreds of wrecked aircraft. Some which had crash landed had simply been bulldozed out of the way. Badly shot-up Fortresses were piled two or three high. It was the first time I had seen a fork-lift truck. They just went into the side of an aircraft, lifted it and cast it away.'

On 12 July Lancaster LM208 EM M-Mike, with Wing Commander John Grey at the controls, bounded down the runway, lifting off at 10.25pm. It was Wallace's fiftieth bombing operation.

The target that night was a railway junction at Culmont-Chalindrey and McIntosh remembers his surprise when they found the town on a map.

'We'd been used to these little short trips and then, suddenly, they sprang this one on us and we got back to another eight-hour flight. The target was straightforward, it was the distance. We were fooled. We had got lulled into a false sense of security thinking all the long hauls were behind us, but this was a long stooge into France and it was the first time we'd seen a German fighter so far down into that country.

'We were attacked by a Messerschmitt Bf-109 after bombing the target. He had been stooging about and came right in behind us at 8,000ft. Tommy Young, the flight engineer, got the best view of him coming in round the side. There were two other Lancasters nearby and I believe the German was caught between the devil and the deep blue sea. Which one should he have a go at? He picked us, not the best of choices because we had become experts at dealing with sitting ducks. It didn't take long to sort him out.

'Larry got the first batter at him because he was slightly above the tail. He just turned on to his back, went down and was seen crashing on the ground and bursting into flames. Two or three of our aircraft reported seeing the combat.'

They touched down at Spilsby at exactly 7am in reasonable time for breakfast after debriefing. They were so hungry they could have eaten a horse apiece, but had to make do with a generous portion of crisp bacon, eggs and mugs of hot sweet tea.

Next morning they saw pictures of the devastation at Culmont-Chalindrey. About twenty severely damaged steam engines stood in the ruins of the locomotive shed. The repair shops were destroyed and the lines cut to Dijon, Chaumont and Belfort. They were also impressed by John Cook's aiming point photographs, taken by the in-board camera, which showed dark smoke billowing from the mangled target and the impact of M-Mike's bombs.

This raid came at the end of the blackest period in the history of 207 Squadron. Five aircraft were lost on the 21/22 June raid to Wesseling, while a total of seven Lancasters went down in the two attacks against St-Leu-d'Esserent on 4/5 July and 7/8 July. Sixty-four men were killed in the three operations.

On 14 July, Spilsby's commanding officer, Group Captain Harris, who had taken over as CO from Cheshire, heard that Grey was flying to Wainfleet Sands for some high-level bombing practice and asked if he could go with him as a passenger. It was a fine day and there was no doubt he would much prefer to be sitting in the front of a busy Lancaster cockpit than at his desk in station headquarters sorting through piles of bumph and drinking pints of tea. He also said he wanted to see how the crew operated.

They attacked a target off the Lincolnshire coast from 20,000ft. John Cook released ten practice bombs. McIntosh heard the bomb aimer murmur: 'Steady, steady. Bombs gone!' At this moment McIntosh furtively eased an eleventh bomb out of the rear turret and watched it plunge out of sight, grinning mischievously. There were no fighters to shoot at but he wanted to play a part in the exercise. It would have been fun to take a small bomb packed with high explosives to drop over Germany, but that would have interfered with his other rather more important tasks.

It was a satisfactory bombing practice and to complete the beaming CO's pleasure a Bristol Beaufighter had been laid on for a session of fighter affiliation. They spent several exhilarating minutes being chased by a pilot who knew the ropes, then pursuing him while Groupie, braying his appreciation, clung to his seat.

'I'm sure he was highly impressed,' says McIntosh, 'because we were attacked continuously by the Beaufighter and we did the commentary as if it was an actual sortie.'

They got back to the officers' mess in time for a good late lunch and Harris, with a story to tell, got outside a few stiff drinks. The affable Harris asked the Scot to bring another air gunner with him to be his guests at an important dinner at the nearby bomber airfield of East Kirkby.

'It was a nice little jolly. But when I arrived I noticed that one of the guests was Sir Ralph Cochrane. He left his party of senior officers to find out how I was getting on. That was the kind of bloke he was. He was interested in anybody who was making news for 5 Group. Rank didn't mean a thing if you were performing well. I had a great admiration for Cochrane, a genuine fellow, who didn't get the recognition he deserved.'

On stand downs, when they were not relaxing in the mess, enjoying fish and chips and mushy peas at Skegness, or wandering lazily through sun-dappled lanes around Spilsby they went to the camp's Astra cinema. The pictures was always good value and for the outlay of a shilling or two the films offered a couple of hours' welcome escape from war into the fantasy world of Randolph Scott's gritty Westerns, the comical capers of Laurel and Hardy, and an opportunity to admire the million-dollar legs and curves of Betty Grable. War films were popular but any sign of a battle being won by a handful of smooth-talking Yanks drew jeers and derisive whistles.

The Astra was packed on the nights when 207 Squadron was featured on Gaumont British News. Cheers rang out, drowning the excited commentary, when 207 Lancasters, clearly bearing the squadron code letters EM, were seen belting down the runway. For a few minutes the boys of 207 appeared on the same screen as their favourite stars. It was something special to put in letters home and talk about for days afterwards. There was nothing fanciful about the Bomber War, however, and it was soon back to business as usual.

In 1945, Joyce Brotherton, now a squadron officer, wrote: 'Life on a bomber station was made up of moments of feverish activity and breathless excitement, followed by suspense and, all too often, heartbreak.' She had stood on countless nights beside the controller's caravan waving off Lancaster crews and often, a few hours later, mourned so many who had not returned. They included the eight 207 Squadron men who were killed when their bomber was brought down at the small village of Lignières-de-Touraine on the night of 15/16 July during the attack on railway yards at Nevers, near Tours.

Three nights later Spilsby was again badly shaken by the news that three more of its Lancasters were missing from a raid over France. A force of 253 Lancasters and ten Mosquitoes had been sent to hit railway junctions at Revigny and Aulnoye. Two Lancasters were lost on the Aulnoye sortie, but fighters were waiting for the bombers heading for Revigny. These included the unfortunate bombers from 207 Squadron which had despatched twelve Lancasters to the French town. Both targets were hit and railway lines were cut to the Front but a staggering twenty-four Lancasters were shot down on this raid, which had promised to be a routine operation.

Nineteen Spilsby men were killed, including two pilots, both aged twenty. The two men who survived, evaded capture and got back to England in September.

John Grey and his crew did not go to Revigny, nor were they involved in the attack against the oil refinery and storage depot at Donges, near the mouth of the river Loire, on the night of 24/25 July. But this was a significant sortie because it was the night when 207 Squadron lost one of its three McIntoshes. Besides air gunner Wallace and pilot John, a quiet and unassuming Scot who survived the war with a DFC and Bar, there was another pilot, Flying Officer Peter McIntosh, who had been posted to Spilsby in the spring.

McIntosh, twenty, had been jettisoning a bomb off the Lincolnshire coast when his Lancaster crashed into the sea, killing all aboard. The young pilot lies buried at Scartho Road cemetery, Grimsby. His was one of only three bodies found. Peter McIntosh had come from the Glasgow area yet spoke without a Scottish accent. He and his sister, Mary, had looked after their three younger sisters after the death of their parents. The youngest girl was only nine.

Four nights later Grey was at the controls of M-Mike when they returned to Germany for the last of three attacks in five nights carried out on Stuttgart by Bomber Command.

Sitting quietly in the briefing room Wallace McIntosh's eyes bleakly followed the tape on the map which stretched across the North Sea into the depths of the hated Ruhr valley. He was reminded of an air gunner who was about to leave 207 Squadron at the time the Scotsman had arrived. The experienced gunner was the sort of man who needed to unload all his bad news on to a sympathetic soul before skipping off without any pressing worries to a week or two of leave and a few months' instructing, leaving his confidante slightly uneasy about the future.

The gunner had shaken his head sorrowfully, recalling past horrors, then lowered his voice and said, confidentially: 'Stuttgart is a deadly bloody place. It's down beside Karlsruhe and there are any number of night fighter airfields in that area. I've been several times and it's never a picnic. Watch out for bloody Stuttgart because the way into it is the most infested alley with fighters that you'll find anywhere. They're crack crews too and should be, the buggers are up nearly every night.'

'I never went to Karlsruhe, but it was on the way to Stuttgart and I never had an easy trip there,' says McIntosh. 'I didn't like Stuttgart and was always apprehensive about going there and tonight that feeling was justified. It was a real baddie. I had had a nasty one there with Fred Richardson in April the previous year and the memory stayed with me. But we had been briefed to go and were not in a position to pick and choose our ops. It was a fairly long trip and you were flying through an awkward corridor with some of the bigger fighter stations on the way down.

'It was just the city we were bombing, make no mistake about that. There was an aiming point on the city at the furthest end of Stuttgart from where we came in because of 'creep back'. A lot of bombs would drop on the aiming point but many always dropped short and the next lot of bombers never went right over so they would also drop short. That was when you got creep back, so they had the aiming point on the far side of the city.'

They left Spilsby in M-Mike an hour after dusk, joining another 493 Lancasters and two Mosquitoes. There was a bright moon, which McIntosh favoured, but a horde of night fighters were waiting for them over France, flexing their trigger fingers. The Lancasters were like pheasants being beaten innocently towards the guns. McIntosh recalls a vast firework display of flak flung at them on the way in but, luckily, they reached the target untouched and bombed from 20,000ft. Stuttgart was burning as they turned for home, but their sortie had only just started.

The German controller was pleased with his fighters which that night shot down thirty-nine Lancasters – 7.9% of the force. Thirty-three bombers had been lost on the previous two Stuttgart raids on 24 and 25 July. In total the three Stuttgart raids cost the lives of 372 bomber aircrew. Another seventy-nine men became prisoners of war and sixty-four avoided being captured. The attacks on the German city were said to be successful. A good deal of damage had been caused on the ground, including the destruction of most of Stuttgart's cultural and public buildings. 1,171 people had been killed and another 1,600 injured.

Coming out of the target it seemed likely that Grey's Lancaster would be added to the mounting grim statistics as fighters were almost queuing up to attack them.

'The first one who found us was an FW-190. He came straight in at the back of us. There was another Lanc beside us which started corkscrewing after we'd shot the fighter down. I suppose he thought he was going to be attacked and didn't want to take any chances. After the fighter went down in flames and we'd straightened up Grey said, anxiously: "Is everything okay?" No one was hurt but we'd lost about 4,000ft by corkscrewing and we slowly climbed up again to twenty thou. You never went straight up because you would lose too much fuel. And if you started revving hard your engines would be sparking like the clappers. They would get very hot and you'd give your position away.

'Another FW-109 came steaming in like an express train, making a pass at us before disappearing. Most of them did vanish if they thought they'd been seen because there were plenty more bombers and there was no point getting involved with an aircraft that might have you in its sights. They only needed a second or so to know if they had been seen. The FW-190 might have seen us take a combat manoeuvre. That could have been a diving turn or Grey might have moved the aircraft up or down on the wings to look underneath. They knew when they risked being hit all right, they were no fools. They would be warned by any aircraft which was not flying straight and level. The German wouldn't normally see me moving my guns to point at him but it was a moonlit night and he might have seen the reflection on them.'

The Germans also knew that some bomber crews were less vigilant than others, just as RAF aircrews knew some enemy fighters were less brave or less earnest to press on with an attack if they fired back. Cats and mice were playing a deadly game over Stuttgart.

A Ju-88 charged in underneath from the rear, guns and cannon blazing. It turned and was picked up moving to the rear by the wireless operator. Bob Jack lost him but the fighter reappeared, spitting bullets and shells.

'He came unstuck on this second attack. Larry and I saw him come in from about 800 yards. We opened up and got him right underneath our tail. Flames and smoke billowed out of him and he went straight down. Another Ju-88 came in just after we'd straightened up after the last combat. He came to within 700 or 800 yards almost straight astern. He just had a quick look before diving away. He knew he'd been seen. I think he had been working in conjunction with the Ju-88 that we shot down. A lot of them worked in pairs. One maybe stood off winking its lights trying to distract bomber crews. They were cunning buggers, trying all the tricks of their trade.'

Bomb aimer John Cook was given the rare opportunity of firing the two Brownings in the front turret when a fighter recklessly attempted a head-on attack. It was a bad moment but a fierce burst was enough to make the German pilot change his mind.

McIntosh's worst shock of the night came as he was searching the sky for more possible trouble. The scare did not involve the Luftwaffe and it was delivered without warning inside the aircraft. He explains:

'We were just flying along rather quietly, hoping the excitement was over. We'd had these attacks and the aircraft had been thrown about quite a bit. It was peaceful in the rear turret with just the normal drone of the engines when suddenly I was struck heavily on my shoulder. For a fraction of a second I thought someone was in there attacking me and I spun round wondering who the hell it could be. You think of all sorts of things, especially on ops and you're always waiting for something which is unexpected and I got the scare of my bloody life. Then I realised that I had been hit by the axe which hung behind me. The strapping which held it had worked loose with the vibration. The axe was there for any emergency in which I needed to hack my way out of the turret. I grabbed it and laid it at my feet where it could cause no more shocks.'

It was always particularly satisfying after a hectic trip to return to base knowing that after landing they would be swept up into a familiar friendly routine which always helped brush away at least some of the violence which they had just encountered. Sitting in the Lancaster tottering round the perimeter track, cocooned in fatigue, they knew their patient ground crew would be waiting at dispersal with a merry quip or two, ready to make a note of any niggling or major problems with the aircraft. The truck or van taking them to debriefing would be driven by a WAAF who usually managed to smile prettily however dead the hour. A girl's smile, however fleeting and innocent, could revive a fellow's flagging spirits. The debriefing would not take long, but in any case a cup of hot tea and a cigarette did wonders to pick a fellow up. The early breakfast was always welcome and now, at the height of summer, they did not shiver as they crawled into bed and drifted into the blessed relief of sleep. Yes, there was a lot to be said for the routine which faced tired aircrews returning after a hairy raid to their airfield.

The Stuttgart sortie, which had taken 7hr 50min, was the last of the long-haul ops for John Grey and his crew.

CHAPTER THIRTEEN

HANGING ON

Although the Third Reich was visibly crumbling by the summer of 1944, the faithful Luftwaffe was defending the Fatherland with an undiminished ferocity. The death toll on the Stuttgart raid had been appalling for Bomber Command and there was no reason to believe that raids against the enemy in the near future would be anything less than severely demanding for aircrews. Newly-trained bomber crews were still coming through to the squadrons but their lack of operational experience condemned many to a short sharp tour.

John Grey led the squadron in a practice for formation flying on the evening of 4 August. It lasted only thirty minutes and was not a great success. McIntosh says scornfully: 'We looked like a gaggle of geese, but it was not easy.'

In the mess that night there were arguments for and against formation flying, but the majority came out against the idea. They were not used to it for one thing. They were terrorfliegers – terror bombers – the droppers of bombs, the scourge of the Boche, not aerial ballet dancers. Besides, the Americans had not done that wonderfully well so beautifully slotted in together, had they? They had also suffered huge losses of men and aircraft.

No one was pleased early next day to learn that they would be flying in formation on a daylight sortie. Wing Commander John Grey was leading a wing which was attacking a large underground flying bomb store in caves in the Oise valley at St-Leu-d'Esserent, just north of Paris. McIntosh describes it as 'an awkward damned place'. That might be considered to be a slight understatement.

Detailed plans of the caves, which had been used before the war for growing mushrooms, had been passed by the French to the Air Ministry.

The first V1 flying bombs had been launched against London on 13 June. Said to be Hitler's revenge weapons in retaliation for the bombing of German cities they were also a desperate gamble to turn the tide.

A large force of 742 aircraft was split between two flying bomb storage site targets: St-Leu-d'Esserent and Fôret de Nieppe.

'It was a sudden change to be flying out there in the daylight after crawling about for two-and-a-half years at night. However, it was wonderful to see the countryside pleasantly laid out and, of course, to keep your eyes on the fellows who were on your left and right, sitting in aircraft we were leading.'

Grey's Lancaster M-Mike lifted off at 11.05am, a time when McIntosh

would often be busily employed in the gunnery section. As the fifteen
Lancasters from 207 Squadron climbed steadily their crews looked down
wistfully upon the spidery maze of Lincolnshire's narrow country lanes
merging into golden fields of ripening corn that swallowed up dozens of small
villages which they used as grey stepping stones to the North Sea.

'People on the ground, especially right through France, must have wondered
what was happening when they saw this gaggle of Lancasters passing
overhead. It was certainly not like the close-knit formations they had seen so
often of the Americans going across France and into Germany. But we were
carrying many more bombs than the Yanks could have managed and that was
what mattered.

'The aircraft were not strung out all over the place but they were not as tight
as experts would have expected. Formation flying with big bombers was totally
different than with fighters. You had four engines to control and sometimes one
or two needed more thrust than the others. Our vic or vee was okay. The next
two vics were not as close as they might have been.

'A tight formation was the best thing for defence if you were attacked
because you could concentrate more fire power and the fighters could not come
in among you so easily, although they would have had no problem with us in
daylight. A bunch of FW-190s would have made a hell of a mess of that lot.

'But none of us was used to formation flying. Practice might make perfect
but we hadn't had much practice. You had to be very careful. If you moved only
a few feet either way you would knock your mate down. It was a bit scary for
some chaps and no one wanted anyone to get too close to one of their wing tips.
Grey's aircraft was close to the two who were next to him but all three were
experienced pilots.'

There was 5/10ths to 7/10ths cloud over the target which made it difficult
for bomb aimers to pick up the aiming point.

'All went well until we got near the target where the heavy flak was intense.
We were flying through great puffs of smoke the whole time. We were in front,
of course, at the sharp end, soaking everything up. We led the mob in at
18,000ft and ran in to bomb as shells were bursting all round us. I remember
two aircraft were on either beam when everything seemed to happen at once.'

The bombs were released and McIntosh heard someone at the front saying
the bomb doors were slow to close. Then a burst of heavy flak exploded like a
massive clap of thunder under the nose. The port inner engine was badly
damaged, but most of the starboard outer Merlin was blown away. A storm of
metal fragments flew into space, some smashing into the rear of the Lancaster,
many becoming embedded in the tailplane. Luckily, there was no fire, but oil
poured out, streaming over the fuselage and wings, and they were embraced by
dense black smoke. For a moment it was like flying through a thick angry
cloud. No one was hurt but John Cook had a narrow escape in the nose when
his maps, fusing switch and fuse box were hit. The engineer struggled to
feather the port inner motor and Grey fought to bring the aircraft back under
control. McIntosh remembers what happened next.

'The aircraft suddenly reared up, turned on to its side and went twirling
down out of the smoke into a very steep hurtling dive, shuddering like hell, the

two remaining engines going like the clappers. We had completely lost control and I could hear Grey and Tommy Young trying to correct the Lancaster as it spun towards the ground. I was lying on my back and thought this was the end, I really did. I thought nothing would prevent us from going straight in. I couldn't see anything and was held fast by G-force. The world was going round and round, I couldn't move and was totally unaware of anything that was happening. There was hardly any time to think and I believe I blacked out for a moment then just waited for oblivion because there was nothing else I could do.

'Nobody called out. There was nothing said by anyone except the flight engineer and I heard him give Grey a few words of encouragement, that was all. The rest of us were just hanging on.'

Any cries or words probably froze in their throats, yet the plunge seemed terminal and words were superfluous. Only isolated thoughts fought to make themselves comprehensible in scrambled minds which had been stunned by the terrible abruptness of the change in their fortunes. They had all seen at different times other bombers falling helplessly out of the sky, touched by the dark stigma of doom and thought, perhaps selfishly: 'Poor buggers, thank God that's not us.' But now it was them and they knew at last what it was like to be plummeting into the abyss, having thought they had been blessed through numerous sorties by the luck of the gods.

Virtually paralysed by the astonishing G-force, they all knew they were close to extinction, but hoped if it came that it would be quick. None thought that they could cope with a future of pain-filled inactivity. They had seen fliers, bright-eyed happy-go-lucky youngsters, who had escaped the tragedy of death only to be unable to function normally in the stumbling wreck of their bodies.

Had they been busy at their positions beating off fighters or coping with the routine maladies of an over-stretched Lancaster bomber they would have had no time to waste on the frivolity of self-pity and doubt. But it was clear to them all that only Grey and Young could save them.

Pilot and engineer worked vigorously at the controls, without panic, ignoring stress, seasoned by RAF discipline and considerable experience. In this dire situation no one could run away from death, they could only seek to force the door shut on it. Grey was a big strong man. Young was stocky, well built. They made a fine team. But there was no time to think except to employ the combined force of their straining muscles to heave mightily on the controls to get the tortured Lancaster back under control. At first it seemed impossible as the altimeter sunk lower and lower. Slowly, wretchedly slowly, the obstinate bomber responded to the taut muscles and prayers of its masters. The dive slackened, the two engines stopped screaming and the limbs of the five men not employed in the impossible mission began to stir weakly after desperate prompting.

'It was touch and go right enough, but Grey and Young pulled her out of the dive and we levelled out just in time at around 2,000ft. It was a great piece of flying. I did not think the bomb doors were properly closed and believed other damage was increasing the drag. Grey said: "I've stabilised her and she's flying reasonably well."'

'I looked out and saw below fields and houses, and above us all the other bastards heading happily for home. When the G-force came off I got my senses back, realised we weren't far above the ground and opened my turret doors. The bomb doors were closed, and we all got ready for the big jump. The port inner had run for a wee while before conking out and Grey said: "Okay, prepare to bale out." We were flying towards Dieppe which was still occupied by the Germans.

'I came out of my turret and joined Larry Sutherland with our Mae Wests clipped on at the rear door. We opened the door and when we peeped out it looked a very long way down, so we hastily closed the door and awaited developments. Everybody else, except the pilot and the flight engineer, congregated at the exit stations, ready to hit the silk.'

As his aircraft wavered at 2,000ft, the wing commander handed over as wing leader to another pilot, Flight Lieutenant Eric Oakes, DFC.

A Lancaster from another squadron, which had also lost height but was in better shape than M-Mike, flew alongside them for several minutes, a thoughtful gesture which they appreciated. It was bad enough to be crossing a hostile France in daylight with an aircraft in good condition, but being in an obviously crippled kite, well behind the formation, a juicy prey to any passing lip-smacking fighter, was an unnerving experience: 'After the other Lanc left we had no company, no escort, nothing. We were at the mercy of any fighter who wanted to have a go at us.'

At this moment he thought of his wise old grandmother and one of her heartfelt pieces of advice which seemed particularly relevant at this time. 'Never be last because they are the easiest caught.'

Contact was made with 11 Group which promised to send out fighters to escort them home, but none appeared.

When he had been sitting briefly at the rear door watching the fields of France fluttering by below, waiting for the word which would make them leap out into the sky, McIntosh wondered, bleakly, why he had allowed himself to be put into this position. He wished he were back on nights believing, perversely, that they would then be in a better position to deal with this emergency.

The port outer and starboard inner engines were purring, although straining at higher revs to do the work of four. Grey's task would have been made more difficult if he only had two Merlins on one side because they would be continually trying to drag him off a straight line. But they now seemed to be limping home, the engineer reported no problems, they had enough fuel, the crisis had apparently passed and the skipper seemed reasonably happy.

McIntosh returned to his turret in case they caught a fighter's eye or appeared on German radar as a faltering bomber, which would be ideal as a target for shooting practice. They were still over enemy territory. He knew if they were attacked seven lives would then rely solely on the accuracy of his shooting for the aircraft was in no shape to go dancing round the sky to avoid a fleet-footed fighter. He recalls the memory which invaded his thoughts at that time.

'Before that night I had only once sat in the rear turret and thought about what I would do if I was in the position of having to bale out. The first thing, I had decided, would be to take off my slip-on boots because as you went backwards the boots could catch under the guns and nearly tear your legs off. In the gunnery section I always told the boys to make sure they kicked off their boots before slipping out.

'The thought of baling out didn't really bother me. As I saw the fields whipping past I thought if I had to land down there I would be in good company with my crewmates. I didn't think about the Germans.'

Settling back in his seat the gunner said: 'Skipper, I think we should start jettisoning as much stuff as possible to lighten the aircraft.'

Grey replied enthusiastically: 'Good show, do that.'

The crew were pleased they had something to distract them from their perilous position, still tip-toeing along at 2,000ft.

'Everything heavy was thrown down the flare chute or out of the back door. That included all the ammunition from the front and top turrets. John Cook got rid of the ammo from the front turret while Larry Sutherland, Happy Hall, the navigator, and Bob Jack, the wireless operator, flung out belts of ammunition from the panniers in the rear turret and the stuff from the top turret.

'We kept a few rounds back in the tail. But anything that was loose and could be moved was chucked out or taken to the back door where Larry was busily throwing stuff out. He was standing there quite casually without a parachute scattering things around the French countryside. The aircraft must have been lightened by quite a bit.'

At 2,000ft they would not become desperate for air so the oxygen bottles were dropped out like small bombs, while axes were used to hack out anything which could be made portable, including some radio equipment the loss of which the wireless operator said would not impede their crawling progress back to England.

McIntosh pointed out that the guns were useless without ammunition so those in the front and top turrets were taken to bits and heaved out through the rear door and McIntosh dismantled two of his four Brownings which followed them.

Approaching Dunkirk their situation became more grave after Tommy Young told his skipper the starboard inner engine was giving increasing trouble and suggested it might not last the rest of the flight. Grey said, mildly: 'Goodness gracious.'

If this seemed an oddly bland remark to be made by a man in charge of a heavy bomber which appeared to be on the brink of being reduced to the status of a bulky and virtually uncontrollable monoplane, this was typically John Grey. He was a man who never resorted to coarse or violent language, even when strongly provoked or in a frightening or stressful situation. Calm, as usual, he added, resignedly:

'The next problem boys is that we are too low to think about baling out. We must now prepare for ditching. Okay chaps, take up ditching positions. You'd better come out of your turret, Mec.'

The pilot would much later tell debriefing intelligence officer Joyce Brotherton at Spilsby: 'I think I could have coped on one engine if it had been one of the inboard ones, but I was doubtful about it with only an outboard Merlin.'

'We were ready to ditch and had no fears,' says McIntosh. 'We knew Grey would bring her down nicely in the water. We had total confidence in that man.'

Young was nursing the malcontent coughing engine as they crept forward at no more than 1,000ft. They stared down into the sea which contrived to look sinister and unwelcoming, even with the summer sunshine glinting off it. The sea was anything but smooth and ditching would not necessarily be the easy and tranquil experience that some men believed. McIntosh thought, without confidence, of his spell of dinghy drill at the swimming pool in Newcastle.

McIntosh was still sitting at the rear door as the aircraft dragged itself across the sea when Sutherland spotted a dinghy with four men in it. Some distance away were two chaps supported by their Mae Wests. Other aircraft flying at normal height would probably not have seen the men who ripped off their shirts and jackets and waved at them excitedly. Some appeared to be whooping with unrestrained joy, having been unwittingly ignored by several aircraft at a much higher altitude. Standing at the open doorway of M-Mike they exchanged waves with the ditched airmen and Bob Jack quickly sent a radio message for help to England.

'It was the crew of a Flying Fortress which had been badly shot up and ditched on the way back that morning. They could see we were in no position to hang around as company or to mark their position and carried on waving to us as we drifted on, still losing height. It was a sobering thought to think that we might soon be ditching ourselves. We heard later that an Air Sea Rescue launch was sent out and rescued them all alive.'

Jack had put through a Mayday to the emergency landing airfield at Manston, Kent, but approaching the English coast the starboard inner engine was coughing and spluttering. They had planned to cross into England over the 533ft-high chalk cliffs at Beachy Head but batallions of great barrage balloons were stationed as a long impossible barrier in front of them. They hung dourly above the cliffs and over the water, attached to boats, protection against incoming flying bombs, forcing them to turn to starboard. They crept along, close to land and safety, continuing to lose height, adding miles to their flight and heightening tension.

'It was pointless trying to get over or through the balloons, so we flew parallel with them along the Channel until Margate where we were able to turn in for Manston who knew we were coming.'

As water was replaced by land the idea of ditching became redundant, but it seemed likely that they would be forced to find a large field in which to crash-land before reaching Manston which was two miles west of Ramsgate.

'We were stuttering about on one-and-a-half engines as we came in over Kent at about 600ft and were now in crash positions. But when we were crawling towards the airfield they told us we could not land on the long emergency runway. Grey told the engineer to join us at the back behind the main spar so the pilot was on his own and had to put her down on grass beside the runway. We staggered down on one engine shortly after the starboard inner, which Tommy had been nursing, conked out. We'd been afraid of the undercarriage being so badly damaged that we would prang on landing, but the wheels held and she came down okay. It was another fine piece of flying and the end of a hair-raising escape.'

The trip had taken 3hr 50min. The Lancaster had, fortuitously, kept them airborne long enough to land safely, but they could measure that luck by a couple of miles and the same number of minutes both of which had prevented them from ditching or crashing. It was good to stand on firm ground at last but there was no relieved shaking of hands, exchanging platitudes, or any other minor celebration. Experienced aircrews were far too stoic to indulge in such tomfoolery.

They did, however, walk stiffly round the battle-scarred aircraft quietly marvelling that it had carried them back unscathed, while reflecting it was a good job they had not been sent that morning to the outer reaches of Germany. The bomber was in a distressed state and included damage to the port inner engine and the comprehensive demolition of the starboard outer, which had shattered that wing's leading edge.

'The kite was in a hell of a mess. The underneath was covered in oil which had been flying back from the engines. There were numerous flak holes and the bomb bay doors were closed, but buckled.'

M-Mike was repaired and sent off on more operations from Spilsby, but it was shot down on the night of 15/16 October 1944 during a mine-laying trip off Denmark.

'A truck picked us up and took us to station headquarters where they asked us where we'd been. We did not have a proper briefing but while we were there we heard a strange: "Swwwwsh!" No wonder we couldn't land on the runway. We'd arrived just in time for the early operational flights of the Gloster Meteor jets. A squadron of them took off while we were there. They were afraid of us buggering them up.

'Grey got on the phone to Spilsby and even as he was put through they were saying there that it looked as if we'd had it. Other crews saw us go down and thought we'd bought it. The skipper asked for someone to come for us and meanwhile we were given a meal.

'They had a fancy mess at Manston which was a lovely big purpose-built station. It had all the amenities which we did not have. We had bacon, sausage and egg, nothing out of the ordinary, but it was in lovely surroundings and there was toast on the table which we never got at Spilsby where we lived in small Nissen huts of very secondary importance. The atmosphere was of some affluence, but to me it looked a wee bit toffee-nosed. Grey and the group captain had a chat during which he told the skipper that flying back to England in a bomber so badly damaged was a remarkable achievement.

'Then we went through to the huge snooker room where Grey and Sutherland had a game while we were waiting for our transport back to Lincolnshire. Real cool. Larry, who was quite a dab hand at snooker – most of the Canadians were – told Grey: "You're a bloody awful snooker player, but you're a bloody good pilot."'

Flying Officer J A Giddens, a Canadian pilot, arrived in a Lancaster, their transport back to base. He asked Grey if he would like to fly them on the one-hour trip to Spilsby. Grey replied: 'No, you carry on, I'll be second pilot.'

Two Halifaxes were lost in the raid against St-Leu-d'Esserent. McIntosh says:

'On the flight back to base I said: "Let's have nights any time", but I'd already done my last night flight with John Grey. We were debriefed when we got back to Spilsby. It really had been a tremendous feat of flying and we had been through all the disciplines on one trip: flying, bombing, being prepared to bale out, getting ready for ditching and then for crash-landing and getting down on one engine. And all the sequences were done very efficiently. Quite an eventful trip, really.'

The attack on St-Leu-d'Esserent was Larry Sutherland's thirty-fifth and last sortie. Until he finished his tour Grey would use spare bods in the mid-upper turret. Sutherland had done thirty-five ops and was supposed to do only thirty, and so was pretty shook up by this time.

Less than a week before his final op Sutherland had cut off one side of Squadron Leader Sidney 'Pat' Pattinson's distinctive handlebar moustache while the burly officer was asleep on his bed. Pattinson, one of the flight commanders, did not discover the wanton devastation perpetrated on his closest companion until later when wandering refreshed into the mess he wondered why everyone was chuckling and pointing. After close examination of the lamentable deed Pattinson hastily retreated to restore order to his upper lip by removing the remaining wing of his moustache. Sutherland left the squadron before Pattinson had thought of appropriate vengeance. Sutherland and Pattinson, (who both had two DFCs), and Grey had been great friends, occasionally going out in the squadron commander's car to pubs well away from Spilsby.

The day after St-Leu-d'Esserent McIntosh was summoned to the adjutant's office where he was reminded that he had already done a large number of sorties, fifty-two to be exact, and if he wanted to finish his second tour without going up on another op he could. The gunner sat there dumbly for a moment as a tumult of emotions passed through him. There was a tingling and a tumbling that could almost be equated to a briefing for a ghastly raid on Essen, together with the smile from a beautiful woman. It was an odd feeling to be told that with just a word he could end it all that morning.

There would be no more terrible warnings at debriefing about a massive presence of fighters packed full of ammunition lurking wolfishly around a target. Quitting now would also mean no more lousy flak which he vehemently hated, no fear of collision with one of his own bombers, no high buffeting winds battling to throw them off course. No longer would he have to punish his eyes and body to remain vigilant during the blackest and most exhausting of nights. There would be no more tangling with the murderous Luftwaffe in any shape or form. To turn down this offer, which held tremendous appeal, might virtually be an act of suicide.

And yet, this was no ordinary job where he could stop working at five o'clock like an engineer, a joiner or a butcher. This had been his life. It had been packed with adventure and camaraderie, there was nothing else like it in the world. He was an experienced top class air gunner, a job that he could do better than anything else. But if he gave up now decisions about his future would have to be taken more urgently than he had feared. He needed time to think. He told the adjutant that he would discuss the situation with Wing Commander Grey and left the office.

John Grey nodded wisely as McIntosh confronted him with his dilemma. He said:

'Well, the decision is yours, Mec. If you want to finish now you must. But I still have another two trips to finish another tour and I want to see them through.' McIntosh, who never liked letting anyone down, says:

'The rest of the crew also had a few ops to do because they were on their first tour. Grey and I had a chat and I decided to carry on. It looked as if the two of us would also help the others finish their tour with us rather than leave them to be pushed around as spare bods with crews who might have lacked experience.'

This was more than a generous gesture. Many pilots would have said 'enough is enough' and quit before they flew one op too many, but Grey recognised the unswerving loyalty of his crew particularly after the post-Amiens foul-up and believed that he owed them something, knowing they would be better off with him. Nor did McIntosh want to split up a good team and he agreed, without hesitation, to stay on for another two trips, although both men knew they were taking a chance. The fields and forests of Germany, France and Holland had all become temporary resting places for numerous considerate men who had embarked on just one more sortie. But two? And as it turned out, for Wallace McIntosh, there would be another three.

CHAPTER FOURTEEN

THE END OF THE TRAIL

With the end of his second tour looming Wallace McIntosh had been more seriously considering his future. It was still his dream to be given a permanent commission. After nearly five years, he could not envisage any other kind of life than with the Royal Air Force. The RAF had provided him with a job that had delivered more excitement than any young man could have imagined. He also had a comfortable home, affable companions and the all-important three square meals a day. He knew he could not be an air gunner popping off at Germans for the next twenty-five years, but believed the country was getting its money's worth out of him and he was prepared to serve the Air Force loyally in any reasonable capacity, and be able to look forward to a decent pension at the end of it. That was more than he could have expected from a lifetime of toil on the land.

He had never been fitter or happier and knew he would be a fool to chuck everything in and return to the uncertainty of civilian life. He had not dwelled much on his youth in recent months but thinking of Civvy Street brought grim memories of his upbringing in the direst poverty sneaking back briefly to disturb him.

Mixed up with the modest plans, which he kept pushing to one side, was a gnawing anxiety that maybe he should be taking advice from someone. He knew of pilots, navigators and wireless operators who talked seriously about one day trying to get jobs on civilian airlines which they expected to be booming in peacetime. But openings for air gunners, however sharp their reflexes and night vision, would be in short supply at the end of the war. He did not want to start a third tour, because his luck was unlikely to last for ever. He was now drawing on resources deep within him to maintain his unceasing vigilance on each sortie. He knew that if, because of desperate weariness he made a mistake and someone died, their loss would haunt him for ever. Yet he had great faith in the RAF and felt sure that something suitable would turn up. And it did. He says:

'Sir Ralph Cochrane was so taken with the work that one or two senior gunners had done he felt they should be retained on their squadrons where they should assess gunners and try to improve them. I was the first one on 5 Group to be given such a job. The first time I heard about it was from John Grey, who dropped a few hints. It became clear later. I would not leave 207 Squadron at the end of my tour; a new job was being created for me – gunnery analysis officer.'

Although part of him was embarrassed by being sought out in this way he was tremendously proud that Cochrane had shown faith in him:

'I had a few drinks in the mess after hearing of the job that was waiting for me. Cochrane was a genuine fellow, a Scotsman and pretty ruthless, but smart and super efficient at running 5 Group which I think was *the* group.'

After the Stuttgart sortie McIntosh was delighted to hear that he would be receiving a Bar to his DFC. This was not specifically for Stuttgart, rather as a reward for good work on several operations and outstanding leadership on the squadron. He was considerably bucked by this and thought it might bring him to the attention of senior officers who would soon be involved in the reorganisation of a post-war Royal Air Force.

The award, promulgated in the *London Gazette*, read:

> *Now on his second tour of operational duty, this officer has taken part in a large number of sorties. Since the award of the Distinguished Flying Cross he has destroyed a further three enemy aircraft bringing his total victories to six enemy aircraft destroyed. On one occasion in July, 1944, Flying Officer McIntosh was rear gunner in an aircraft detailed for an attack on Stuttgart. While over the target area his aircraft was attacked five times by enemy fighters. In co-operation with the mid-upper gunner he succeeded in destroying two of the enemy fighters and in driving off the remainder. In times of stress this officer has invariably shown great coolness, courage and a fine fighting spirit. Both in the air and on the ground he has set a high standard of efficiency.*

John Grey took his rear gunner to East Kirkby when he was called one night for a meeting of senior officers to discuss ways of flying in better formations than they had on the attack against St-Leu-d'Esserent. McIntosh remembers:

'Bomber Command knew bugger all about formation flying and never did. The meeting was virtually to ask people if they had any suggestions. Grey took me because we would be the lead aircraft on the next raid and I was in the rear turret watching closely what was happening behind and reporting to him. That was the only reason I was there. Everything was discussed at great length, about the heights the different vics that would be flying on the next daylight op and how bomber crews could improve signalling to one another.'

A stand down was announced at Spilsby early on 12 August 1944 and that night aircrews were gleefully scattered through the East Midlands. Wallace McIntosh with some of his crewmates had not gone far. They were quietly drinking their first pint at a pub in Spilsby village when service police and orderlies suddenly burst in shouting: 'All aircrew from 207 Squadron out. NOW!'

After the initial shock, followed by touching protests and a little good-humoured cynicism the men reluctantly obeyed the compelling instinct of their training, tossed down the last throatfuls of ale and shuffled into the street, where other chaps were milling about in confusion and buses were waiting with their engines running. McIntosh grunted in alarm, to no one in particular: 'Jesus, what's happened?'

Buses and trucks had also been sent elsewhere, including Boston and Skegness, for SPs to trawl through bars and restaurants, winkling out men who had thought they could let their hair down for a decent night out. Instead, they were returned abruptly and complaining to their squadrons, without being told the reason, in variable states of sobriety. By the time the coaches had trundled into RAF Spilsby and tipped them out at the briefing room rumours had multiplied and, fanned by the fumes of alcohol, had become so fanciful that everyone was rather relieved to discover that Britain had not been invaded by mighty squadrons of Martian spaceships.

Instead, an emergency bombing operation had been set up and they were met by Groupie, Wing Commander Grey and the adjutant, who were hastily making up crews. Grey would be based at the control tower, the officer in charge of flying that night. But several pilots were looking for volunteers to make up a crew.

Men were being asked if they had been drinking heavily, several said they had not but were clearly unsteady on their feet. Eyes were then cautiously examined for any sign of glazing while breath was being half-heartedly sniffed by a flinching Grey and others assisting him. Some men, cheerfully floating in a dense mist of alcohol, not fit to be in charge of their own feet let alone a Lancaster loaded with bombs, were told they were not required and tottered away. Others, like McIntosh and his crewmates, who only drank in moderation, were obviously good candidates to join a show on the other side of the Channel. It was a curious reminder of crewing up long ago. McIntosh remembers the jostling crowd of aircrews, some still not knowing what was going on.

'There were some complete crews and others who were trying to make up crews. We had known Grey was not flying that night and that we would normally not be required for an op, but they were short of people. Apparently the Germans had broken through at a place we learned later was known as the Falaise Gap, France.

'One of the pilots, Flying Officer L L Goff, who I'd flown with to Ford in West Sussex three days before to pick up some equipment, had only two or three of his crew available. Goff hadn't a flight engineer and asked Tommy Young if he would fly with him. Tommy said he didn't fancy flying without his own crew and we decided we would fly with Goff, provided we all went with him. Eventually, four of us decided to go. Grey was not too chuffed but he said: "Okay then lads, on your way".

'Then one or two of Goff's crew wouldn't fly with him because we did. When I look back it was all very silly agreeing to fly with somebody else when I didn't have to while sitting on fifty-two operations.

'There was no meal for us before the trip that night because it was a real rush job. We went with Goff into the briefing room where they were sorting out which crews were flying and out to one of the aircraft that had been bombed up at short notice. After the run up we were chatting about one thing and another and the pilot tried to familiarise himself with who was there.

'He said: "We'll just have to work things out." Tommy Young said: "Yes, we will. You steer it and we'll do the rest." As cool as that. Tommy was a flight sergeant at that time. Goff didn't say a lot to that, but he knew who was boss. He was in an awkward position, really. Here he was with the most senior crew on the squadron. But he was a nice chap.'

But Goff was no whey-faced sprog. This was his fifteenth bombing operation. Tall, slim, with a dark moustache, the pilot decided to say nothing and put the mild insubordination down to experience. They left Spilsby at 12.30am.

Goff's Lancaster, LM263 N-Nan, was one of six 207 Squadron aircraft with makeshift crews which joined another eighty-five Lancasters, thirty-six Halifaxes, twelve Stirlings and five Mosquitoes which were to attack a concentration of German troops and a road junction north of Falaise. The raid was later said to have been very effective and no aircraft were lost. McIntosh recalls it as being an easy target to hit.

On 15 August 1,004 crews were briefed to take part in a massive attack on nine Luftwaffe night fighter airfields in Holland and Belgium before Bomber Command resumed its night offensives against Germany. It was an important raid for 207 Squadron whose target was the Dutch airfield of Deelen. The weather was fine and clear and they were to bomb from 17,500ft. Grey's Lancaster, PD220, carried a bomb load of eleven 1,000-pounders and four 500lb bombs.

'This was another daylight op with Wing Commander Grey in the pilot's seat and leading the attack. We took off at 9.59am and the others formed up behind us over Lincolnshire. We set course for Deelen, and were supposed to be flying in close formation, from near Cromer, Norfolk. From time to time Grey said: "What are they like at the back, Mec?" And I would reply: "A bloody mess, skipper." We were never any good at formation flying.

'We climbed high until we were flying between 17,000 and 18,000ft. I didn't care for the daylight. I would have preferred to go out there at night, but the trip out so far was uneventful. It was quite different to be sitting in my turret in daylight, seeing all the other aircraft. At night we might not see another bomber from the time we took off to when we got back to Spilsby.'

Flight Lieutenant Geert Adrianus Cornelius Overgaauw, a Dutch pilot, from Amsterdam, known more informally on the squadron as Johnny, was flying next to Grey on the starboard side, no more than thirty or forty feet between the wing tips of the two Lancasters. Most chaps from 207 Squadron knew that Johnny's sister was getting married in Holland that day. Although the Dutchman could not be in church to support his sister he regarded the flight over his homeland that afternoon as a symbolic gesture, embracing his love for her and his warm wishes for her happy future. McIntosh waved to the men in the aircraft on either side, including Sergeant Ron Coaker and Pilot Officer Alick Watt, a Canadian, Overgaauw's gunners.

Grey had a rather illustrious spare bod in the mid-upper gunner's seat now Larry Sutherland had finished his tour. The squadron's gunnery leader, Flight Lieutenant Jimmy Wardle DFM, keen to add another op to his second tour, thought that in such experienced company this should be a reasonably safe trip if luck flew with them. He was a small man of about 5ft 5in, who rarely flew and was probably more comfortable sitting in his office in the gunnery section. This was his last operational flight.

The most horrifying moments of a sortie were often those which occurred during a placid period when nothing seemed to threaten the progress of bombers streaming towards their target. McIntosh recalls such a moment:

'We were coming up to Utrecht when, all of a sudden I got the shock of my bloody life. There was this burst of bright orange flak, a flash, a big puff of smoke and I said, over the intercom: "Overgaauw's gone." His aircraft had blown up and disappeared. That was all that was said.'

The Dutchman's aircraft literally vanished as if it had never existed. Some men saw fragments of the bomber scattered about the sky. There was no time for the crew to scream, feel pain or suffer in any way. All seven men aboard would have been killed instantly. Debris from the aircraft was thrown to the rear of Grey's aircraft which, astonishingly, registered no more than a stately tremble. McIntosh stared in disbelief at the gap where seconds before he had been exchanging grins and waves with young men who were now dead. It was impossible to imagine the nothingness of death. The split-second transition from the bubbling zest of a good life to the coldness of a corpse. Still touched by the awfulness of the moment McIntosh says:

'That was the first time I had actually seen one of our own squadron aircraft shot down. I had seen plenty of Jerries go down, and other bombers, but not one from 207. I'm convinced that Johnny Overgaauw's aircraft received a direct hit from a shell. There was a lot of controversy about it with people surmising this and that, but they weren't there to see it. I was and I saw what happened. Some fellows said he was hit by bombs from above, but there were no bombers above us. There are still people today who say bombs struck his Lanc, but this is just bullshit because they were definitely hit by flak. I had seen enough bloody flak to know what it was that day.

'It was a shattering blow, and so close to us. It was only our second daylight raid and someone else had got the works. The fact that we had had a narrow escape on our first daylight op brought it home to us. And we were very lucky not to have been caught up in this explosion. We were going forward and moving away from the other Lancaster as it was reduced to smithereens. It was a terrible end for them, but that was happening all through the war, although you were less aware of it in the dark. The next aircraft moved up to take Johnny's place beside us. We were alive and, for us, the war continued.'

It was a ghastly moment but it had to be wiped from their minds. They had a job to do. There would be time later to reflect on the sudden death of men they knew and had been talking to cheerfully earlier that day.

Grey's Lancaster, flying at a steady 155mph, approached Deelen airfield. The target was identified visually and by yellow target indicators. John Cook pressed the bomb tit, their bombs cascaded down at 12.09pm and they turned for home.

'We went straight in and bombed. I remember looking down and seeing German fighters sitting on the dispersals and the runways. We released a beautiful stick of bombs that went straight up the runway. It was great bombing and the airfield was knocked out. It was one of the raids leading up to the Arnhem invasion on 17 September.'

Overgaauw's aircraft had crashed near Arnhem. All seven bodies were found in the vicinity of the wreckage. Five, including the twenty-six-year-old pilot, now lie buried at Moscova General Cemetery. At the end of the war the two Canadians from the crew, Flying Officer Bill Swinton, twenty-two, the bomb aimer, and Alick Watt were taken to Groesbeek Canadian War Cemetery. The others who died were Pilot Officer Anthony Brett, the navigator, and Ron Coaker, both aged nineteen, the wireless operator, Pilot Officer Huntley McKay, twenty-four, and Sergeant Percy Wildsmith, the flight engineer, who was twenty-five. Their aircraft was one of three bombers lost on the raids that day.

McIntosh was not a close friend of Johnny Overgaauw, but remembers him as a tall, smart, pleasant fair-haired fellow. He visited his grave many years after the Deelen raid.

The loss of the Dutchman and his crew had been a blow to the squadron but it did not prey on their minds. McIntosh had learned to detach himself from such events, however harrowing they might seem: 'There were many worse things happening those days. If we allowed ourselves to dwell on something like that we'd never have won the war.'

Flying Officer Wallace McIntosh, still only twenty-four, left Spilsby for his fifty-fifth sortie on 3 September 1944, the fifth anniversary of the outbreak of war. They had another spare bod in the mid-upper turret, Flight Sergeant Alec Copsey, a young Australian.

McIntosh climbed into the Lancaster's rear turret, wondering about the trip ahead, hoping the Germans would not be on the ball. They took off at 3.40pm and roared belligerently into the autumnal sky.

Six airfields in southern Holland were successfully attacked that afternoon by a force of 675 aircraft. Grey was again the formation leader for another strike against Deelen airfield.

McIntosh had always hoped he could finish his second tour on a high. He was not looking for glory with opportunities to shoot down more German fighters, but the young Scot had looked forward to winding up his operational career with a good solid display of alertness in the rear turret which would make the blighters think twice before attacking them. Although he was coming to the end of the trail he did not know that this would be his last sortie. It was another attack against the enemy in which he would be on the boil from the moment they left Spilsby to when they returned.

To say that he was disappointed when the hydraulics feeding his turret began leaking as they were crossing the Dutch coast was an understatement.

'Each crew had been briefed in the areas they should watch. We were at the head of the formation so everyone at the front of our aircraft was watching above because we could have had a head-on attack instead of the usual stuff from the rear. When my turret packed up I was facing dead astern because I was watching the formation behind. It was important what happened there. I told Grey from time to time what the formation looked like. It was never anything but a gaggle. I don't know how much formation flying training the others had been given, but we'd managed thirty minutes of it, if the others had done no more it was clearly not enough.' He reported his problem to Grey in a dismayed growl.

'A hydraulic leak can happen at any time, often from normal wear and tear. There was nothing I could do about it once we were away. I centralised the turret with the hand-winding gear and could still fire my guns in short bursts. But I couldn't rotate the turret and fire at the same time, my guns were now in a fixed position. Normally I could rotate, elevate and depress my guns in one movement.

'The main thing was to watch for any approaching fighters. Had they come in daylight you couldn't dodge about because we were sitting in a vic of three aircraft. You couldn't corkscrew three at a time or you'd all be in a heap on the ground. But if a fighter did attack there would be more fire power from each vic in the formation to direct at him.

'We got over Deelen and saw that the Germans had been busily working on the airfield, filling in craters. We dropped 1,000-pounders to penetrate the runways. I saw our stick of bombs falling. It was like a repeat of our previous raid. We had another 100 or so Lancasters around us and some of our Mustangs playing about. I just sat there and watched as the airfield was given another good working over. It was a pleasure seeing the bombs rip down the runway.'

Two days later Grey told his rear gunner: 'Right, that's us finished.' A post was waiting for the wing commander elsewhere and he was required to take it up soon.

A significant glance, encompassing relief, gratitude and pride, may have passed between the pilot and the men who had served him so loyally since that first raid on Frankfurt in March. It had been a long traumatic trail.

McIntosh did not feel any regret that he would not be flying again. There was always a chance that they would be attacked by an old hand who would despatch them without thought, or a youngster who got lucky.

'I had known I was living on borrowed time and had no inclination to fly again. The longer you went on the more uncertain it got, it was as simple as that. I used to think more about it as my sorties went through the forties and into the fifties: "Christ, if I get knocked down now." I had been keen to see the others through as far as possible and would not have jockeyed out from Grey with one or two to do, but he was well over his time and this was a good time for him to go.

'There was no party, we just split up. Some guys had piss-ups at the end of their tours, but we didn't have one at Spilsby. I was being kept on the squadron anyway and the others finished their tours as spare bods. And Grey just got into his aircraft, an Airspeed Oxford, and buggered off, which was a sad day for 207. None of us exchanged addresses. In those days we didn't think about it. It was only later, when chaps were of retirement age, that we thought about getting in touch with old comrades. We had had a great rapport among us and yet you just parted company and never heard or saw one another again. That was war, I suppose.

'Grey was electric, a special kind of man. He certainly set me an example on how to live and how to make quick decisions. He was an inspiration to anybody. He never dithered and liked people around him who were of a similar nature. He had no time for wimps. He regarded me as his Number Two, occasionally asked what I thought and expected me to answer him straightaway.'

McIntosh lay quietly in bed on the night after John Grey told him they were finishing and for the first time in nearly two years knew that he was a survivor. He had a future. With ordinary luck he might survive into old age. With extraordinary luck he had got through two tours totalling fifty-five sorties. The Germans had not managed to shoot him down although he had experienced more narrow escapes than Harry Houdini.

Bomber Command did not keep a record of enemy aircraft shot down by its air gunners, but with Wallace McIntosh's confirmed eight 'kills' and a probable, and the one-eyed Larry Sutherland's seven, they were among the top scorers. Some believe they were first and second. What cannot be disputed is that the skill and alertness shown by these two men and the other gunners who flew with Fred Richardson and John Grey were major factors in helping prevent their aircraft from being shot down.

McIntosh went home by the first possible train to that tiny house at Errol in Perthshire, with a pass for three weeks' leave. He was still getting used to the idea that when he returned to Spilsby he would never again be flying into battle with four Browning machine guns at his finger tips when the Errol postman delivered a mysterious package, wrapped securely in brown paper and cardboard. The covering label carried the name of Mappin and Webb. He turned it round and round in his hands, puzzling over what it could be before his grandmother urged him to open it. Inside was a one-pint pewter tankard bearing the inscription: 'Good shooting, Mac. From Wing Commander J F Grey DSO, DFC. 1944.'

The tankard remains one of Wallace McIntosh's most prized possessions.

After the war John Grey was sent to Argentina to help set up its Air Force. Invalided out of the RAF with a heart condition in November 1957 he died on 21 March 1961, aged forty-eight. He was survived by his second wife, Doreen, and the three children from his first marriage to Austrian-born Lotte.

CHAPTER FIFTEEN

BETRAYAL

McIntosh returned to Spilsby from leave to take up his new non-operational position with mixed feelings. He was excited about the prospects of the job and what it might lead to after the war, but knew he would never again experience the thrill of leaving on a sortie. Thinking positively he told himself that he no longer had to face the constant threat of sudden annihilation. He had no intention of starting a third tour yet two or three times the restless Scot found himself wandering up to the runway to wave a bunch of lads off on a raid, but this soon lost its appeal. His eyes were always drawn to the men in the turrets bolted on to the rumps of the big bombers while knowing that many a Lancaster had returned from an op with a gaping hole where the rear turret had been.

He felt no envy or regret, merely a little sadness because he knew that some of these boisterous youngsters would not come back. While war was largely a brutal lottery for the participants he hoped that at least some of his advice had sunk in and they might be better equipped to cope with the fierce battleground in the sky. He says:

'I didn't like trailing away down there and watching chaps screwing themselves up before taking off, so I stopped going. I didn't meet them coming back after a night sortie as I was too fond of my bed and getting back into the routine of a normal night's sleep. But in the mornings I called in at the gunnery section and had a look at the board to see if they had all safely returned.'

It was difficult to settle because he was now on the far-flung fringes of the war. Having been a professional warrior he was now an instructor, a role he had been happy to fill as a part-timer, but one without the other was difficult to handle. Although he had the security of having both feet firmly on the ground his head and spirits were still in the clouds at 20,000ft experiencing the excitement of the bombing run, the adrenaline rush of detecting and dealing with fighters and the comforting hammering of his Browning machine guns. Long-term security without the occasional frisson of danger somehow lacked zest.

Then one day, soon after returning from his end-of-tour leave, McIntosh had the chance to go back to war. A pilot whose rear gunner had gone sick before that night's raid on Königsberg, asked if he would consider flying one more sortie. The offer was very tempting.

'Initially I said I would, but I was soon more or less told that I should not.

My friends' better counsel ruled and I pulled out at the last minute. I would have looked bloody silly having done fifty-five trips and landing up in Danzig Bay on the fifty-sixth. It would have been stupid not to give him one of the spare gunners, which is what I did. They got to the target and returned safely but I didn't regret my decision, I'd had my luck.'

Wallace McIntosh's most stimulating activity immediately after finishing his second tour was the formation in a Spilsby pub of The Chopper Club with Jimmy Wardle. It was a club exclusively for air gunners who had completed a minimum of five sorties. McIntosh observes laconically:

'We didn't have a lot of members because so many poor devils were getting the chop. Our new officer commanding 207 Squadron, Wing Commander Black AFC, was our patron and he had the special membership cards made. It was something different and we had beers together occasionally.'

It is entirely possible that the design of the club's membership card might have acted as a powerful deterrent against a clamouring of air gunners to join, especially those who clutched at superstitions to get them safely through the war. The club crest included two air gunners' badges and two fearful axes in the process of falling.

McIntosh was sent on a two-month gunnery leaders' course to the Central Gunnery School at Catfoss, north-east of Beverley, Yorkshire, on 24 October 1944. Five miles from the coast, the airfield was ideal as a training station. Its air gunnery and bombing range was in the North Sea in an area between Skipsea and Hornsea, but McIntosh had few good words to say about Catfoss.

'The course was a waste of time, much of which was spent firing ammunition into the sea. We did some drogue firing and a bit of photographic stuff, but to be firing about 400 rounds into the sea at the end of a course was a waste of bloody time and money. It was just air to sea firing. The first time I did that was in a Botha at the gunnery school at Morpeth when we were taken out to sea for two or three bursts to get used to the feel of the guns and the noise in the turret. After two tours I was being told to do it all over again.'

It was like sending a university graduate back to primary school to learn to read. Not surprisingly, the entire system at Catfoss irritated McIntosh: 'Most of the chaps with me on the course had done a tour, and those who hadn't might have been lying about on the squadrons and were pushed on to this course to become instructors without any operational experience.'

Battle-hardened veterans like McIntosh could not see how gunners without operational know-how could be gunnery instructors when their country was at war. Perhaps they could in peacetime when there was no war to sharpen their teeth on because gunnery manuals were available to sift through. But after five years of war surely enough tour-lapsed gunners were available to teach sprogs the rudiments of air gunnery?

They flew in Wellingtons at Catfoss where most of the drogues were pulled by single-engine Miles Martinets. 'The drogues were towed by a thin wire rope and I shot down two of them,' he says with relish. 'That saved the other guys having to fire at them and also meant we had an early return to the station for a bite to eat.

'It was probably more difficult for me to accept because I had been in charge of the gunners on an operational squadron at Spilsby with Jimmy Wardle. Then I had to go off on this course, which was essential if I wanted to remain in Bomber Command. I had put off going there several times and certainly wouldn't have gone in the middle of my tour with Grey.

'I went through the motions at Catfoss, but I wasn't at all keen. Other experienced gunners and myself had more discussions in the mess with chaps on the course than with the instructors. I had nothing against the instructors because they had an agenda which they had to stick to, but it was already getting out of date.

'They were lecturing us about a turret which I had sat in for the last two years. It was a bit boring to be told that this turret was the FM120, it is hydraulic electric and has four Browning machine guns. It drove me up the wall. It was all right for the sprogs who were put on the course because they hadn't a squadron to go to or were surplus to requirements. For people like me it was supposed to be so I could become a gunnery leader and pass on my expertise to young chaps for their benefit and make them more proficient as crew members. Because of my experiences at Catfoss I tried to make my courses more interesting as an instructor at Spilsby.'

Qualifying as a gunnery leader on 6 December, he returned to 207 Squadron, his opinion of the RAF a little blemished, but nevertheless plunged back into his job as gunnery analysis officer which he found increasingly interesting and satisfying.

'I took the young gunners under my wing for a while, spoke to them, finding out their attitude, what they were doing in the aircraft, comparing it with what I had done, and discovering what they knew. You didn't always get a lot of that because some would go missing next day.

'There was a criterion of efficiency and I graded them from A to C. I tried to get them all to be As. The idea was not to have a C. I had two Cs. One of them didn't like the squadron anyway but I said no one would leave Spilsby with a bloody C to bring discredit to me, my training and the squadron. So I gave him extra tuition and he was posted to another squadron as a B. The other C went missing.

'Gunnery analysis was a big job and I think a lot of squadrons could have followed it. Certainly I think that's why 207 had a very efficient gunnery section. I passed a tremendous amount of information on to the lads, including aircraft recognition, fighter tactics, incidents they were liable to come up against and what to do in an emergency. It wasn't just a question of shooting down fighters. It was experience and what I call being with it, knowing the gen. It was great to see these lads and I loved to see a crew finishing their tour.'

That winter, Elizabeth Hendry took her uniformed grandson to see his mother. They had been visiting his Uncle Jimmy and Aunt Susan in Aberdeen and left the granite city, heading north by bus, rattling grimly through cheerless country roads past damp crouching villages and round the squat lumpy bases of glowering hills which were topped by snow. Over twenty miles was a long way to travel on public transport which was at its bleakest in wartime, and McIntosh did not enjoy any of the thirty uneasy minutes spent at their destination.

It was a journey which his thoughtful grandmother had been quietly planning for some time and she understood her grandson's reluctance to make the journey to the village of Rothienorman. She felt the time was right for a belated attempt at reconciliation and wanted her daughter to see what a fine young man he had grown into. A son of whom she should be proud.

Wallace McIntosh's parents lived at an out-farm on a hill where his father was the foreman: 'It was cold and bloody miserable. I felt that if Granny wanted her to see me that was fair enough, but it didn't give me any other incentive. My mother was there, but she didn't really register. I was not very chuffed about being there. I felt more a Hendry than a McIntosh and can't remember anything that was said, but I recall three or four young sisters I had never seen peeking round corners at me. I had a glimpse of my father but didn't have much to say to him. My two brothers, Gordon and Edward, were away at war.'

McIntosh admits that his mother, still a pretty woman, was nervous, but says he could understand that. After all, she had given him as a baby to her parents to bring up. Years after the war when she was a widow, following his own retirement, his feelings towards her mellowed and he visited her comfortable flat in Aberdeen near the beach, overlooking the golf course, where she spent her happiest years, supported by her daughters, Frances and Rose, who lived nearby. A keen member of the Salvation Army all her life she died in 1993 aged ninety-three. She had been a widow thirty-one years.

'She had done a wonderful job bringing up her family considering many difficulties. My father was always changing jobs, never thinking about housing or schools. They had probably moved homes twenty times before she was sixty, but he was a good worker, capable with horses. He got away from the land when he was about fifty and worked as a labourer laying the runways at Dyce airfield, which is now Aberdeen airport. They moved to Margaret Street, Aberdeen, where they had two adjoining rooms, no running water and an outside toilet.'

Wallace McIntosh did not go out with the lads to celebrate the end of the war in Europe. On VE Day, 8 May 1945, he was stretched out sourly in a bed at Spilsby's sick quarters, suffering badly from quinsy. One of his visitors was his squadron commander, Wing Commander Black, the successor to John Grey.

McIntosh knew that 1660 HCU, Swinderby, was looking for a gunnery leader and was interested in having him. 'Black pleaded with me to stay at Spilsby, saying I was part of the establishment there. He said: "When we lose you we will lose the legend that 207 Squadron created."

'I had been lying there feeling a little insecure with the war ending. It seemed to be an anticlimax and I wondered what the future held. Black was a decent and pleasant man, but I decided I had to go. The war had finished, I was hoping to get a permanent commission and needed to move on.'

McIntosh, not a man who took kindly to being ill, told Black he would meet people at Swinderby when he was well. 'I saw the training commander there after I'd returned from sick leave and although I wasn't impressed by him decided to go. It seemed to be a move in the right direction.'

Perhaps Black knew intuitively that McIntosh would not be happy at

Swinderby and realised he might be better advised not to make impulsive decisions until the peacetime RAF had sorted itself out. Certainly, had he stayed with 207 Squadron, which had become his whole life, it was likely that his future would have been quite different. He left Spilsby on 12 May, heaving his kit and himself into the Airspeed Oxford in which he was given a lift to Swinderby.

He hated Swinderby almost from the moment he arrived and within a day had applied to be posted into Transport Command with the idea that he might at least give himself the chance of seeing the world. The pointlessness of Catfoss closely followed by an ill-advised move to Swinderby was the beginning of Wallace McIntosh's bitter disillusionment with the RAF.

'I saw at Swinderby quite a few of the old guys I had known from way back. They were all going redundant. There were so many people there no one knew what they were doing. There was a bad atmosphere and a couldn't-t-care-less attitude was creeping in. I did a little instructing but the gunners realised there was no future for them in the post-war RAF and so were not interested in being taught anything. It was obvious to me that becoming the gunnery leader was like putting a rope around my neck. I thought I should have stayed on 207, although the squadron's operations had finished and I would have had a bogged-down job in the gunnery office again.'

A young man who had fitted smoothly into the discipline of war, he could not so easily cope with the indiscipline of peace. He was sent to the Aircrew Allocation Centre, Catterick, the week he was due to meet the King at a Buckingham Palace investiture to receive his medals. He joined his wife, Betty, and daughter, Frances, on their train at York station on 3 July and travelled with them to London.

'About 300 of us were waiting in a long queue. An orchestra was playing and when you were about sixth in line a flunky stepped forward and put what we called a meat hook for the medals to be hung on the top of my pocket. The King was a little man and had on his face what appeared to be rouge,' says McIntosh. 'He didn't look well. We had been told not to shake his hand too briskly because he was seeing several hundred people that day. He just said: "Well done."

'We had all wondered who would come away with a meat hook but nobody did. When you were out of sight of the King a flunky took your medals off the hook, put them into a box and went off with the hook. The only souvenirs to be had were two or three sheets of Royal toilet paper whipped when you were having a widdle in the loo.'

No photograph was taken of him after he stepped proudly outside the gates of the Palace wearing his medals. Within a week he was back at Catterick and discovered he had been promoted to flight lieutenant.

'There seemed to be thousands of people going through Catterick at that time. It was very sad because a lot had been made redundant against their wishes, some were lost because the RAF was all they had known since leaving school while others, like myself, were just fed up with the whole bloody system.

'I was told that they were looking for people at Swinderby, but I said: "No thank you." I was then given two alternatives. One was to become a passenger and freight officer. The other job was MT officer. I chose passenger and freight because it sounded a little bit more exciting. I was sent on a three-week course to St Mawgan, Cornwall, but found when I got there that the course was full so several other chaps and I spent three weeks in a hotel, all expenses paid. At the end of the next course, packed full of knowledge about documentation, stewardship, emergencies, how to balance an aircraft, passenger manifests, and a good deal more, I was posted to 1665 Heavy Transport Conversion Unit, Linton-on-Ouse.'

Much to his surprise, McIntosh, who had believed his beloved Royal Air Force had drifted away from him, found himself enjoying his new job. He had a staff which fluctuated between ten and twenty: former air gunners and pilots. There were training exercises in the Dakotas and Halifaxes which were used to fly RAF freight, passengers and diplomatic bags around the country, and to France, Malta and Libya. Slowly, he began adapting to living in peacetime Britain.

McIntosh recognised a familiar glowering figure who had, years ago, loudly torn him off a strip for not saluting an officer. Flight Lieutenant McIntosh was pleased to acknowledge a salute from the former service policeman, Sergeant Casling, now Linton's station warrant officer.

His future seemed more assured when he took a four-year short service commission and in August 1946, the unit moved to Syerston where McIntosh continued as passenger and freight officer. The Transport Support Training Unit was also here with Dakotas and Horsa gliders. He got friendly with Captain Waldron who offered to take him up for a fifteen-minute flip in a Horsa. 'I liked it so much that I went up again, this time for half-an-hour and at night. It was funny to be in the air above the towing aircraft which was still running along the runway.'

Occasionally, when members of the passenger and freight office were returning from abroad carrying goodies like alcohol, cigarettes, watches or chocolates a phone call was put through to Customs and Excise to say the time their aircraft would be arriving in England. The call was often made late so the booty could be removed before the Customs man arrived at the airfield.

There were lighter moments among the routine work at Syerston where several airmen and WAAFs were encouraged to display their latent talents as entertainers. McIntosh explains: 'We had a marvellous concert party at the station including comedians, singers and conjurors. Being the passenger man I was responsible for seeing they were flown to a lot of different British airfields where they gave shows which were well received.'

Britain shivered in the harsh winter of 1947 when the country, covered by deep snow, almost shuddered to a standstill. Heavy flooding followed the thaw and an SOS went out to the RAF to help feed stranded farm animals.

On 17 March McIntosh was in charge of a load of baled hay which had been packed into a Dakota. They took off from Syerston at 10.35am with Flying Officer Warburton DFC, at the controls. There was something touchingly ironic about two hardened veterans of World War Two now flying on a goodwill mission to starving sheep in Wales. They had to drop the hay on the side of a mountain, Plynlymmon, near Devil's Bridge. The 2,465ft Plynlymmon, standing on the borders of Cardiganshire and Montgomeryshire, was the source of five rivers, including the Severn and Wye, and it was no great surprise to anyone that land around it was badly flooded, but it was not easy to deliver emergency rations in an aeroplane to animals high above the water line.

'It was very dicey flying between the peaks of mountains at around 1,000ft to get to the right spot. There was a swirling mist and we'd been told that farmers would light fires to guide us to the dropping points. We saw a lot of sheep lying dead before spotting the smoke rising from the beacons.'

A Nottingham newspaper which had heard of the mercy mission, instantly recognised a good story, and persuaded the station commander to let them send a photographer on the flight. He took shots of McIntosh heaving bales of hay out of the rear door. The former air gunner and the photographer wore parachutes, just in case of difficulties.

Next day Syerston received a call from High Bentham, south of Kirkby Lonsdale, Westmorland, where an isolated stable of race horses was in urgent need of feeding. This time McIntosh's pilot was his unit CO, Wing Commander Warner DFC, AFC, who had seen action of a very different kind a few years ago, dropping bombs. Tossing out hay was a less hazardous operation although he found the principle was more or less the same, but this time he had a former rear gunner guiding him to the aiming point.

It was a clear day with a hard frost and the stable lads' fires were quickly spotted. The press photographer was again in action, getting another series of action shots of McIntosh with bales of hay flopping on to the Lancashire countryside.

McIntosh's fortunes should have taken a considerable leap forward while he was at Syerston when he received an unexpected but powerful endorsement of his worth. He recalls:

'Sir Ralph Cochrane was made Commander-in-Chief of Transport Command. The first thing he did was have a parade of everybody on his stations so he could have a look at them. Everyone lined up at Syerston. The adjutant, Flight Lieutenant Courtenay, who had a ripe plum in his mouth spoke of "the h'officers" who were there.

'Cochrane in his full regalia, with the group captain who was CO of Syerston, followed by all the flunkies, walked slowly along the front line where I was standing with a nice row of ribbons. Cochrane stopped in front of me and said: "Pull that man forward."

'I stepped forward and he said: "You are who?"

'Flight Lieutenant Wallace McIntosh, Sir. Ex-Grey and -Richardson's crews.'

'He nodded, he had a great memory. He said: "Yes." Then, turning to the group captain, told him: "Have this man recommended for a permanent commission immediately."

'He shook my hand, I saluted him and stepped back, very proud. At that moment I remember seeing the adjutant looking down his nose. The CO called me in next day. He looked at me across his desk as if I was no more than a feather duster and had no inclination even to give me a proper interview. He only spared me two or three dozen words. He didn't like me, I don't know why, he was an odd fellow. He said: "I see you knew that man." He didn't even have the courtesy to mention Cochrane by name.

'I said he had been my operational chief. I know the CO hated Cochrane taking over as Transport Command chief and he didn't show any enthusiasm or give me any encouragement. He just said: "I'll see about it. You'll be hearing." I'm still waiting. I had a few forms to fill in and don't know what happened to them. Maybe he thought I was not an interesting sort of fellow, possibly not an officer who should have a permanent commission, I don't know. But Cochrane did think I was worth it, otherwise he would not have bothered pulling me forward on a major parade like that and telling the group captain what he should do.'

Although McIntosh did not leave the group captain's office with anything remotely like a kindly pat on the back or propitious words ringing in his ears, Cochrane had remembered him and that, surely, was what mattered.

'I then volunteered to go back to Bomber Command, thinking that this might enhance my chances. I went on a short camera-gun course that May flying Wellingtons at the Central Gunnery School, which had moved to Leconfield, just outside Beverley, Yorkshire. It was like a refresher course and I flew with different pilots while getting my hand back in.'

McIntosh and his wife separated in 1947, five years after their wedding. He had become increasingly anxious about their marriage and thought there was a chance the comforting presence of little Frances would help he and Betty overcome any difficulties, including his long absences fighting the war, but it didn't work. In the end, they just drifted apart.

Betty McIntosh took their daughter with her but, aged three-and-a-half, Frances returned to live with her grandparents. Leaving school at fifteen, she went into digs and started work with the *Perthshire Advertiser*, as a junior reporter.

McIntosh focused on furthering his career in the RAF.

'In June 1947, I got the prime post: gunnery leader with 50 Squadron which was re-forming at Waddington on Lincoln bombers. It was a bit of a disaster really, I was there a very short time. A lot of people were leaving the RAF. No one seemed to know much about Lincolns and there was always a shortage of someone in a crew. You either had a pilot and a navigator but no engineer, or you had an engineer and no pilot. Out of the half-dozen aircraft we had we were lucky if we could put one in the air. I had about thirty air gunners, although plenty were leaving.

'I did four trips from Waddington, including testing at Farnborough and landing at Lyneham. Then the RAF decided to centralise things and have all aircrew bomber training done at 230 Operational Conversion Unit, RAF Lindholme, near Doncaster. It was a major unit and needed a gunnery leader and that became my new job which was very difficult.

'I and ten instructors trained nearly 200 air gunners, including those who had been on operations, and Canadians who were re-enlisting because they couldn't get a job at home. So they came back to the RAF and assembled at Lindholme. There were air gunners all round the bloody place, it was bedlam.

No one knew where they'd come from or where to put them and we had been told to instruct them on Lancasters, aircraft that were becoming obsolete. I was becoming very disorientated, but I didn't let that rub off on anybody because I always gave of my best as an instructor.

'I went up sometimes in a Mosquito during fighter affiliation with Lancasters, assessing the gunners. My pilot was always Flying Officer Cox. Coxy was a great pilot, I liked flying with him and used to say: "Get underneath them" as we pretended to attack the Lancaster, trying all the old tricks. The de Havilland Mosquito was a beautiful aircraft, it was fast, climbed high and could carry a Cookie.'

McIntosh's dismay in his perceived peacetime disintegration of the RAF continued as he observed disorganisation and disquiet seething all round him. Disorganisation had not won the war and the RAF he knew seemed to be in disarray. For months he had observed a growing resentment by regular pre-war officers – 'the shiny-arsed brigade' – of himself and other aircrew attempting to stay on in the service. While there seemed to be no one who was in the position to press a button or turn a handle to get the RAF moving again McIntosh, who had never been a skiver, saw people with nothing to do keeping out of sight and volunteering for nothing.

Worst of all was the attitude of high-ranking administrators, with shiny seats to their trousers, who knew little about fighting a war but a lot about bureaucracy, bullshit and self-aggrandisement. McIntosh recalls, bitterly:

'The old peacetime farts were beginning to feel important again. They wanted to return to the old days. They were happy and comfortable, nicely protected in their own little cocoons. My old gunnery friend, Ginger Bale, had also spoken of this resentment they had and a fear that we would take over their jobs.

'Maybe half-a-dozen newspapers came into the mess in those days. Their arrival led to one great scramble. When we were at Syerston after the war some of these old officers came into the mess early, had their lunch, got a newspaper and fell asleep with it on their heads. They objected to the flying boys asking if they'd finished with it so we could look at the sports pages. The racing pages were popular, everybody had a wee gamble at that time. Once Ginger set fire to a glossy arse's paper. That woke the bugger up.'

McIntosh thought these men should have been put out to graze. Instead they were given important positions and many of the men who had won the war were cold shouldered, sometimes treated with contempt, while being feared in case their heroics were rewarded by being given well-paid jobs the desk-bound men coveted.

The regulars felt that because they had signed up for a number of years any jobs which remained should go to them, not to volunteers who had only joined the service to fight a war. And still there was no word about McIntosh's application for a permanent commission. He was sure that he had been betrayed by the Syerston commanding officer.

Although he might have written to Sir Ralph Cochrane to inquire politely about what had happened to the permanent commission which the great man had recommended he shrank from putting pen to paper.

McIntosh needed something to distract him from thoughts of this.

'It was easy to get fed up during my days at Lindholme and that summer I used to take a dozen fellows with me clay pigeon shooting at the back of the station. One warm day when we were setting everything up the chap who was going to be first to shoot, had his gun broken. While I was kneeling down setting up the trap an adder came out of the grass a few feet from me and this chap, four or five yards away, picked up his twelve-bore gun and shot it. The snake might have bitten me, it was very quick thinking. If there had been a war on he'd have been very good. I remember the others picking up pieces of the snake's skin.'

But these little excursions were taking him no further forward into a worthwhile future. Longing for the stability of the war years he had flitted hopefully from one job and one station to another in search of something into which he fitted comfortably. He was hopeful of finding something challenging, but hope was trickling away. Perhaps his standards were too high?

McIntosh was highly decorated and, although he and his wartime comrades hated the expression, in the eyes of the public he was a war hero. But there were too many decorated war heroes seeking a permanent career in the services. The country was broke and could not afford to create jobs for these veterans of a conflict they had all had a part in winning. Gloom, embarrassment and disappointment became outrage when it gradually sank in that they might more easily save face and help unclog the system if they just went away.

The RAF had given McIntosh pride, dignity and purpose. Now, having used up all his courage and steadfastness, it seemed to be snatching away everything that it had so willingly given him and he felt miserable, shabbily treated. Perhaps if he had curbed his impatience he might eventually have got his permanent commission and found a job in which he could have spread his wings and brought his personality, natural enthusiasm and organisational skills to bear. He says:

'I was very disappointed after all the encouragement I had got from Cochrane and if I had pursued that with him it may have had a different conclusion. I phoned Bomber Command headquarters and spoke to a group captain. I told him I was very dissatisfied. I had been asked to go to Lindholme to be gunnery leader because of my experience but everything was so disorganised I might as well go back to Transport Command where at least the job I had was interesting. I got no satisfaction from him so I decided to quit. I thought it couldn't be any worse outside than it was inside.'

Many men who had flown in bombers just wanted to put distance between killing and normality, and get back into civilian life where they could lay down the foundations of a decent future they had not expected to have. Others continued to feel lost.

Although he was only one of thousands of lost souls McIntosh was appalled by the general indifference to his situation. Having survived being shot at by German fighters and enemy anti-aircraft gunners, dragging himself and others through numerous traumatic incidents he was finally defeated by bureaucracy. Stunned, terribly hurt and drained of any ambition to continue his RAF career, he sat down sadly and composed a letter resigning his commission.

He had been used to having nothing, but after such a spectacularly successful career with Bomber Command he now expected more. Yet even with the completed letter in his hand he had doubts about whether he was doing the right thing. Still clinging to a life he had once loved and had seen disappear he was reluctant to quit in such a bitter fashion.

Any lingering thoughts that he might in a short time change his mind were demolished in the station orderly room in May 1948 when he sadly put his bulky holdall down beside the desk where a limp and unhelpful clerk was dealing with his railway warrant.

The Scot asked the clerk to make his warrant out for a return in case he wanted to come back for a job. He stared in disbelief at McIntosh who was suggesting that he should flagrantly flout King's Regulations. He could be put on a charge. The young man, part of the glittering future of His Majesty's Royal Air Force, simpered: 'I only make them out one way.'

McIntosh regarded him stonily and thought: 'Christ, all he had to do was write an "R" instead of "Single".'

Immaculately turned out as usual in his uniform, Flight Lieutenant Wallace McIntosh, proud holder of two Distinguished Flying Crosses and a Distinguished Flying Medal, strode with sinking heart towards the guardroom. Still walking, he glanced through the window where, inside, the 4 Group Cricket Rose Bowl was standing. The rose bowl had been won by the gunnery section on the station. McIntosh, who started the team, had been appointed non-playing captain. His deputy gunnery leader, Maxie Bacon, organised the players and opened the batting. There had been some good times, even at Lindholme.

'That rose bowl was the last thing I looked at as I left the station. I just walked out of the gate with my holdall, and jumped on to the liberty truck which was giving me a lift out of the RAF and to the railway station.'

CHAPTER SIXTEEN

CIVVY STREET

Wallace McIntosh had plenty of time to brood on what he had done as he sat quietly in a first-class carriage, probably for the last time, steaming north. Sliding past were towns and cities, some of which, heavily pockmarked, were being rebuilt, and the countryside where the spring had once again gently taken possession. Although the brutal war had altered many features of Britain, not even that could change the regular passing of the seasons. Alone with his thoughts, very little outside the carriage taking root in his awareness, he sighed resignedly at the sudden unfortunate change in circumstances.

For most of his life he had had nothing, a situation which he had been able to deal with satisfactorily when nothing was all he had known. But now, aged twenty-eight, he seemed irrevocably to be returning to nothing and after nearly nine years of comparative plenty this was not what he wanted. No longer content to have empty pockets, an aching belly and a barren future he firmly believed that what he had achieved made him as good as anyone, and nothing would stop him being successful in another career. He did not want to lose for ever that sweet taste of success.

Had he completed the four years of his short service commission he would have received a gratuity of £500. He patted his tunic pocket and grinned ruefully. He was not entirely penniless. He had received an extra £111.2s.2d from the RAF for his war service, but had since dipped into that, leaving very little in his Post Office Savings Bank book. Apart from last month's wages from the RAF, that was his entire life savings. It would have to keep him going until he found a job.

The former air gunner began making vague plans for his readmission to Civvy Street and what he might do for a living. At least, he would be assured of a warm welcome from his grandparents and could look forward to some good honest home cooking and the thought perked him up a little as he pictured them eyeing the old clock on the pine dresser as the train drew nearer to Scotland.

The first thing he did after setting foot in the house in Errol was accompany his grandmother on a bus to the Royal Infirmary in Perth to see his grandfather who had been admitted for a prostate operation. Grandma said she had not let her grandson know because she had not wanted to worry him. They arrived expecting to be told he was asleep and comfortable. Instead, a nurse said the old man had died during the operation, shortly before they arrived. Sandy Hendry was eighty, but his death had been totally unexpected. It was the worst possible homecoming and Elizabeth Hendry was devastated.

Normally tough, resourceful and cheerful, she found it difficult to accept that he had gone. Her grandson, also badly shaken, made the arrangements for the small funeral service at the house and cremation in Dundee. Although by comparison his own troubles were insignificant, keeping busy helped steer his mind away from them. He wore his uniform for the last time at his grandfather's funeral which was on Derby day.

He spent several days with Grandma talking about old times, both finding comfort by remembering how much better the old man had been in recent years, having overcome the crippling rheumatism by the simple expedient of becoming too old to work. An ingenuous uncomplaining man, sustained by an adoring wife and the most modest of pleasures, having only found simple comfort and security in retirement, he died as quietly as he had lived.

They also spoke about the success found in the RAF which had been brought crashing down by the peace, and Mrs Hendry persuaded her grandson to talk about his plans. He did not have any except to find a job; any job, however menial, that would bring in money, put food on the table and help preserve his dignity. That was his current overwhelming plan. Ambition for something better would come in the fullness of time.

Although bitter about how he appeared to have been eased out of the RAF he nonetheless continued to think of the earlier years with enormous affection, especially while desperately searching for work.

'I missed the RAF terribly and was very miserable. I didn't have a job and missed the camaraderie of my mates, the crew room, the gunnery room and the debriefings, things like that. There was an air of expectancy when you entered the briefing room and had a look at the map. The fellows laughing, talking, smoking and joking. It was an adventure to go off on those ops. In some chaps, you could see fear. But I always had complete faith in the crews I was with. Only two things bothered me: coming down in the sea, because I couldn't swim. And getting hit by flak.

'We shared good times and bad, joys and disappointments, excitement and tragedy. But in all the years since the war I have never found the camaraderie which we had on a bomber station. We formed close relationships that could never be repeated in Civvy Street. I felt this more because, although my mother had eleven children I was brought up as one child by my grandparents.

'I never came to terms with being at Lindholme because it wasn't like the real Air Force. There were a lot of people who were square pegs in round holes and many others, pre-war chaps jockeying for positions, wondering how they could get rid of those fly-by-nights, those smart arses, who included me, I suppose.

'But I was philosophical. It was the start of a new era. Life must go on and I had to earn a living, it was as simple as that. I would probably have to get stuck into jobs that two years before I could not have dreamed about because I had no qualifications apart from the skills I had learned in the RAF.'

He thought briefly about applying for a commission in the Royal Australian

Air Force and, more seriously, considered joining the crew of a whaler.

'I made some inquiries and could have got a job on a whaler without any trouble through Salvesen's in Leith. Then I thought how bloody cold it had been flying in a Lancaster and it would probably be even worse on a whaler, so that idea went very quickly out of my mind. I also thought of emigrating to Canada. I had a brother, Gordon, who was there, although I had not even met him. I decided, instead, to try my luck in Scotland and started door knocking.'

On his way to the Labour Exchange in Perth he was attracted to the electricity board's grand offices and persuaded the uniformed commissionaire to let him have a word with the boss.

'The boss asked me why an RAF officer like me was looking for a job and I told him. He asked me to go back next day and when I did he said they were creating a job for me. I was to be the wayleave officer for Tayside. It sounded good and promised to be a decent job.'

The board was putting up pylons and poles to carry electricity across the countryside but, said McIntosh, land owners were becoming greedy and wanted to be paid so much a year for them standing on their property. Each one was being given a reference number and would be marked on maps that were being drawn up. It would be his job to make sure the wayleaves were paid.

'It was early summer and I was given a big office at the top of the building overlooking the river Tay and the pleasure park. The office was beautifully furnished and there were four pretty girls and me in it. We were not very busy because surveyors were still plotting pylons across the maps and I spent my days looking out of the window watching women walking in the street wearing their summer dresses, people swimming and boats going along the river. I suffered that for about two months.

'I had learned to drive after coming out of the RAF and soon got a job as an agricultural representative to sell feeding stuffs to farmers. The boss in Perth, Mr J C W Simms, had told me: "You are just the chap we are looking for. A country type." He was in his fifties, well-fed, with sleek hair full of Brylcreem. I thought: "I'm more of a country type than you could imagine, being laid about the side of the roads as a boy".'

After training with animal feed nutritionists Silcocks in Liverpool, and a spell as a probationary assistant salesman in Mid Calder, West Lothian, he was given his own territory to develop in the Inverurie area of Aberdeenshire. He discovered that his gift of the gab, delivering patter with a cheerful smile, gave him clear advantages in the selling business. He made a lot of farmer friends, was a good salesman and loved the work. But he was on a fixed weekly wage while his immediate boss, the local agent, was earning a fat commission. This grated with McIntosh who believed he was worth more. But there was an exceptionally bright spot on his horizon.

He met twenty-five-year-old Christina Cooper, who was brought up with five sisters and a brother on their parents' farm at Bourtie, a little village near Inverurie.

'We met through a dare,' he says, grinning delightedly. 'She was dared to ask me to go to a basket whist drive at Inverurie town hall. Basket whist is where the women take a basket with cakes, scones and things. You play whist, then have your tea.' It was a long courtship, but Christina had infinite patience with a boyfriend who had an obsession with making a success of his life, to be someone important of whom she would be very proud.

When McIntosh threatened to quit selling seed and feed, Simms split a territory in Ayrshire of which the former RAF officer was to get half.

'I was delighted. Ayrshire was full of dairy cows that would be eating up all this feed earning commission that would go into my pocket. I was made a fully-fledged salesman and given a little Austin Eight. But when I arrived in Ayrshire I discovered that instead of getting part of the lowlands I had been given the high moors where there were not a lot of dairy cows nor even many farms. There were more bloody grouse and rabbits on Fenwick Moor than beasts and there wasn't a living to be made. I left the following weekend and thought: "Now what am I going to do?" I had no money and no car, but I was very good at getting on buses.

'After delivering the car to Simms in Perth I called in at the Labour Exchange. I said: "What have you got? Any jobs?" They only had labouring work, but I could handle a pick and shovel. At that time they were building a lot of big dams for hydroelectric schemes. I was asked: "Would you mind going to live in a camp at one of these sites? There's quite a bit of money can be made there, but you've got to work twelve-hour shifts, seven days a week."

I said: "I'm your kid".'

A contractor with 3,000 men was building the Clunie dam near Blair Atholl in the district of Erochty. McIntosh was not exactly welcomed with a lively skirl of pipes, three cheers and a wee warming dram. The site agent looked him up and down suspiciously and growled: 'Ah, another man looking for a job. Have you run away from your wife or something?'

'I need work.'

'We're looking for an assistant storekeeper.'

'You've found one.'

'You start tomorrow morning. You'll get a pair of wellingtons, a donkey jacket and a cloth cap.'

Thousands of tons of sand, cement and all the building materials were daily coming into the site's big batching plant and McIntosh's job at first was checking the lorries and marking them on a sheet at night, not his idea of storekeeping. The money was good but he was not sorry when he was withdrawn from his chilly open position in persistent heavy rain and admitted to the stores.

Asked if he knew anything about machinery, McIntosh said: 'Nothing, but I used to sit in the rear turret of an aeroplane.' His intriguing reply led to another job.

'I finished up as a banksman on a digger. I greased it and sat in the cab drinking tea with the driver who spent hours doing nothing simply because there was nothing for him to do. I was getting around 4s (20p) an hour, better than the ordinary man in the street.'

He worked on three dam sites in Scotland, including one at the Glen Devon reservoir near Auchterarder, Perthshire.

'Glen Devon had very good billets and an excellent dining hall with such tasty food, it was like being back in the RAF. They needed to train staff on the site. I was taken on and they seemed to think I was a semi-intelligent sort of a guy. Over several months I saw how the towers were built, how ropes were coiled, how the winches were in and how the operating levers and everything were fitted in the winch house, while the chap who operated it taught me all the fundamentals.

'I was made assistant cable way operator earning big money, on a bonus for each cubic yard of concrete put into the dam. I loved it and within three months had bought a Morris Minor tourer for £40 with a roof that folded up and down. It was a grand little car, I wish I had it today.'

After two years he was tempted down to Devon in 1952 working on the South Brent dam. 'It was a beautiful place on the edge of Dartmoor. I was put into excellent digs in the sleepy little village of South Brent and given a subsistence allowance of £3.10s (£3.50). As the digs were only £3 I was already in profit, but I worked long hours.

'They hadn't even completed the roads to the site. My job involved starting work three hours before everyone else and finishing three hours later than them at night. Driving a Land Rover I picked up engineers all over the place, including Teignmouth, Torquay, Babbacombe and Brixham and took them home after they'd finished. These engineers were all toffs with collars and ties, carrying theodolites and pencils, not shovels. I did this for eight months. The average national wage at that time was between £7 and £9 a week. I was earning big bucks, sometimes as much as £50, and saving hard.'

He got into a routine of leaving his digs at 5am, returning at midnight. He had little sleep, nor did his landlady who looked after him as well as Mrs Cribbes at Cockburnspath, for she was always there to provide him and three others from the dam with a large breakfast and a hot dinner of good plain food.

McIntosh was in the constant grip of a compulsive energy which was motivating him to succeed and to be seen to be a success. He had observed so much failure and misery there was no way he was going to fall into the trap of poverty and squalor. Because of this he put in many more hours than he needed, but the fear of failure drove him on. His mind was sharp and receptive, able to quickly pick up the rudiments of a job for which he had enjoyed no long apprenticeship. He needed to be told something only once, having rediscovered the enthusiasm for his work which he experienced as an air gunner. He caught the eye of site agent Jack Diamond, became involved with building the cable way and was soon put in charge of it.

At this time he wondered where he would be and what job he would have had if he stayed in the RAF. Certainly, the money was better at South Brent and he was happy to be climbing ladders. 'The cable way had to be working twenty-four hours a day, stopping only for maintenance on Sundays. I had very little knowledge about engineering, but I knew how to operate this cable way.'

'It was tough work and people got thirsty. You got paid on a Friday. Dam workers queued up outside South Brent's three pubs that night, drinking whisky, gin and vodka. Same again on Saturday. On Sunday and Monday they were reduced to beer and Tuesday and Wednesday when money was getting short, you saw them sitting with pints of scrumpy at about fourpence a pint. It was nothing to come driving through the street at night and see two or three men absolutely shit marack (drunk and incapable) in the streets. A lot were hoboes, on the move all the time, rough diamonds with no prospects, some had run away from their wife, or were supporting two wives, and had opted out of society for a while. They weren't all like that, of course, there were excellent engineers, Welsh and Irish miners who did the pick and shovelling down at the base of the dam and vibrating the concrete, hard-working tradesmen, and others, but everyone enjoyed making good money.'

Scams boomed at the dam. A bookmaker paid the timekeeper, a little man from Kirkaldy, £10 a day to let him have an office at the camp to which his runners swarmed from all over the vast South Brent site. Cans were filled from company tankers to keep employees' cars topped up during the Suez crisis when petrol rationing was re-introduced. Their employers turned a blind eye.

McIntosh rarely took holidays but occasionally snatched time to drive a Land Rover to the horse racing at Newton Abbot or Buckfastleigh, and fishing patiently in the Avon or Dart when he remembered easier pickings he had enjoyed years ago from the river Farg in Perthshire.

After three years at South Brent McIntosh bought a brand-new Sunbeam car for £600 with cash he took out of his hip pocket, but when the concrete had all been laid, the bonuses dried up and McIntosh began looking for new challenges.

He was offered a good job building the cable way at another dam being inserted into the picturesque Vale of Taunton Deane near the market town of Wiveliscombe, Somerset. It was here the following Easter that he unexpectedly met the seed and feed salesman he had worked with in Inverurie, still looking prosperous from the steady flow of his commissions. McIntosh recalls:

'He told me: "There's a company in Aberdeen looking for a chap like you." It was Barclay, Ross and Hutchison, well-known agricultural engineers, millwrights and manufacturers, among other things, of threshing boxes, grain cleaners, ploughs, harrows, turnip cutters, fertiliser spreaders and hay rickers.'

With his heart still rooted in the country, McIntosh liked the sound of the old-established company and even before accepting the post of trainee salesman thought that if he was lucky, he would get to revisit the haunts of his youth.

The romance between him and Christina Cooper which had shown healthy signs of blossoming in the late 1940s had been virtually put on hold during his frenzied work pattern in Devon, although he had had no other girlfriends. In 1956, following his move to Aberdeen, their friendship was rekindled.

Still married to his first wife, Betty, he had kept her waiting for a divorce until early 1957 after Christina had accepted his proposal of marriage. The divorce completed, Wallace and Christina were married on 7 December 1957 in the church at Bourtie. It was a quiet ceremony for although McIntosh got on well with Christina's parents, especially Janet, her mother, others in the Cooper family frowned at the notion of the young woman marrying a divorced man.

Despite everything that had gone before, that day was when his life really started. At thirty-seven he was more mature than when he and Betty had stood holding hands in church in 1942 and the war had quickly drawn him back to do his duty. Not until now did he realise that Christina was the perfect soul mate whom, almost unknowingly, he had always been seeking. 'I felt really secure and comfortable for the first time in my life. I could see a future and felt I was going places. We did very well and always had a reasonable standard of living.'

Christina, pretty, with light brown hair and a fine figure, was a warm gentle woman, the perfect foil to a man who had been to hell and back many times with Bomber Command, and who was known for being impulsive. Their first home was at Fyvie, near Turriff. In 1982 they moved to Dyce, a mile from Aberdeen airport.

Now he was settled within one company it was no surprise to anyone when one promotion followed another. A hard worker, resourceful and a good organiser, people trusted him, often turning to him in emergencies. He became senior salesman, then branch manager in Montrose where he later added the Arbroath and Brechin operations to his little empire. The firm was taken over in 1974 when he was made a director of the parent company. Another promotion followed in 1978 when he became managing director of the shops division.

He was a Rotarian, a member of the Chamber of Commerce and had done good business with people from 'Big Hooses' all over Scotland. My God, who would have thought it possible? The end of all this was less distressing than leaving the RAF. He explains:

'The slow wind down of the company started in 1982. It was sold off in bits and pieces and dissolved. I retired in 1985, the day we closed the agricultural division.'

The war in Europe had been over for forty years when Wallace McIntosh, in company with hundreds more war veterans, now retired, thought more than fleetingly about what had happened to his former comrades. He received a letter in 1985 with the news that an association had been formed for anyone who served with 207 Squadron. He made a telephone call and quickly enrolled as a member. Memories flooded back, reunions were organised and old friends got together to talk through their experiences.

Wallace and Christina McIntosh had three children: Anne, who became a nurse in Saudi Arabia, and now lives with her family in Florida, Mary who went into business management, and James who joined the Royal Artillery.

His mother and grandmother were eventually both living in Aberdeen. McIntosh occasionally visited his mother, who told him she had never been happier, while knowing her large family had all tasted success. His children only twice visited their grandmother. Mrs McIntosh was not part of the closer family they had known while growing up.

They more regularly saw their great-grandmother. The old woman's rented former fisherman's cottage was small but picturesque, standing at the north side of the river Don on the edge of Aberdeen. McIntosh's grandma spent several happy years here until she died on 28 December 1965, aged ninety. She was buried in the churchyard at Kineff which is also the last resting place of McIntosh's mother, and his little friend, Alistair Chalmers, who was drowned at the age of five.

As his children grew up and became aware of their father's extraordinary job during the war McIntosh decided to take them on a guided tour of the airfields where he had been stationed, while trying to rediscover old haunts in Nottingham and Newark.

His family saw little at the former RAF Spilsby that reminds anyone of the violence of war or of the hundreds of people who passed through this now tranquil corner of Lincolnshire nearly sixty years ago. One hangar remains, used by a farmer, and a short stretch of runway can be found. Visitors occasionally stumble over foundations of buildings, but they will see the memorial to those who were based here, specifically mentioning the ten men who were killed in the terrible explosion in April 1944. Unveiled in 2001, the memorial stands on the base of the station fire tender house.

A parachute school now uses the old Langar control tower where there is a display of 207 Squadron photographs. Men and women are taken up to a maximum 13,000ft in propeller-driven aircraft and jump out to float serenely down to the old airfield, clinging to billowing square-shaped coloured parachutes.

McIntosh found his old dispersal where he, Fred Richardson and their crewmates regularly climbed into a Lancaster, set off for distant targets with a load of bombs and were always lucky to return. Young James McIntosh dug into the old crumbling dispersal concrete and produced a handful of pebbles which he gave to his father who had them polished and kept safely ever since in a small cardboard box.

He opens the box occasionally and dreams wistfully of a long-lost age when boys became men almost overnight and life was frighteningly precarious as Britain was poised on the edge of an abyss. He mourns the dismal truth that few people today are aware of the sacrifices made by bomber aircrews and all servicemen in the name of freedom. And if they do know, how many really care? He also wonders how Britain, comfortable and well-fed, would cope if it had to fight another major war, which could drag it back to the miserable austerity of the 1940s and 1950s. Having less would be more daunting now after decades of plenty.

The McIntoshes enjoyed many holidays abroad visiting places he could not have dreamed about in the 1920s and 1930s when poor people in Scotland struggled to fill their bellies. Despite these trips to foreign parts the couple's hearts really belonged to Scotland. One of their favourite spots was Glenbuchat, which is one of the attractive tributary glens of the upper Don. They came here to drink in the pure sweet air and enjoy the tranquility of the valley which, over the years, has sadly become drastically depopulated. McIntosh says:

'Glenbuchat was an area heading into the hills where I did a lot of business with farmers. It used be a thriving community with dances every other week. It had seventeen good farms when I was making my way as a salesman and I dealt with them all. I often came home with a leg of venison or a fine salmon. The venison would have come from a poached deer and the salmon was caught by a friend. They were all poachers up there. Now I think there are only three farms and a few houses in Glenbuchat, which is very sad. It was a lovely place to go for a run on a Sunday.

Christina became ill in August 1990. Operated on for stomach cancer she became extremely ill. Then she improved, was able to get out of the house and seemed back to her old self.

'She liked motoring, and always had her own Ford Capri. She used to drive to Bourtie sixteen miles up the road to see her mother. She also saw her sisters most of whom had married and settled within a stone's throw of the family farm. She was quite active up to the Christmas of that year, but deteriorated in January. February she wasn't too well, then she was taken back into hospital at the beginning of April. Anne was in America and Mary had left her job to look after her mother. I had a part-time job driving executives around for an oil company.

'I don't know whether they told Christina but the hospital called me in and said she wouldn't last a month. I came home absolutely shattered. She was my life, my best friend. We had travelled a good part of the world together. There always seemed to be somewhere to visit, another place to explore. We were always on the move. The hospital couldn't do any more and she was sent home.'

Christina McIntosh died on 18 April 1991, aged sixty-eight. The family took her ashes to Glenbuchat and tearfully dropped them into the River Buchat beside which she had spent many happy hours. During this distressing time it was a comfort to her family to think that she would be carried through the countryside she knew and loved.

CHAPTER SEVENTEEN

A PILGRIMAGE

One night in the summer following the death of his wife, Wallace McIntosh was sitting alone at home reminiscing. His had been a full and busy life, but now at seventy-one, he contemplated the future, which not only seemed bleak and empty, it had begun closing down, excluding him. Wondering what he could do to cope more easily with his sorrow, his mind trailed back across the happier RAF years and dropped abstractedly into his spell at Morpeth where he trained as an air gunner and discovered for the first time what he thought of as the real and exciting wartime Air Force.

He remembered the good-humoured daredevil Polish pilots with their strange unpronounceable names whose antics at the controls of the Blackburn Bothas frightened some youngsters but excited the young adventurous McIntosh. He recalled their enthusiasm when they talked about their homeland and, in particular, the Tatra Mountains, whose ruggedness they had compared to the Scottish Highlands. They told him that he should visit the mountains after the war. It was a corner of the world which had taken root in his mind forty-nine years before and had recently assumed the proportions of a fabled country where he could find peace and absolution; a sort of Shangri-La. In his diary on 12 August 1991 he wrote: 'May visit Poland.'

He had, years before, considered taking a holiday there, but Christina had refused to go. He did not know why unless his wife was afraid he might want to visit Auschwitz and she would be forced to learn about the sickening brutality the Germans had inflicted on the Poles. The impulsive bug stirred.

'I thought I had nothing to do and a lot of time in which to do it and, suddenly, felt like escaping for a while. I needed to do something, go somewhere. Next day I phoned the Polish embassy in Edinburgh to make inquiries about the visa. It cost me £20 and I got it in the morning. I asked my neighbour to give me a lift into Aberdeen the following day, 15 August. The bus left with me on it for London at 6.30am.

'I had not even looked at a map, didn't take one with me and only had a vague idea of my destination. I just packed a shoulder bag. I was well prepared but didn't know how long I would be away. My idea was to hitchhike to Poland at minimum cost and see as much as possible. I didn't do much planning, I never had unless it was in sales. I just swung the bag on my shoulder and went. I suppose I was running away.

'I bought a ticket for the ferry to Calais, looked around the trucks and buses aboard and spotted a Wallace Arnold coach that was heading for Belgium. I spoke to the courier and told her my plan. She said with a wee bit of luck I could get right into Poland by bus. Her bus was three-quarters full and she agreed to take me but would not let me pay a penny for my fare.'

In Brussels she introduced him to the courier on a bus from the same company heading for Berlin and McIntosh repeated his story. He was invited aboard but his offer of payment was again refused. He learned he could be transferred in the German capital to a bus which would take him to Kraków, in the south of Poland, near the mountains he wanted to see. His trip was in the year following the unification of Germany.

'I'd had nothing to eat since leaving home and bought a huge sausage roll in Brussels which I guzzled with a can of Coke. We had a problem on the way to Kraków. We were stopped at Görlitz at the Polish border. There was a hold-up. We saw a queue of traffic stretching ahead and were stuck there for hours. It was very difficult, especially as I was not on the coach's manifest. When we started moving at last, I didn't have a ticket and had to get off the bus and walk across the border alongside the bus. The border guards saw me walking, but that was all right. I didn't have a ticket for the bus, but I had a visa for Poland.

'We arrived in Kraków at four in the morning. I looked out of the bus and found that we were in the biggest square I had ever seen with the most beautiful buildings around it. I was feeling bloody manky by this time after sitting about in buses. I hadn't slept or had the opportunity to get a bath. I was told plenty of buses would be going to Zakopane in a few hours and advised to find a hotel for a meal.

'I went to a huge hotel where a receptionist could speak very good English. I was taken to a room where I changed my clothes, had a shower and enjoyed a hearty breakfast, but when I came to pay I was asked for Polish zlotys. I had none, but waited for the hotel's exchange bureau to open and found I was a zloty millionaire. The exchange rate was about 22,000 zlotys to the pound. I came away with one hundred pound's worth in my pocket, which was a lot of zlotys.

'When I left on a bus going south for Zakopane the square in Kraków was hotting up. People were milling about, bands were playing, and there were conjurers and singers and a huge open-air market. There was music and gaiety everywhere, although people were so poor. I found a hotel and explained that I wanted to stay for some time and was given a huge room. It had a good view of the Tatra mountains, a large television and a hi-fi unit, neither of which worked, but it had a bath and a massive bed and I laid out on it with my clothes on and slept soundly for several hours.'

Before going out to explore McIntosh found a member of staff who spoke English and asked if it was possible for his clothes to be laundered.

'A stout buxom hard-looking woman in her fifties with a striped apron and great muscular arms agreed to do it. I laid my dirty clothes out on the bed and went into the town to look round. When I came back everything was there on the bed, looking nicely laundered and ironed. I went in search of the woman but she wasn't interested in money. All she wanted was a big Marks & Spencer plastic bag I had. I was told she would take that as payment, they were that bloody poor. When I left I gave her a bag of toiletries and some zlotys. The hotel cost £3.50 a day which covered my room, a good breakfast and a big dinner at night, amazing value.'

The garrulous Wallace McIntosh met a party of teachers and students from near Manchester and was invited to join them.

'Plans were made each night in the hotel bar for the next day. We got a bus into Kraków and went shopping. I bought silver and amber bracelets for the girls, pieces of crystal, and beautiful walking sticks from a wood carver for my farmer friends, slippers and jerseys, all for peanuts.

'We went horse trekking and white-water rafting, visited salt mines, and went up the mountains where time seemed to have stood still. We sat eating chunks of bread and cheese, drinking wine, watching a crofting farmer cutting hay with his scythe and a woman loading it on to a cart pulled by a horse. It was brilliant, very much like the Scotland I knew as a boy. It's undulating interesting country and I would like to go back one day, although next time I would fly. The Polish pilots had been absolutely right about these mountains, the scenery is spectacular.

'It was warm and therapeutic, bringing back many childhood memories. I was always looking to see what they were doing in the fields. They cut hay with scythes on the side of the mountains and smaller farms, but big modern machinery worked the plains.

'When I said I was going to the death camp at Auschwitz the others did not think it was appropriate but they came with me. It was a sombre day out. We saw the fences, ovens, and toilet blocks about fifty yards long which were holes in concrete with water gushing underneath. There was an execution wall where many people were shot by the Germans, it was a very nasty place. There was a restaurant for tourists, but I can't imagine how anyone could have eaten there.

'We were told that some gold from the Jews' teeth, which had escaped the Germans' attention, had been washed with the ash of their corpses into the river Vistula and could be seen glinting on the banks after rain.

'I won't forget the stupid remark made by a teacher who said to the guide: "You have told us about the atrocities and how primitive everything was, but what did these people use for toilet paper?" He looked at her and said: "They used their fingers Madam, or somebody else's hand that was spare".'

McIntosh did not try to find any of the Polish pilots he had met at Morpeth quite simply because he had not brought their names and would not have known where to look for them if he had. He was content to walk in the towns of which they had spoken so warmly and in the mountains they had loved, the memories of which had sustained them in the fight from England against the Germans who had devastated their country and people.

McIntosh's Manchester friends displayed no interest in his stories about the war and he was unable to communicate with the Poles who might have known men who flew with Bomber Command. 'But I was moved by the many memorials dedicated to Polish people who died during the German occupation and thought Christ! 207 Squadron had 1,000 men killed and bugger all to remember them by.'

He returned to England in the Manchester group's coach, more relaxed, enriched by his experience, but exhausted. His friends from Lancashire would not let him pay for his seat on their coach which meant, surprisingly, that his journey across Europe had cost nothing. 'I rode in a taxi from Aberdeen the seven or eight miles to my home in Dyce. It cost £7. I had travelled through Europe for less.'

In March 1993 he was ready to embark on a sponsored marathon solo tour of over sixty former Bomber Command airfields, a punishing drive of around 3,300 miles in a month from Yorkshire into Lincolnshire and East Anglia in which he met former aircrew and serving officers and airmen. His plan was to augment funds of 207 Squadron Association which wanted to erect memorials at the four wartime airfields where the squadron had been based. These would be lasting tributes to nearly 1,000 men who were killed. His first call was on Teesside airport, formerly RAF Middleton St George, which had been a base for Halifaxes and Lancasters.

Squadron survivors, relations of those who were killed, and senior RAF officers attended the poignant unveiling ceremony of the memorial stone on the former airfield at Langar. Unfortunately, not enough money was available to commission memorials to stand at Waddington and Bottesford. A memento plaque bearing the squadron's crest was erected in Bottesford control tower which had been renovated and turned into offices. A memorial book paid for by 207 Squadron Association was placed in Great Steeping church.

Nearly sixty years after the end of the war bodies of aircrews and the wrecks of aircraft are still being found all over Europe, clearing up mysteries which have haunted families of men lost when their aeroplanes disappeared.

In October 1996 Wallace McIntosh joined old comrades at a Cambridge graveyard to pay their respects to a former 207 Squadron air gunner who had died in a tragic accident over fifty-one years before. The remains of Sergeant Bob Banks were laid to rest with full military honours. McIntosh, on behalf of the squadron, laid a wreath on Banks' grave.

He had been killed in the early hours of 2 March 1945 when his Lancaster, ME473, on fighter affiliation, piloted by Flight Lieutenant Ted Lawson, an Australian, collided with another Lancaster, ND572, from East Kirkby-based 57 Squadron over Ruskington Fen, near Sleaford, Lincolnshire. Both crews were killed, but one body from the 207 Squadron aircraft could not be identified and another could not be found. Fifty years later Banks' remains were found by Lincolnshire Aircraft Recovery Group five feet under a ploughed field. He was identified by the pay book in what remained of his tunic. A year was spent searching unsuccessfully for relatives of the dead man, a divorcee, before his funeral the following year.

The discovery of Banks, thirty-three when he died, cleared up a mystery which had lingered since 1945. The RAF was able to positively identify another body which, coincidentally, had been buried in the same Cambridge cemetery, in a grave marked 'unknown airman', in the military section, near where his former crewmate now lies. He was the crew's bomb aimer Flight Sergeant Arthur Henderson, twenty-one.

On the day of Banks' funeral McIntosh, who had known the air gunner at

Spilsby, told a newspaper reporter: 'It is most important that they should be remembered because some of these men went through horrific ordeals in the sky.'

In April 1998 McIntosh fulfilled a dream to visit Deelen airfield. He had twice been in formations of bombers from 207 Squadron which attacked the airfield in 1944. He also wanted to visit the grave of pilot Flight Lieutenant Johnny Overgaauw whose Lancaster had been shot down on the first of these raids. McIntosh stood on the runway and imagined the moment when his aircraft's bombs struck the great expanse of concrete with mind-numbing explosions as the Germans cowered in their shelters.

He and two other veterans from 207 Squadron who had not flown on the Deelen raids, pilot Bill Verrals and air gunner Alec White, were invited into the new control tower, and also shown the actual film which had been taken of the first RAF raid on the airfield, with British bombers surging in to bomb. McIntosh, shaking his head in delight, picked out the leading aircraft, which had been piloted by Grey, with himself in the rear turret. It was a curious feeling to be unexpectedly confronted by a fragment of his traumatic past.

At Moscowa cemetery, near Arnhem, McIntosh laid a wreath on the grave of Overgaauw and the British members of his crew.

Further north in Dronten the Burgomaster gave the little group a fine lunch and showed them a special room in the town hall which had been set aside as a tribute to air gunners. It contains many photographs of men who were shot down, paintings and considerable wartime memorabilia. The room has become a place of pilgrimage for air gunners of all Groups.

While in Dronten they were invited into the house of an elderly couple who were among civilians risking torture and execution by bravely sheltering airmen on the run from the Germans. The Dutch couple gave them soup and sandwiches and, still disturbed by their suffering during the war, wept when they left.

Three years later McIntosh was invited to visit France for a service and the unveiling of a stone bearing 207 Squadron's crest at Margny communal cemetery where lie the remains of Flying Officer Norman Weekes and his crew, killed on the Revigny raid in July 1944. McIntosh realised the cemetery was not far from Mailly-le-Camp, the graveyard for many bombers shot down in May 1944 during the raid which went spectacularly wrong. He was dumbstruck to find the beautiful memorial to the men who were killed that night while struggling to bomb the German military camp. He says: 'We were so lucky to escape, puttering about on three engines when the fighters were going crazy.'

When McIntosh looks back he is reminded how tough it was in Bomber Command. No one could afford to relax even during what were considered routine flights which were occasionally punctuated by moments of tumultuous terror and the certainty that death was nigh.

'In 1942 and 1943 if you were among those chaps taken at Dunkirk or had been shot down, and were now lying in a prisoner-of-war camp and heard the sirens going you knew we were up there bumping away at something and it gave you hope that we were still operational. And as our sorties grew in intensity we became great morale boosters for them.'

Many old pals who disappeared at the end of the war failed to show up after the formation of squadron associations and annual reunions.

'I would particularly love to meet Happy Hall, Bob Jack or Tommy Young again. I've tried in vain to find them through numerous channels, including the Ministry of Defence. They may have emigrated or died. I haven't given up hope of seeing them again, but it's been a long time.'

He still gives talks to groups and at airfields where anyone who has a fondness for history can learn the truth about what happened around sixty years ago from someone who was one of thousands of courageous young men employed to fight Britain's war in the air.

When his rumbling braw consonants start switchbacking evocatively over his hushed audience like a skirl of bagpipes, he gets into his stride, effortlessly conjuring up vivid and horrifying images of his war in the air. As he talks the former air gunner can almost smell the fumes from the blaring Merlin engines drifting across the airfield before takeoff, and the pungent cocktail of paint, dope, metal, sweat, oil, bombs and fear inside the Lancaster. He remembers so well peering deeply into a succession of cold black nights continually searching for the flitting evil shadow of a German fighter. And he can hear the satisfying loud rattle of his Browning machine guns as he tries to blow it out of the sky.

Occasionally, Wallace McIntosh looks up into the night sky from his home in Dyce and watches a big jet, navigation lights flashing, taking off from Aberdeen airport a mile away. Instinctively he gets it into his sights, squeezes his trigger fingers and grins to himself.

'Ay, another sitting duck.'

WALLACE McINTOSH'S OPERATIONAL RECORD
[extracted from his logbook]

First tour with 207 Squadron from Langar. All sorties in Lancasters, most as dorsal [mid-upper] gunner.

No	Date	Takeoff time	Aircraft	Duration	Pilot	Target	Remarks
1	4.2.43	18.20	R5504	7h 40m	Sgt Pete Evison	Turin	Landed at Exeter. Trailed by Bf-109 for 10 min.
2	13.2.43	19.15	W4171	6h 55m	Sgt Fred Richardson	Lorient	
3	16.2.43	19.00	ED418	3h 40m	Richardson	Lorient	Abortive.
4	26.2.43	18.55	ED554	4h 30m	Richardson	Cologne	
5	28.2.43	18.45	W4120	5h 50m	Richardson	St Nazaire	
6	3.3.43	18.50	ED554	5h 40m	Richardson	Hamburg	
7	22.3.43	19.30	ED550	4h 55m	Richardson	St Nazaire	
8	26.3.43	19.00	ED550	3h 15m	Richardson	Duisburg	Early return.
9	27.3.43	19.55	W4171	7h 55m	Richardson	Berlin	Me-109 destroyed and 1 Me-109 damaged.
10	29.3.43	21.35	ED550	8h 20m	Richardson	Berlin	
11	3.4.43	19.30	ED364	4h 05m	Richardson	Essen	Abortive.
12	4.4.43	21.00	W4120	6h 20m	Richardson	Kiel	
13	8.4.43	21.00	ED600	5h 50m	Richardson	Duisburg	
14	9.4.43	20.20	ED600	4h 40m	Richardson	Duisburg	
15	13.4.43	20.20	ED600	10h 30m	Richardson	La Spezia	
16	14.4.43	22.15	W4938	6h 20m	Richardson	Stuttgart	Ju-88 probable. Attacked 4 times.
17	20.4.43	21.30	W4962	8h 10m	Richardson	Stettin	A Ju-88 sighted 700 yards.
18	26.4.43	00.15	W4962	4h 50m	Richardson	Duisburg	

No	Date	Takeoff time	Aircraft	Duration	Pilot	Target	Remarks
19	27.4.43	21.15	W4962	5h 55m	Richardson	Mining off La Rochelle	
20	30.4.43	21.35	ED586	4h 30m	Richardson	Essen	
21	13.5.43	21.20	ED550	7h 25m	Richardson	Pilsen	
22	23.5.43	22.00	ED550	5h 5m	Richardson	Dortmund	
23	29.5.43	22.10	ED550	5h 40m	Richardson	Wuppertal	Bombed on 3 engines.
24	11.6.43	22.30	ED550	3h 15m	Richardson	Düsseldorf	Aborted. Starboard outer feathered.
25	12.6.43	22.40	ED569	5h 30m	Richardson	Bochum	Dorsal turret holed by flak. Port outer feathered.
26	20.6.43	21.50	LM326	10h 10m	Richardson	Friedrichshafen	Landed Blida, North Africa.
27	23.6.43	19.30	LM326	9h 05m	Richardson	La Spezia	From Blida to base.
28	8.7.43	22.20	ED550	5h 35m	Plt Off Richardson	Cologne	
29	9.7.43	22.25	ED550	5h 40m	Richardson	Gelsenkirchen	
30	12.7.43	22.30	ED550	10h 00m	Richardson	Turin	Ju-88 sighted. Shot out 2 searchlights.
31	16.7.43	22.00	LM334	9h 45m	Richardson	Cislago	Shot up target, 5,000 rounds from 500ft. Landed at Blida, North Africa.
32	24.7.43	21.05	LM334	8h 00m	Richardson	Leghorn	From Blida.
33	29.7.43	22.15	ED550	5h 05m	Richardson	Hamburg	

Second tour with 207 Squadron from Spilsby. All sorties in Lancasters, as rear gunner.

No	Date	Takeoff time	Aircraft	Duration	Pilot	Target	Remarks
34	22.3.44	19.05	ME631	5h 40m	Sqn Ldr John Grey	Frankfurt	Scared off an FW-190, 50 rounds.

No	Date	Takeoff time	Aircraft	Duration	Pilot	Target	Remarks
35	26.3.44	19.50	ME631	5h 20m	Wg Cdr John Grey	Essen	Bombed aircraft repair factory from 6,500ft.
36	5.4.44	20.20	ME681	7h 55m	Grey	Toulouse	Landed at Little Horwood.
37	18.4.44	20.45	ME631	4h 45m	Grey	Juvisy	Marshalling yards.
38	20.4.44	22.05	ME667	5h 05m	Grey	La Chappelle	Bombed from 8,900ft.
39	22.4.44	23.10	ME631	5h 45m	Grey	Brunswick	Marshalling yards.
40	29.4.44	22.10	ME667	6h 45m	Grey	Clermont-Ferrand	Aircraft repair factory. Bombed from 6,900ft.
41	3.5.44	21.55	ME667	5h 50m	Grey	Mailly-le-Camp	Military depot. Bombed from 6,000ft. Round trip on 3 engines. Shot down Me-110 over target in flames. Claimed destroyed. 1,000 rounds.
42	19.5.44	23.10	LL973	4h 05m	Grey	Amiens	Recalled by R/T on target. Did not bomb.
43	25.5.44	21.10	ND567	1h 20m	Grey	Stuttgart	Recalled.
44	27.5.44	23.40	NE678	3h 20m	Grey	St Valéry-en Caux	Target: Big guns. 6,900ft.
45	4.6.44	01.25	LL973	4h 10m	Grey	Maisy	Big guns.
46	5.6.44	01.35	LL973	4h 15m	Grey	La Pernelle	Big guns. Invasion. D-Day.
47	7.6.44	23.30	LL973	4h 10m	Grey	Forêt de Cerisy	Shot down Junkers 88 (0156). Shot down Junkers 88 (0157). Shot down Me-210 or 410 (0233).

No	Date	Takeoff time	Aircraft	Duration	Pilot	Target	Remarks
							Quiet trip?
							W/T Controller.
48	14.6.44	22.15	LL973	4h 30m	Grey	Aunay-sur-Odon	Panzer concentration.
49	27.6.44	23.25	LL902	2h 30m	Grey	Mimoyecques	Flying bomb site.
50	12.7.44	22.25	LM208	8h 35m	Grey	Culmont-Chalindrey	Shot down Me-109.
51	28.7.44	21.55	LM208	7h 50m	Grey	Stuttgart	Shot down FW-190. Shot down Junkers 88. Attacked 5 times.
52	5.8.44	11.05	LM208	3h 50m	Grey	St-Leu-D'Esserent	Daylight. Formation leader. Hit over target by flak. Returned on two engines. Landed at Manston.
53	12.8.44	00.30	LM263	3h 25m	Fg Off L L Goff	Falaise	Troops and supply columns.
54	15.8.44	09.59	PD220	3h 25m	Grey	Deelen airfield	Daylight. Formation leader.
55	3.9.44	15.40	LL968	3h 25m	Grey	Deelen airfield	Daylight. Formation leader. Rear turret u/s.

207 SQUADRON SECOND WORLD WAR CASUALTIES

Killed: 955, of whom 201 had no known grave. Prisoners of war: 171. Evaders: 39.

The Squadron carried out 4,563 sorties, in which 148 aircraft were lost. Nineteen Lancasters and eight Manchesters were also destroyed in crashes. Often regarded as an unlucky squadron, 207 suffered the highest percentage losses in 5 Group and the fourth highest overall percentage losses in Bomber Command.

A PAGE FROM JOHN GREY'S LOGBOOK

YEAR 19....		AIRCRAFT		PILOT, OR 1ST PILOT	2ND PILOT, PUPIL OR PASSENGER	DUTY (INCLUDING RESULTS AND REMARKS
MONTH	DATE	Type	No.			
—	—	—	—	—	—	— TOTALS BROUGHT FORWARD
APRIL	20	LANCASTER I.	X	SELF	F/O CASEY, F/O HALL SGT JACK, SGT YOUNG F/O MACKINTOSH SGT CHARLESWORTH.	OPERATIONS PARIS (LA CHAPELLE)
	22	LANCASTER I.	K	SELF	CREW.	N.F.T.
	22	LANCASTER I	K	SELF	F/O CASEY. F/S HALL SGT JACK SGT YOUNG F/O MACKINTOSH SGT CHARLESWORTH	OPERATIONS - BRUNSWICK.
	29	LANCASTER I	X	SELF.	F/O CASEY. F/S HALL SGT JACK, SGT YOUNG F/O MACKINTOSH SGT CHARLESWORTH	OPERATIONS - CLERMONT - FERRAND
	30	LANCASTER I	X	SELF	CREW.	H. L. B.
MAY	3	LANCASTER I	X	SELF	F/O CASEY, F/S HALL SGT JACK, SGT YOUNG F/O MACKINTOSH. SGT CHARLESWORTH	OPERATIONS - MAILLY - LE - CAMP. ME 110 shot down. CLAIM CONFIRMED.
	14	LANCASTER I	K	SELF	CREW	BASE - SYERSTON.
	14	LANCASTER I	K	SELF	CREW.	SYERSTON - BASE
	19	LANCASTER I	K	SELF	F/O CASEY. F/S HALL SGT JACK. SGT YOUNG F/O MACKINTOSH SGT CHARLESWORTH	OPERATIONS - AMIENS. A/B LOST EYE.

GRAND TOTAL [Cols. (1) to (10)]

.................Hrs..................Mins.

TOTALS CARRIED FORWARD

SINGLE-ENGINE AIRCRAFT				MULTI-ENGINE AIRCRAFT						PASS-ENGER	INSTR/CLOUD FLYING [Incl. in cols. (1) to (10)]	
DAY		NIGHT		DAY			NIGHT					
DUAL	PILOT	DUAL	PILOT	DUAL	1ST PILOT	2ND PILOT	DUAL	1ST PILOT	2ND PILOT		DUAL	PILOT
(1)	(2)	(3)	(4)	(5)	(6)	(7)	(8)	(9)	(10)	(11)	(12)	(13)
58.00	976.15	1.00	64.00	38.10	681.45	3.15	18.05	146.35		758c	15.20	
								5.05				
					40							
								5.45				
								6.45				
					1.15							
								5.50				
					.30							
					.10							
								4.05				
58.00	976.15	1.00	69.00	38.10	684.20	3.15	18.05	174.05		75.30	15.20.	
(1)	(2)	(3)	(4)	(5)	(6)	(7)	(8)	(9)	(10)	(11)	(12)	(13)

207 Sqdn.   JUNE   1944.

Date	Hour	Aircraft Type and No.	Pilot	Duty	Remarks (including results of bombing, gunnery, exercises, etc.)	Day	Night
					Time carried forward —	161.20	312.25
						473.45.	
4/6/44	0125	Lancaster "H"	W/C Grey Pfc.	REAR GUNNER	OPERATIONS:- "MAISY" BIG GUNS (45)		4.10
5/6/44	0135	Lancaster "H"	W/C Grey Pfc.	REAR GUNNER	OPERATIONS:- "LA-PERNELLE." BIG GUNS. (46)		4.15
7/6/44	23:30	Lancaster "H"	W/C Grey Pfc.	REAR GUNNER	OPERATIONS:- "INVASION. 1) DAY. "FORÊT-DE-CERISY." (47)		4.10
14/6/44	22:15	Lancaster "H"	W/C Grey Pfc.	REAR GUNNER	OPERATIONS:- "AUNAY-SUR-ODON." "PANZER CONCENTRATION." SHOT DOWN JUNKERS 88 (0150). SHOT DOWN ME 210 or 410 (0233). "QUIET TRIP", w/t Controller. (48)		4.30
17.6.44	10.55	Lancaster "H"	Flt. Cunningham Pfc.	GUNNER PASSENGER	BASE TO SYERSTON.	.30	
17.6.44	16.30	Lancaster "J" w/o Player REA	P/O Grant.	PASSENGER.	SYERSTON TO BASE.	.45	
18.6.44	14.55	Lancaster "J"	W/C Grey Pfc.	REAR GUNNER.	LEVELLING MK. XIV BOMB SIGHT.	.50	
20.6.44	13.10	Lancaster "H"	G/C Cheshire	GUNNER REAR	TO NORWICH.	.40	
20.6.44	15.50	Lancaster "H"	G/C Cheshire	REAR GUNNER.	NORWICH. TO BASE.	.40	
					TOTAL TIME ...	164.45	329.30

204 Sqdn. SPILSBY

JULY 1944.

Date	Hour	Aircraft Type and No.	Pilot	Duty	Remarks (including results of bombing, gunnery, exercises, etc.)	Time carried forward :— 164hrs 333. 497.45	
						Flying Times Day	Night
4/7/44	12.25	Lancaster "M"	W/C Grey D/FC	Rear Gunner	BOMBING.	2.00	
6/7/44	16.05	Lancaster "M"	W/C Grey D/FC	Rear Gunner	Base to Woodbridge. U/S. Base. To Woodbridge.	.50	
6/7/44	19.40	Lancaster "H"	F/L Cunningham D/FC	Rear Gunner	Woodbridge To Base.	.35	
12/7/44	12.03	Lancaster "M"	W/C Grey D/FC	Rear Gunner	Base To Market ~ Harborough.	12.30	
12/7/44	14.04	Lancaster "M"	W/C Grey D/FC	Rear Gunner	Market- Harborough To Base.	.30	
13/7/44	22.25	Lancaster "M"	W/C Grey D/FC	Rear Gunner	OPERATIONS:- CULMONT- SHOT DOWN. ME 109. HIGH LEVEL BOMBING (50)	2.00	8.35
14/7/44	11.15	Lancaster "K"	G/C Harris	Rear Gunner	OPERATIONS:- STUTTGART (51) SHOT DOWN:- FW 190 SHOT DOWN:- JUNKER 88. ATTACKED 5 TIMES.		7.50
28/7/44	3.65	Lancaster "M"	W/C Grey D/FC	Rear Gunner	DAY FLYING 6.25. NIGHT FLYING. 16.25. w/c		

Summary for JULY 1944.
Unit 204 Sqdn.
Date 1-8-44.
Signature ...

1 LANCASTER

O.C. A Flt.

O.C. 204 Sqdn.

TOTAL TIME ... 171.10 34.9 1/25

FLYING OFFICER WALLACE McINTOSH'S DFC POSTAGRAM

Wt. 25617/Bt434 100,000 Pads 9/43 H.P. 51-7341

R.A.F. Form 1924

POSTAGRAM.

Originator's Reference Number:—

BC/S.23191/P

Date :—

18th June, 1944.

To: F/O W. McIntosh, DFM (149980),
No. 207 Squadron,
R.A.F. Station, SPILSBY.

From: The Commander-in-Chief, Bomber Command.

My warmest congratulations on the award of your

Distinguished Flying Cross.

A.T. Harris

Air Chief Marshal.

Originator's
Signature

Time of
Origin

A message from Bomber Command Chief Arthur Butch Harris.

FLYING OFFICER WALLACE McINTOSH'S
CHOPPER CLUB MEMBERSHIP

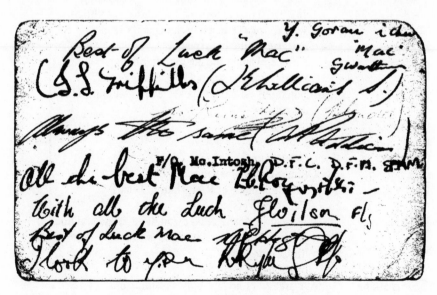

You needed a lot of luck to belong to the Chopper Club.

GLOSSARY

AC2	Aircraftman second class
AFC	Air Force Cross
AOC	Air officer commanding
ATS	Auxiliary Territorial Service. Set up in 1941 for women serving in the British Army
Bomb tit	The bomb release button
Bull's eye	A precision bombing exercise
CO	Commanding officer
Con	Condensation
Coning	Held in a cone of blinding light by searchlights, directed by a radar-operated master searchlight
Cookie	4,000lb impact-fused high-capacity bomb
ETA	Estimated time of arrival
Evaders	Airmen evading the enemy after baling out
FTS	Flying Training School
Funnel	The lights on tapered posts leading aircraft on to the runway
Gardening	Mine-laying
Garry	15cwt truck
Groupie	Group captain
Gee	Radio-based navigational aid
Halton brat	Boy apprentice at RAF Halton, Bucks
HCU	Heavy conversion unit
H2S	A radar device reading through darkness and thick cloud, giving a picture of the terrain and places below
MT	Motor transport
NFT	Night flying test
Oboe marking	A precise radio bombing system using transmissions from two ground stations
OTU	Operational training unit
Pitot head	The inlet for the air speed indicator. At dispersal it was always covered to keep oil and muck out of it
QDM	The magnetic course to steer for base, assuming zero wind
R/T	Radio telephone

Second dickey	A pilot going as second pilot on his first familiarisation sortie with an experienced skipper
Schräge Musik	Jazz music – a pair of upward-firing machine guns or cannons mounted behind the cockpit of a German fighter.
SPs, or Snowdrops	RAF service police
Sprog	A new recruit
WAAF	Women's Auxiliary Air Force
Wimpey	Wellington
Window	Strips of aluminium foil dropped by Allied bombers to confuse German radar

BIBLIOGRAPHY

Barrymore Halpenny, Bruce, *Action Stations 2. Military airfields of Lincolnshire and the East Midlands; Action Stations 4. Military airfields of Yorkshire* (Patrick Stephens, 1981 & 1982)

Bowyer, Michael J F, *Action Stations. 1 Wartime military airfields of East Anglia 1939-1945* (Patrick Stephens, 1979)

Boyle, Andrew, *No Passing Glory* (Collins, 1972)

Brotherton, Joyce, *Press on Regardless*, 1945

Chorley, W R, *RAF Bomber Command Losses of the Second World War, 1943; RAF Bomber Command Losses of the Second World War, 1944* (Midland Counties Publications, 1996 & 1997); 'The Raid On Mailly-Le-Camp 3-4 May 1944', *Aviation News*, 3-16 October 1986

Cooper, Alan, *Beyond The Dams To The Tirpitz* (Goodall, 1991)

Cross, Robin, *The Bombers* (Grub Street, 1987)

Dick, David and Glynne-Owen, Raymond *207 Squadron RAF Association Members' Memorial Book* (1993)

Fairhead, Ralph, *An Airman's Diary* (New Horizon, 1982)

Garbett, Mike and Goulding, Brian, *The Lancaster At War; Lancaster at War 2* (Ian Allan, 1974 & 1979)

Hammersley, Roland A, DFM, *Into Battle With 57 Squadron*, 1992

Hammerton, edited by Sir J A, *The Modern Encyclopedia*, edited by (The Amalgamated Press, 1930s)

Hastings, Max, *Bomber Command* (Michael Joseph, 1979)

Hinchliffe, Peter, *The Other Battle* (Airlife, 1996)

Jane's Fighting Aircraft of World War II (Studio Editions Ltd, 1992)

Jones, R V, *Most Secret War* (Wordsworth Editions, reprint 1998)

Middlebrook, Martin, *The Bomber Command War Diaries*, with Chris Everitt (Viking, 1985)

Otter, Patrick, *Lincolnshire Airfields in the Second World War* (Countryside Books, 1996)

Price, Alfred, *The Bomber in World War II* (Macdonald and Jane's, 1976)

Smith, David J, *Action Stations 7. Military airfields of Scotland, the North-East and Northern Ireland* (Patrick Stephens, 1983)

Weal, Elke C, Weal, John A. and Barker, Richard F., *Combat Aircraft of World War Two* (Arms and Armour Press, 1977)

INDEX